D0853940

The Bedside 'Guardian' 29

THE BEDSIDE 'GUARDIAN' 29

A selection from

The 'Guardian' 1979–80

Edited by

W. L. Webb

With an introduction by

Shirley Williams

Cartoons by

Bryan McAllister

COLLINS
St James's Place, London
1980

William Collins Sons & Co Ltd
London · Glasgow · Sydney · Auckland
Toronto · Johannesburg

First published 1980 © Guardian Newspapers Ltd, 1980
ISBN 0 00 216285 7

Photo-set in 10/11 Imprint
Made and Printed in Great Britain by
William Collins Sons & Co Ltd Glasgow

Introduction

It's a rainy morning and the milk's gone bad. The whole morning's post is a circular about fabulous prizes to be won if you've got a lucky number, which you haven't, and a letter from the tax inspector asking if you're ever going to reply to a letter whose contents you don't recall and which is anyway interred in a pile of clamorous unread public relations handouts and shiny magazines. Each of them is shrieking for attention, like the hot tap in the kitchen and the damp patch at the corner of the ceiling. If you ring, no one will come, and if somebody does, it will be just when you're at the office, so why start? The news is as awful as ever, the boy's been playing very loud rock for an hour in the bathroom, and you wouldn't stay afloat at all without *The Guardian* to start this dog-eared day.

Except of course the blasted rag hasn't arrived because the printers are cross, shaking oily rags at the bland dials of the new machines, or the distributors are snarled up, or the *Daily Telegraph* has been delivered instead, a tasteful recognition by the newsagent that you are a Serious Reader. So you'll have to find your tranquillizer and your shot – or what Auden more elegantly called 'my evening prayer, my morning song' – in *The Bedside Guardian*, scrabbling to dislodge it from the duvet and the dust, its nightlong neighbours.

Reassuring? No, not really. It parades the world's leaders, the pocket-size Jimmy Carter with his 'death defrosted smile' (I hadn't realized it before, but of course), grinning with blank eyes through a score of primaries while the world rumbles and tumbles round him. And Brezhnev, a craggy side of beef, bulldozing Schmidt and Giscard and the other elegant subtle Europeans out of their intellectual redoubts on détente, arms control, Afghanistan and all the rest of it. *The Bedside Guardian* also, like its more peripatetic begetter, digs out the leaders you hadn't heard of before, tomorrow's world-shapers.

The problems those leaders have to confront get grimmer

all the time. Through the year Peter Niesewand, dodging the helicopter gunships in the orchards near Jalalabad, has described the warriors of the Mojahadin, cloned from Kipling's Gunga Din. Martin Woollacott charted the ebb and flow of human flotsam in Thailand and Kampuchea: photographs of skeletal children in the Sahel bruised the casual eye; one month Somalia, one month Uganda, one month Vietnam, the never-never-ending tale of human despair. Much of this won't surface in *The Bedside Guardian*: it was nightmare reading.

What does surface is a world hooked on arms, £212 thousand millions of them last year. Even the British Army preening itself in the regimental silver and dreaming of coups, of Edward Heath in the guardroom and Harold Wilson on jankers. Thank the Lord for Lord Carver, as reported by David Pallister. He always seemed a controlled sort of man.

Mind you, the zombie-like existence of the world's leaders is penetrated from time to time. At the Dublin summit, the limousines screamed to a stop and out got the blanched politicians, not enjoying playing at Al Capone. 'Clearly national virility,' said Simon Hoggart, 'is somehow tied up with the speed at which each car storms through the gateway.' Other glimpses of the way our leaders live: Denis Thatcher erupting into visibility at the Conservative conference to cheer the arrival of the South African rugby team, and then uneasily subsiding into invisibility again; Jimmy Carter strangled by his pants when a Baltimore ward heeler at a White House party seized the President's belt from behind. Mostly, of course, *The Guardian* attends upon the great, but occasionally the great attend upon *The Guardian*. James Cameron rates a personal 3.00 a.m. visit from Fidel Castro, throbbing with eloquence in his Havana hotel bedroom.

It's a great place, *The Guardian*, though some of the fresh-faced high-minded austerity we used to associate with it isn't what it was. But then it isn't what it was in Britain either. Up in the Lake District, the tradition goes on unmarred, I'm glad to say. Harry Griffin used to soak his boots in goose grease and nowadays soaks them in Rydal water; it's painful as hell, but in the end they fit perfectly, an analogy for a good *Guardian*

6

life. That's real stoicism for you, but it's going, going. The Glasgow lads with the tar-puddle eyes aren't looking for tern and trout in Erlend Clouston's Shetland Isles, but for fast bucks and reeling booze; Polly Toynbee's young ladies are all out of manuscripts and into boardroom kitchens feeding top piggies; and Stanley Reynolds left the sharp chat and beer-marinated pubs of Liverpool a long time ago for lusher fields. Louis MacNeice summed it all up acidly in his 'Bagpipe Music':

> It's no go the Yogi-Man,
> It's no go Blavatsky,
> All we want is a bank balance
> And a bit of skirt in a taxi.

We want a bit more than that, and *The Guardian* gives us a lot more. There's the Guardian Arts to be our surrogate at operas and concerts and plays we meant to get to and didn't, to listen to the broadcasts and watch the television programmes we missed. *The Bedside Guardian* catches the moment Joan Sutherland met the Queen Mother at Covent Garden: 'if their tiaras had met, they would have fused the lights'. Guardian Education helps its readers to agonize over whether to keep kids in State schools, with no books and motorway meals, or to prepare a hundred reasons why they have to be moved. And Guardian Women raises the paradox why a sex so richly gifted is, by other newspapers, so under-described.

The Bedside Guardian's a better bedmate than many you may meet. As for *The Guardian* itself, qwertyuiops and all, it does get you through the week.

Shirley Williams

The invisible man at Number 10

It is Sunday lunchtime in the Home Counties and your host for the weekend has taken you for a drink at his golf club. After a while you are joined by a trim, balding man in his early 60s. He is wearing cavalry twill trousers and a chunky knit sweater. His voice has a surprising drawl, as if the vowels were having trouble escaping from his throat; it is the voice developed by some middle-class officers during the war as a medium for addressing the other ranks. However, he seems amiable and without any pomposity; he suggests that it is 'time for a tincture or two' and inquires 'what's your poison?'

Conversation does not range widely. The game of golf he has just finished is exhaustively discussed, as is a rugby match he recently watched on television. There is a good deal of talk about cars, big ends, petrol injection and so forth, and he mentions his Rolls-Royce. Other people at the bar begin some routine banter about wives, who are referred to as 'the boss' or, in mock cockney, 'the trouble and strife,' but he does not join in. He seems slightly in awe of his own wife.

His politics are clearly right wing – more right wing than the present government. But it is not the reactionary chic of some young monetarists; instead it has a faintly old-fashioned, nostalgic air. At one point he asks 'we all pulled together during the war, so why can't we do it now?'

He particularly dislikes the Labour Party, which he seems to believe consists entirely of craven cowards or else paid-up members of the Politburo. You are more puzzled by this ingenuous view when he leaves for home and 'mid-day re-fuelling' and you learn that he is the Prime Minister's husband.

There are two things which everyone who knows him says about Denis Thatcher. The first is that he is extremely nice, a view even shared by his first wife who was also called Margaret. She said he was 'one of the kindest men I have ever known'. The second is that he is perfectly captured in the

Private Eye column 'Dear Bill,' which is presented as a fortnightly letter from Thatcher to one of his golfing chums and drinking companions.

The column is so accurate about his language and tastes that there is some gossip in Westminster that there is a Mole in the Thatcher camp who reports to the author. John Wells. Recent columns about the trip to Lusaka and a disastrous holiday on the island of Islay have particularly delighted those in the know. One associate says that the real summer holiday was actually worse than the *Private Eye* description. 'It's exaggerated, of course, and it doesn't catch his real affection for Margaret. But he really does use phrases like "don't like the cut of that man's jib".'

People tend to see him in terms of small vignettes, flashes which illuminate the man. He actually does say 'tincture' when he means a drink, and he is given to the extensive use of golfing metaphors. At a formal dinner for the Kenyans this summer he sat next to to the Zambian High Commissioner, a strikingly handsome black woman. The dessert was pineapple chunks served in a scooped-out pineapple. Thatcher helped himself, and left two chunks joined together hanging over the lip of the fruit. 'There you are, nicely teed-up for you,' he said to the baffled diplomat.

At a dinner for Hua he was placed between Lords Carrington and Soames, old friends from Eton days. 'They talked behind Denis, they talked in front of Denis, they did everything except talk to Denis,' someone who was sitting nearby says.

He is intensely and emotionally involved with his wife's public appearances. At the big confidence debate in March which led to the Labour Government's fall, Denis could be heard muttering to himself, egging her on from the gallery, though she could not possibly have heard him.

There is a tradition that nobody applauds at press conferences, but in April surprised reporters at Central Office occasionally heard a loud burst of clapping from the back of the room whenever the lady gave a particularly trenchant answer. When they looked round they saw it was Denis.

He accompanies her on most of her set-piece trips, and

during the election could be seen constantly with her, a respectful few feet behind. As she plunged into crowds he would cry 'get her out of there or there'll be an accident!' On the embarrassing occasion when she cradled a new-born calf he said grimly, 'If we're not careful, we'll have a dead calf on our hands.'

All this is, no doubt, wise advice, yet nobody seems to pay any attention and the caravanserai of aides, detectives, journalists and TV crewmen moves remorselessly on.

Only rarely does he let his own views become public. At the Tory conference this year one speaker praised the arrival of the South African mixed rugby team. The delegates burst into loud applause, as did Denis until he noticed that the whole of the Cabinet was silent, when he too suddenly froze.

Like a lot of people with strong political views, he is not terribly interested in politics as such. He has an almost unbounded admiration for his wife, and will excitedly praise a speech or a Commons performance. Then, realizing that he is not the most unbiased judge, he will add diffidently 'you have to remember, I'm a fan.'

He rarely speaks ill of individuals; not surprisingly, Ted Heath is one of the few people he is unpleasant about. He tends to believe that all Labour MPs are unrepentant Marxists, unless they prove themselves innocent by, say, joining the Conservative Party. Among the men he most admires are Reg Prentice, Lord George-Brown and Frank Chapple.

They met in 1949 when he had been invited to make up the numbers at a dinner on the night she was adopted Tory candidate for Dartford. He gave her a lift back to London that night, and they began their courting more or less in secret. Their engagement leaked out just before polling day in the 1951 election.

He was $10\frac{1}{2}$ years older than her and was joint general manager of the family firm, the Atlas Preservative Company of Erith. This was the subject of successive takeovers and was the reason why he ended his business career on the board of a Burmah Oil subsidiary. His compulsory retirement at the age of 60 was within two months of her election as Tory leader.

Friends say that he was 'staggered' at her elevation, which came as suddenly to him as to everyone else including her. 'You must remember that Denis is the kind of chap who would never imagine that a woman might become leader of the Conservative party,' one associate says. 'He was shattered. For a year he was like a man in a trance; he simply didn't have the faintest idea of what to do.'

He has recovered remarkably well. One of the people closest to her says 'he does a frightful job in a more conscientious way than it is reasonable to expect.' (The Prime Minister's spouse, almost uniquely in the West, has no financial or secretarial help and has to do everything for himself.)

The moment she became leader the decision was taken to keep him right out of the limelight. The one press interview he has given was to *The Financial Times* on the subject of railway sleepers – he is still a director of a firm that makes them. It was felt that it would be quite unfair to expose him to publicity and to the crafty tactics of journalists. Interviews with Denis would end up as goodies to be tossed out to Tory papers in exchange for favours. Last but far from least – and her people tend to skate round this – was the fear that his blunt right-wing views might prove embarrassing.

He now seems to enjoy the round of trips and has achieved a certain social relaxation. At factories and businesses he will linger behind occasionally to chat with evident genuine interest.

He is, those close to Mrs Thatcher say, highly influential but not in a direct political sense. In other words she doesn't ask for his views on immigration or the unions or monetary policy, though she might consult him on business matters. But he is good at persuading her to delegate – her neurotic belief that nobody can do a job, from running the country to washing up, better than she can means that she takes on more work than is good for her.

She also depends on him at times for judgements about people. The Tory party runs to a large extent on the kind of opinions formed in the clubs and smoking rooms. It's a world which she knows nothing about, and ignorance has led to some woeful choices as personal aides. 'But Denis can spot a wrong 'un, one MP says, 'and she seems to trust his advice about people.'

At home he is entirely supportive, buoying her up at her lowest moments. 'When she gets back for those famous little weeps he's always there to console her,' one former aide says. George Gardiner's biography of her quotes him at the time of the 'milk-snatcher' row which caused her intense unhappiness and anguish. He said 'to hell with this, why not pack it up?' though she gritted her teeth and carried on

Visitors to the various Thatcher homes say that he plays a Johnnie Craddock role, fixing the drinks and the wine while she does the food. He is successful in this task: 'Denis has a sharp eye for the refill,' one guest says appreciatively.

One visitor complained tentatively that cooking dinner was perhaps not the best use of the Leader of the Opposition's time. 'Oh, don't stop her, it's her form of therapy,' he explained. But he is not spared her infuriating habit of putting people down in small ways.

Another dinner guest, this time in Kent, says that Denis was pouring the wine at lunch and remarked 'I think you'll rather like this claret.' She replied crisply: 'How do you know? You only bought it at the off-licence this morning.'

'He's had to learn how to be married to the Prime Minister, after 28 years of being just married to Margaret Thatcher,' a friend says, 'and there's no doubt he's learning fast. She doesn't like being disagreed with, and so instead of just leaping in with his opinion, he'll start by saying "You're probably right my dear, you usually are . . ."'

'The odd thing is that in some ways Denis is the archetypal old-style Heath man,' another associate says. 'He really does believe in free enterprise, letting the chaps who know about it get on with it. But he's not terribly interested in the nuances, he'd rather be out playing golf.'

Shortly after the election a reporter overheard him say 'We're going off to Portugal for a holiday next week' and the paper promptly printed a big exclusive story about Margaret Thatcher's secret holiday. In fact Denis was just off for a golfing trip with his old friend Bill Deedes, the editor of the

Daily Telegraph, who bears such a close physical resemblance to him.

His relations with the press are prickly. Like the spouses of many leading politicians, he has not developed the same tough hide as the MPs themselves have, so that criticism which she can just about shrug off he takes painfully to heart. He has brisk views about certain journalists, particularly political ones. There was an incident in the first year when he got into a row with a reporter who had written something disparaging about her, and onlookers thought (wrongly) that Denis was going to hit him. Since then he has become somewhat calmer.

'It has been a very happy marriage,' one close associate says, 'and he deserves great credit for keeping the family together and united. Sometimes I think she might have preferred someone a bit more dashing, a bit more politically sophisticated – say Peter Carrington with John Biffen's views. But really, you know, she couldn't have done any better than she has.'

12 November 1979   **Simon Hoggart**

Your friendly neighbourhood terrorist

Above the house a chopper buzzed and circled, a robot mosquito too big to swat. 'My mother,' said the housewife, frowning up through a bent Venetian blind, 'was a real Christian woman, the kind that never wanted to upset anyone. But I remember a peeler coming to the door and she wouldn't let him in. She told him stay there, son, if you don't mind, because the likes of you bring bad luck on the house. And she sprinkled him with holy water.'

'When I was fourteen,' said another housewife, 'me and Eileen and Tom were coming home one night and Eileen knocked over these milk bottles. A peeler came up and shouted at us and we ran round the corner and Tom yelled 'Up the Rebels' and we were lifted for that, taken down to the barracks.'

The stories are endless and the very words used – peeler, barracks – show that long before this decade of trouble

trouble, Ulster Catholics saw the police as an alien occupying force. At the end of the sixties that always strained relationship snapped. Now the police are considered a straightforward arm of the military. Brits in black uniforms. 'Last time they were up here after some man about social security, they all came rushing up in their cars, spilled out and flattened themselves over there and here, behind there with their guns, just like the Brits. We never see them without the Brits, they must be trained by them too.'

So today the people of the Catholic ghettos feel they have no resort in official law and order, even for everyday motoring problems. 'If someone crashed into my car here,' said one man, 'we'd just have to sort if out for ourselves, we'd neither of us report it.' Women nodded agreement. Nothing, they said, would persuade them to call the police, not even if they were raped. Especially not if they were raped. Thus they live in Ulster: whole communities as effectively lawless as America's Wild West or the Deep South after the Civil War, China post-liberation or Sicily after countless invasions.

Yet despite colonization, war, liberation or invasion, crimes and disputes continue and must be dealt with by some group in some way if total chaos is to be averted. In the American West, the people appointed sheriffs; in the Deep South the Ku-Klux-Klan took over. In China, Communist cadres set up People's Courts and struggle meetings; in Sicily the Mafia was born – the word itself means 'place of refuge'. And in the Catholic areas of Northern Ireland, the Irish Republican Army and its sympathizers do the job. This is a message from one of their posters, headed 'Crackdown on Criminals' and signed by the Belfast Brigade of the IRA:

'In the weeks of September the IRA on request from you, the local Republican population, cracked down on Thieves, Vandals, Sex Offenders and Muggers within the areas. The Summary Justice meted out was, because of the war situation, harsh punishment, and in that one Month, the crime rate sharply declined. Our Political Opponents and other Bodies in the areas condemned us, despite the fact that you, the Local People, were aware that known Criminals were being punished. These Criminals in the past were punishing you, by breaking into working-class homes and stealing, mugging old-age-pensioners and sexually assaulting young people. We have canvassed opinion and are happy that you realize the necessity for this short-term though imperfect Policy of dealing with criminals. Our enemies have called for the reintroduction of the hated RUC, as if that would solve things. Areas like the Shankill and Newtownards Rd, where they do patrol, have a crime rate five times ours: so clearly they are not the answer. Crimes reported to us by the People, and demanding action, will be dealt with. First offenders will be given an initial warning. Ideas from you for a less arbitrary method of adjudication (People's Courts etc) will be studied.'

That message, or words to its effect, must have been duplicated thousands of times across time and the world. This time, it applies to a part of the British Isles. At the moment, Sinn Fein – the political arm of the IRA – operates five Belfast advice centres open six days a week and four smaller centres open only at night. To their shabby barricaded doors come the people of the area with their complaints: an old woman has water coming through the ceiling, a wife isn't getting her family allowance, kids setting bonfires are frightening an elderly couple, a woman has had her handbag stolen, another woman wails of her battering husband.

Sinn Fein also run crêches for working women, three People's Co-operatives for cheaper food, transport for prisoners' families, and the People's Taxis – eight passengers crushed into old London taxis for 10p each. They spearhead ring road protests, tennants' associations, demolition demands, and environmental enquiries. They organize children's bands and children's holidays in the South and when new groups need help to organize, they teach them anything necessary from how to run off stencils to the writing of press statements. And they are, for better or for worse, the law.

In any country, in peace time, criminal statistics are tricky figures, capable of being interpreted in many different ways. In Northern Ireland, an outstandingly law-abiding community until the end of the sixties, any attempt to separate 'ordinary' crime from that connected with the troubles is well-nigh impossible. Of the 55 women currently serving sentence, 51 have committed apparently 'ordinary' crimes. Yet 32 are presently involved in demanding political status and the Northern Ireland Office reckons the nineteen left have all had something to do with the troubles.

Male connections are even more inextricable. Of 1,859 convicted during 1978, only 48 are imprisoned for offences unlikely to be anything but 'ordinary' (sex offenders, drugs). The rest, whether guilty of dangerous driving, burglary, riotous behaviour, or malicious damage, could well have done what they did for the cause. Even the destruction of telephone boxes, a common vandals' crime in London, could, in Ulster, be done to prevent informers telephoning out.

The police, sealed off in the outside world, cannot pin down motives with any certainty. British law denies the existence of political crime on the grounds that, in a democracy, wrongs should be righted by the vote and not by violence. The men and women in Ulster prisons demand political status because, among many other grievances, they resent being treated as common criminals when they are arrested as uncommon criminals, under the Emergency Provisions Act. Confusion reigns.

But on the inside, in the areas, it is easier to mark out the motives for crime, easier to distinguish the ordinary from the political. Partly because of this, anger is endemic – they *know* who does what and why, or doesn't do it. Because they know, back doors are still left trustingly open, car doors remain unlocked. Nevertheless, ordinary crimes are committed and problems arise. Who copes? Your man, the Godfather, the paramilitary, the IRA.

'This woman down the road, her boys are getting drinks at the local pub, under age. So she went to your man. The pub got two warnings and then it was blown up.' 'This woman, her husband kept beating her up, wouldn't give her any money. She went to your man and he got a good lacing.' A man rapes a girl and gets a concrete block dropped on his feet. Another mugs an old lady and gets kneecapped (these days, more generally a flesh wound in buttocks or calves). Your man visits lads making trouble and they don't make trouble again.

Am I saying, then, that the IRA and its cohorts are some kind of gun-toting social workers? Do I pretend that men who maim and kill children with random bombs are actually Clark Kents, always ready to strip into Supermen and zoom off to avenge the weak? The myth of the vigilante, the Robin Hood, the Jesse James, is ancient and seductive and, in everyday life, grim; a lot nearer to the real Mafia than the surreal Superman. The heart may leap up to hear of one crime avenged and sink with horror to hear of another, far murkier, execution.

Whatever you get, you pay for, and the price of unofficial justice is high. Under-age drinking may be stopped in one place only to be encouraged at another, run by the paramilitary. Random juvenile vandalism may be prevented but the same lads may then be recruited for far more destructive and lethal jobs. Battered women may be protected one day and battered by their protectors another for stepping out of line. The paramilitary look after their own on the understanding that their own will look after them.

This arrangement is, at best, rough justice, but what other options are there when, for whatever reason, official justice has been rejected? If all the normal barriers have broken down, they must be rebuilt in some form, however rough, and at least in close communities, forced in upon themselves and clearly identifiable, a great deal is known about each individual member, a fact that offers short-cuts to decisions on guilt that, in London, would require a vast organization to establish. Even then, mistakes are made. Even then, some would say, justice is often rough enough.

The community role of the IRA is the acceptable face of terrorism and there always is one. Guerrillas turn monstrous faces to the world, murderers' masks, the black visages of psychopaths. But the faces turned inward, towards their own people, are different; and unless we recognize the human beings beneath the masks we shall never understand how they gain and keep support, and so never resolve the war.

19 February, 1980   **Jill Tweedie**

The Law on us

*The People of Britain v. the Judges, Ex parte Peach.

Before Lord Mugger, Lord Dunnem, Lord Void of Tax, Lord Shortcut, and Lord Vox of Populi.

Four out of five Lords of Appeal upheld the decision of the Lord Chief Justice (*The Times* Law Report, November 15, 1979) that the possibility that a member of the public might have been killed by a severe blow on the head from a weapon wielded by a police officer did not amount to 'Circumstances' the 'continuance or possible recurrence' of which was prejudicial to the safety of the public.

Their Lordships refused an appeal by the People of Britain, on application by the relatives of Mr Clement Blair Peach, to order the coroner, Mr John Burton, to summon a jury of inquest.

Lord Mugger said he regarded the matter as straightforward and raising no question of public interest. If the British people had been killed by a blow from a weapon wielded by a police officer, it might have cause for complaint. But what were the facts in this case? Not the British people but a foreigner, a New Zealander, was the deceased. It appeared that the deceased had brought himself into a position of danger by entering a precinct where police officers, in the course of their duty, were wielding weapons. Was it probable that such circumstances would now recur? One might be confident, after the example given to Mr Peach, that New Zealanders would keep out of public precincts.

His Lordship said that the relevant statute admitted of one interpretation only. Section 13 (2) of the Coroners Amendment Act 1926 provides:

If it appears to the coroner . . . that there is reason to suspect . . . (e) that the death occurred in circumstances the continuance or possible recurrence of which is prejudicial to the health or safety of the public . . . he shall proceed to summon a jury.

The relevant words of the statute are *'appears to the coroner'*. It does not say 'appears to the British people'. That would be an extraordinary construction. Was public opinion to be placed above the coroner or even above the House of Lords? (Laughter in court.) His Lordship hoped that a jest would be excused.

In any case, how could it be argued that *any* action of the police in due execution of duty could be 'prejudicial to the . . . public'? He would invite the Director of Public Prosecutions to institute proceedings against the British people for flagrant barratry.

The Coroners Amendment Act 1926 was passed by the legislature at a time when government had a proper respect for law and order. It is true that this Act, by some oversight, explicitly excluded from its provisions cases of death by murder, manslaughter or infanticide. And that in such cases the summoning of a jury had remained mandatory.

However, this was taken care of in that excellent piece of modernization, the Criminal Law Act 1977, section 56 (2):

Without prejudice to the power of a coroner under subsection (2) of section 13 of the Coroners Amendment Act 1926 to summon a jury if it appears to him that there is any reason for doing so, paragraphs (a) and (d) of that subsection (which require him to do so if it appears to him that the deceased came by his death by murder, manslaughter or infanticide . . .) shall cease to have effect.

This clause was a model of lucidity. His Lordship could not praise the parliamentary drafting enough. Indeed he had had a small hand in drafting it himself. One might say that in this clause the ancient right of inquest by jury was Mugged. (Laughter.) But he would not take all credit on himself. The law officers of the Crown, in 1977, disliked the jury system and had helped the measure on. As for MPs, it was no business of this House to inquire into them. His Lordship supposed that they did not know what they were doing. They rarely did. It had perhaps gone through 'on the nod'. He thought it would be injurious to the public interest to discuss the

'*What I don't understand is why everyone is concerned about who shot J.R. when we still don't know who killed Blair Peach.*'
29 May 1980

matter further. He would accordingly dismiss the appeal.

Lord Dunnem concurred, but wished to enter other arguments. Counsel for the British people had cried a long and tedious list of cases and precedents, and had grounded their appeal on the common law and on the antiquity of the custom. His Lordship had not looked far into these cases, but it was true that juries of inquest could be found at very distant times. And what did we find then? In the 13th century an inquest jury was constituted of every male over the age of 12 in four or more neighbouring townships (*Stat. of Marlborough, 1267*). What kind of a precedent was that? Were we to assemble every male from Southall and adjacent boroughs as a jury? (Laughter.) Where? How would a verdict be found? How could irresponsible persons, Asians, persons who had also received blows from the police, be excluded? And how would we be able, now, to exclude from the jury persons of the gentle sex? If we were to have 15-year-old schoolboys might we not have 15-year-old schoolgirls also? (Consternation and laughter in court.)

His Lordship went on to look at other precedents. Fourteenth-century juries did not submit to the orders of the coroner, but went out and inquired into matters themselves. In one case (*K.B. 27/476, King's membrane, no. 31*) the sheriff and coroner twice sent the jurors out into the streets to inform themselves before finding a verdict on the third attempt. What kind of a precedent was that? (Great laughter in court.) His Lordship was aware that there were one or two judges still about who supposed that case law and precedent still had effect, and constituted some part of the common law His learned colleague, Lord Devlin, still argued in this wholly concervative way, but happily his arguments were confined to books which the public was unlikely to read. In these days of modernization it could not be stressed too solemnly that case law was a fetter on the public interest. What common law means is the commonsense of judges, and judges are the only proper persons to determine what is the public interest. He hoped that arguments from antiquity would not be offered to Their Lordships again. He would dismiss the appeal.

Lord Void of Tax was happy to defer to his learned friends.

He only understood about money. Was any matter of money involved here? Was it suggested that compensation be offered to Mr Peach? What good would that do him? (Laughter.) He would dismiss the appeal.

Lord Shortcut said that he had never heard so much rubbish in his life as had been argued by counsel for the British people. If a police officer had executed his duty on Mr Peach, surely that was an end to the matter of Mr Peach? How could a jury help? A jury would be a waste of time. Appeals were a waste of time. Speaking of time, surely Their Lordships were already late for dinner? He would dismiss the appeal.

Lord Vox of Populi, in a dissenting judgement, adverted to several score of cases in the 18th and 19th centuries in which juries had inquired vigilantly into deaths occasioned by military or police action; as, for example, the case of John Lees, the case of Calthorpe Street, &c (*New Society*, 8 & 15 November 1979). He supposed that these cases had established a constitutional principle. He supposed that it was a matter of common law that the British people had established the right of a jury of inquest, a right which had existed in all sensitive cases such as this for 700 years: and that it was a point of constitutional principle that the police were to be placed under the civil power.

His Lordship argued that over-zealous actions by the police were very clearly 'prejudicial to the health and safety of the public' and decidedly came within the meaning of the Act; that he did not know why the legislature struck out this ancient right in 1977, but that he supposed that MPs were unaware of the construction that might be put upon the clause; that in view of other pending cases (as *Kelly v. Merseyside Police*) there was every reason to anticipate the 'continuance or possible recurrence' of such regrettable episodes; that . . . (but the other four Lordships had retired to dinner, and His Lordship's words were held, by the coroner's officer, PC Crackem, to be in contempt of court).

19 November 1979   **E. P. Thompson**

Minor character

An inoffensive character in *Henry IV Part I* (BBC-2) is called Sir Walter Blunt. It is a nice little part somewhere between 'I will, my lord' and the full blooded railway announcements beginning 'My cousin Paddington and change at Crewe' which are such a trial to an actor's memory and sense of direction. Neither Shakespeare nor the BBC could anticipate the appreciation this simple soul would cause.

Blunt pops up quite early – 'Here is a dear and true-industrious friend' – and is embarrassingly busy T 'How now, good Blunt, thy looks are full of speed' – until he mercifully snuffs it at Shrewsbury. 'A gallant knight he was. His name is Blunt.' Giving Falstaff occasion for some particularly telling thoughts. On honour.

Apart from dear old Blunt, 'Friend to the king', another unexpected eye-catcher was the king himself. You can never be sure that the title part of the play is the juiciest. I bitterly remember being cast as Julius Caesar and, after a few abortive forays in a night gown, having the whole cast fall on me and thump me mercilessly, like a scene out of *Murder on the Orient Express*. As the regicide Henry IV, Jon Finch is, like Lady Macbeth, for ever washing of his hands.

Everything in this beautifully balanced play has its alter ego. The great Irish thinker – no, thinker – Patrick Campbell, wrote a persuasive piece explaining that Prince Hal and Hotspur were the same man, more or less. Falstaff, the second father figure, was I thought rather innocently played by Anthony Quayle, like a big, blue-eyed baby or a teddy bear Hal could throw away, outgrown. There is something of pagan Christmas in Falstaff, or Hogmanay. Hal even calls him 'Old Acquaintance.' Burns never says specifically whether Old Acquaintance should be forgot, leaving it an open question. Some, Prince Hal among them, would argue that the more old acquaintance is forgotten the merrier.

A little more elbow room and breathing space would have

improved the robbery at Gadshill and the battle at Shrewsbury. Despite the Prince's forecast of blustery weather, fog came down impenetrably at Shrewsbury, blocking out the cast of dozens the BBC had, no doubt, assembled for the battle.

10 October 1979   **Nancy Banks-Smith**

Crashing out in Castro's cha-cha

Poor President Carter accumulates egg on his face thicker than any President since Eisenhower. He is now held responsible for everything from the energy crisis to the Middle East to Hurricane Harriet to the impending extinction of the snail-darter fish, imperilled by the building of the new Tennessee Dam. I admit I know little of the snail-darter fish, nor specially care, but wherever it is going it looks like taking President Carter with it.

Now he is lumbered with Cuba once again. It is not exactly a re-run of October 1962 but there are some who would like to see it develop into a promising crisis, even graver than that of the snail-darter fish.

I cannot quite understand why it is so heinous for the Russians to keep their soldiers in Cuba while it is quite acceptable for the Americans to keep theirs in Europe, including this semi-sceptred isle. That is to say, I think it is ridiculous and provocative for either of them to do it, and I could wish for both sides to get the hell home, but if it is all right for one I cannot see why it is otherwise for the other. In any case it always seems to be forgotten in this context that the Russians have for years been openly maintaining a naval base at Cienfuegos in Cuba, and the Americans have had their military establishment at Guantanamo in Oriente province since 1903, no less. This produces the nice paradox that the two main actors in the cold war deal both retain quite powerful forces within the territory of a third nation, and only appear to notice the fact about every 15 years.

This business of mutual electronic keyhole-watching is, I

suppose, inevitable and forever, but my, what a waste of time and money is this folk-dance of the free-booters. Russian soldiers go to Cuba, Cuban soldiers go to Africa, American soldiers go to England, English soldiers go to Ireland, hands down, turn about, follow round the middle, ring-a-roses and we all fall down.

I know it is very wrong of me, but I find it quite difficult to take Cuba seriously. The ghost of the musical comedy crook Batista still haunts Castro's Havana for me. For one thing, Cuba was the first People's Democracy I ever experienced in a decent, not to say lush climate; hitherto I had always associated a somewhat cheerless Communist system with the somewhat cheerless conditions of East Europe, where it always seemed to be four o'clock on a November afternoon with everybody shutting up the bars. Not so in Cuba. The inter-reaction of didactic socialism with Caribbean-Latin temperament was in the early days almost hilarious. I had known the place very slightly in the corrupt old days, when it had seemed rather like a West Indian Soho. After Castro I turned up again (to my great surprise one didn't need a visa; maybe you do now) in a terribly clapped-out old Constellation filled with slightly tipsy trades-unionists from the North of England, I would suppose Party members to a man, to whom this was the daddy of all outings.

Havana greeted them – and indeed me, since I was inextricably by now a TU groupie – in great style, with gallons of rum punch and a little guitar band playing in our honour what they must have supposed to be the British social-democratic Hymn, the Red Flag. After a shaky start the tune within a couple of bars turned into a cha-cha-cha. 'Let cowards flinch – cha – and traitors sneer – cha – we'll keep the cha-cha flying here.' It was much better fun than Blackpool. Anyone who can turn that rather dismal melody into cha-cha-cha, said I, has my vote.

I turned to find that my typewriter had been nicked before I ever got to the Customs. Not that it mattered much; I got to do little work in Cuba. I was supposed to be interviewing Old Faithful, the great Fidel, for a rather stern American journal called *The Atlantic Monthly*. He gave me at least half a dozen appointments all over the island, and stood me up for every one. In the end I abandoned the project and turned in for my one and only early night in the Hotel Habana Libre, which had transformed itself from a Hilton into a sort of Gulag.

At about three in the morning I awoke from a deep sleep to find the bedroom full of bearded bodyguards, and among them the great man himself. He sat on the end of the bed and said: 'We shall talk, no? I have much to say.'

And indeed he doubtless did, since Sr Fidel Castro has rarely been known to utter a sentence less than two hours long. But what it was I know not, since I had taken the precaution of swallowing two deep narcotics, and by the time I awoke again in the morning the audience was over and the room was empty.

I have never seen Fidel Castro since, and I greatly doubt if I ever shall. One does not trifle with history.

As far as that goes, I feel a kinship with the snail-darter fish, about to be rendered extinct by President Carter's Tennessee Dam. Surely one day we shall all be reunited in that great Habana Hilton in the sky.

17 September 1979   **James Cameron**

Piggy at the top

Allegations about the Lucullan dining habits of top London Transport executives were confirmed by independent auditors last week. They found that executive meals were being subsidized by up to £16 per head and fleets of chauffeur-driven cars were being used unnecessarily. Tales of this kind about senior managements leak out from time to time.

In the City and big companies all over the country, good eating is part of the rich fabric of everyday top management life. In recent years there has been a great boom in directors' dining rooms. This is partly because our peculiar tax laws make meals in the boardroom tax deductible, whereas if they take guests out to restaurants (unless they are foreign guests) there are not tax advantages.

To meet the demand there are now many new agencies providing mainly female cooks to cater for the boardrooms. One such agency, M and N, has about a hundred upper class girls on its books, many of whom work permanently with a company. Philippa Novis, herself an accomplished cook, founded the agency.

'My girls have to be very presentable,' she says. 'And they have to be excellent cooks.' She started the agency by selling her service to City firms, knocking on doors, and hoping to get past hall porters through to a director. 'They are so astonished to see a girl in the City that they are usually jolly friendly. Anyway men love talking about anything to do with their tummies. I show them all our girls' menus, and it usually works.'

Boardroom cooking, in fact, has become the fashionable thing for smart young girls. 'They used to do secretarial courses, or go into antiques, after finishing school. But now they all want to cook. I have thousands of girls to choose from.'

Caroline Johnstone is 26 and has been cooking for the boardroom of one merchant bank for five years. She is the daughter of a retired Army officer and first learned to cook at a convent school in Newbury. She cooks for between eight and 16 people a day in the boardroom. 'They have three courses each day. They love their puddings,' she says. 'They like a lot of messed-up starters too.' She listed some of last week's offerings: blinis with caviar, smoked salmon and sour cream to start, followed by steak, kidney, mushroom and oyster pie, then meringue piled high with strawberries and cream. During the week they also had Lamb Cutlets Reform (rolled in egg, breadcrumbs, chopped ham, and fried), with gherkins in port, cheese soufflé, bœuf en croute, Armenian lamb, whitebait, fillet steak, home-made ice cream, loin of veal in cream and brandy.

Caroline has an unlimited budget for food, and can spend whatever she likes. 'I order it all from the best butcher in Smithfield and the best greengrocer and fishmonger. They just send it round. I suppose it costs about 20 per cent more that way than if I were shopping for myself. It does mean that if there's suddenly an extra person for lunch my suppliers will rush round some extra at the last moment. The firm that supplies our meat gives me a free joint for myself each week.'

She doesn't choose the wine, but orders it up from the firm's cellars each week. They have a drink before lunch, and then between 1/3 and 1/2 a bottle of wine each.

'The kitchen is lovely,' she says. 'I can have whatever equipment I want. I just go and tell the directors I need something or other, and they always let me have it.' She has her own waitresses, four of them in black dress, white apron and black bow tie. 'They're all hand picked by *moi*,' she says. 'They have to be of the highest appearance. I also have the most delicious Irish girl who does the pots and pans and vegetables. I've trained her myself.'

The boardroom, she says, is heavy oak panelling. 'Very masculine, with great heavy chairs. I've just persuaded them to add some plants which they seem to like. They are served from silver salvers, beautiful silver coffee pots, silver cigar and cigarette boxes, and lovely cut glass.' But, she says, this is not the grandest dining room in the building. The chairman has an even grander one, with grander food, a butler, and Georgian furniture.

Miss Johnstone says that usually there are guests for meals. 'It makes me a bit wild if they don't have guests,' she admits. 'It's important guests should be well-fed. If they over-eat it's their fault. There's an enormous choice and nothing's forced on them.'

She says she has cooked for firms in the past who run their directors' dining rooms on a much grander scale. Her present firm, she says, is relatively modest. 'With one firm of stockbrokers I cooked for about eight directors. They had to have a choice of three items each day. That meant I had to prepare two different hot dishes, two vegetables, two sorts of potatoes, and a complete cold table as well.

'They were awfully piggy. They used to eat the lot! Three courses, and then the alternative two dishes as well. There was never a scrap left.'

These days weren't businessmen more worried about heart attacks, cholesterol and being over-weight? 'Oh well, my lot, in my dining room don't seem to fuss at all. Though once a year for a couple of days they don't finish up their puds, so I know something's up. I send in a message and ask if they've got their medical check-ups that week, and they say "How did you guess?" But they forget all that in a day or two.'

Phillipa Novis also provides cooks for companies' special sprees. She sends girls with hampers to Ascot, Wimbledon, Glyndebourne, and Twickenham.

'We had such fun at the Varsity match!' she says. 'They ate masses and masses of food. We gave them something we called Scrum Half Soup.' She also sends cooks to company holidays - chalets in Switzerland, shooting parties in the Highlands, trips to villas in the Bahamas. One or two girls have got married as a result of these occasions.

'One girl went to a shooting lodge in Scotland for the weekend, and now she's Lady So-and-So, married to the deliciously eligible bachelor who was organizing it. Perhaps we should start a marriage bureau too!'

She says she vets her girls very carefully. 'I look at the way they dress, and I look at their fingernails.' 'Sloane Ranger' gear is almost *de rigueur*: the little black patents with a gold strap round the heel, the black velvet hair-bands, the silk scarves knotted under the bottom lip like a guardsman's chin-strap.

Companies are rightly wary of talking about their lunching habits. Approaches to press officers in 20 or so top firms in London met with remarkable frostiness. At Rothschild's Bank a manager said he would be delighted to let me talk with the boardroom butler, but next day the butler had been given strict instructions from 'the very highest grade' that he was not to say a word to me. The National Westminster Bank, renowned throughout Fleet Street for its dining facilities, wouldn't let me talk to their chef. 'We don't wish to go into it in detail. It's not something we wish to talk about.' Unilever became a little hysterical and warned me that the whole conversation had been recorded, so I had better not misquote them.

Lunching facilities at companies at all levels are a touchy subject. Most companies have about three separate dining rooms for different grades of staff, and it's often a vital matter of status. It is a class indicator, and a class divider.

Hospitals tend to divide up their dining rooms. At one London teaching hospital, for instance, there are actually four different rooms for different grades, one for all staff, another for staff nurses, sisters, and technicians, another for doctors, and a select one for the consultants.

Most organizations have dining rooms for staff, middle management and senior management, with a boardroom for directors. But when I asked companies about this odd practice, they became extremely defensive. 'It's just an administrative matter,' or 'There isn't room to seat everyone together,' or 'I'm sure more junior members of staff would feel uncomfortable eating with senior grades.'

Guardian City journalists, occasionally lured into these dens of iniquity, report on the changing fashions in food. The smart thing is to provide food not readily available elsewhere. Avocado pears used to be smart, but now that *hoi polloi* eat them in wine bars, king size prawns have taken their place. Quails are popular at the moment, but Chicken Kiev has become vulgar. Since smoked salmon remains expensive it stays popular.

Exotic fruits, specially flown in, are coming into fashion: Chinese gooseberries, passionfruit, and persimmons. Profiteroles, pineapples in kirsch, and gooey gateaux are still favourites.

Banks rate as the biggest eaters. Nat West are voted the most lavish, and the Midland as a respectable worst with 'horrible dry quiche'. Equitable Life is reported to provide excellent sole, and the British Insurance Association has a special line in delicious Old English-style cooking. ICI has its own house in fashionable Smith Square, where executives entertain lavishly. Sperry Rand is reported to have had the best New Year party, a buffet with big prawns and fillet steak.

Since so many companies have a problem with top heavy management, it's probably as good a way as any to kill off excess directors.

11 February 1980 **Polly Toynbee**

Charity begins with the vicar

Inflation is no respecter of the dog collar. Nor, it would appear from a new charity scheme in the diocese of Guildford, does it take account of the costs clergy face in acquiring more secular types of clothing.

The Dorking branch of the Women's Royal Voluntary Service, mindful of how vicars' salaries have fallen behind those of many of the laity, has launched a discreet service to pass hand-me-down clothes to hard-pressed clergymen and their families. The scheme has been announced to the parsons of the diocese in a note sent to them by the Vicar of Dorking, the Reverend John Lamb. The notice tells them that high quality 'nearly new' clothing of all kinds has been set aside by the WRVS for those clergymen in need. Already, two vicars have responded to the offer, Mr Lamb said yesterday. One has asked for clothing for his children, the other has requested a suit for himself.

He said it was obviously embarrassing for clergymen to have to ask for second-hand clothing in this way, but many were finding it difficult to make ends meet, especially those with young children.

Mr Lamb said he knew clergymen in the diocese who were receiving supplementary benefit. 'Until lay members of the Church, some of whom are earning £10,000, wake up to the financial problems of the clergy this sort of thing will be necessary,' he said.

He was not worried that vicars in the diocese might be put in the embarrassing position of wearing cast-off shoes or sports jackets that could be recognized by members of their congregation. 'Most of these clothes are off-the-peg, Marks and Spencer items that everybody wears,' he said.

24 March 1980   **Paul Keel**

Initially amateur

I fancy the last summer of the 1970s will be remembered by cricketers only for India's vain but glorious last-day try and the fact that Essex and Somerset together ended a barren century by sharing the four trophies.

By the time Essex had won the Benson and Hedges final in July their lead already looked so unassailable that the Bow bells pealed plaudits for a good six weeks as only mathematicians refused to join in the dance. Somerset, typically, hesitated until the last weekend of the season to put themselves and us out of our misery.

Might there be a tiny grain of logic in my theory that honours came latest to Essex and Somerset because they were, weren't they, the last two counties to climb out of the old boy network and forgo the amateur 'No 6 all right, vicar?' 'Take the top end, my lord' – traditions that used to so decorate the County Championship with Harlequin colours?

I listed in these columns a few weeks ago a lovely litany of old three-initial men who used to play for Essex. If anything Somerset were even more keen in my boyhood to perpetuate the cult of the 'come and have a game in the vac, old boy, and we'll have a spot of shootin' on the Sunday.' Certainly that August Bank Holiday game was always a cinch for Gloucester when Somerset's batting order between Gimblett and Hazell was autocratically sprinkled with the hyphens and preceding initials of those who donned striped blazers for the tea interval and wrote autographs with disdain as if they were signing school reports or their card in the President's putter.

I can close my eyes and rattle them off still without a crib (but as I do I realize at last that some of them were fine players too: perhaps any theory's already blown): R. J. O. Meyer, N. S. Mitchell-Innes, E. F. Longrigg, B. G. Brocklehurst, M. M. Walford, G. F. S. Woodhouse, C. J. P. Barnewell. A. T. M. Jones and, before my time, two of the most gorgeously named chappies of them all, Mr C. C. C. Case and Mr J. W. Seamer.

On Saturday morning at Lord's when Rose and Denning set off with such a dash I thought of Bill Andrews, four times sacked by the county and four times reinstated, who was one of the stalwart pros who played when the amateurs joined for all those Augusts long ago. As county coach Andrews 'discovered' Rose and Denning and put them in his famous county under-15 XI in the 1960s. He found half the team on Saturday. I hoped Andrews was sucking his pipe somewhere near the Tavern flushed with pride as two of his boys went forth.

Then at tea time the BBC, give them their due, actually asked him up to their eyrie and there he was airing his views to the nation. In itself that interview was a deserved tribute to a man who has so revelled in bucking the established amateur order of things with far more nagging accuracy than he ever managed with those old inswingers of his. He has been Somerset cricket's fifth columnist ever since the morning, 50 years ago next May, that he joined the county team for the first time at Bristol Temple Meads to travel up to Edgbaston. The senior pro, Tom Young, was sitting in a corner of the compartment. Nervous and wanting a boost, young Bill had asked, 'Mr Young, am I the worst cricketer ever to play first class cricket?' Said Young: 'No, son, there is one worse who plays for Glamorgan.'

Bill used to write a column for one of my papers, the *Bristol Evening World*. That's when I first met him. Before then, when Bill had been dropped yet again by the county and was playing league cricket in Scotland of all places, he would ring down his latest Perthshire bowling analysis to the sports editor, who would dot the ground where Somerset were playing that day with placards screaming More Great Bowling By Andrews. So soon he was reinstated again! One of his sackings, so the rumour went, was because he stuck a Labour poster in his window during the 1959 election. I only saw him bowl once. I cannot even remember his action, probably because we Tizered Gloucestershire children were still rolling uncontrollably about the grass after watching the amazing elastic tangle of limbs that Bertie Buse required to unravel before he could propel a cricket ball.

Once, went the joke on the other side of the Avon, R. J. O. Meyer thought to liven up morale by buying a piano for the Somerset dressing room. He went to a reputable second-hand salesman in Bath and asked 'May I have a piano for my team?' Replied the ivory dealer: 'A fair swap, guv, a fair swap!'

But now at last they have done it, and like Essex, with a rare vengeance, and to us behind the ropes at any rate they have done it with a team of professionals who have continued to play up in the same amateur image of their county's cricket that Sir Neville logged long ago – 'fresh and gusty and smacking of the land.' Why, even their smiling champion from the Caribbean won them their day of days, with a warm West Country breeze of an innings. But, now I come to think of it, doesn't the great I. V. A. Richards always insist that the scoreboard carries all his three initials? And if anyone's in line for a knighthood, he is. Somerset's amateur roots grow deep.

13 September 1979   **Frank Keating**

Too cruel to be condoned

I had never before been inside a prison. My reason for visiting Walton Prison in Liverpool and Brixton Prison in London was to obtain some first-hand idea of the conditions which the authorities themselves expect will explode into new prison riots before long and probably before this year is out. This is not journalistic panic-mongering but the almost fatalistic foreboding of the Prison Service itself from its political master, the Home Secretary, downwards.

It may be that an explosion is needed to open the way for the emergency measures to relieve the overcrowding which Mr Whitelaw funked when he made his statement to the House of Commons on April 30. It is an open secret that he had failed to persuade the judges to accept an increase in remission or any other interference with their sentencing and that he was unwilling to defy them. So perhaps nothing short of serious prison disturbances can restore the judiciary to its senses or bring home to a law-and-order-minded public that a nation which wills the end must will the penal means.

The Home Office and the Prison Service are throwing open their gates to reporters and television cameras in the hope of alerting the public to the true and abominable condition of the prisons and in the more slender hope of making the public care. For the crisis in the prisons goes deeper than the over-population of rotting Victorian gaols. The Prison Service has lost its purpose and imprisonment itself a good deal of its precious moral rationalization, and the result is that there is no longer any means of justifying prison conditions in Britain; they are, quite simply, uncivilized and inhumane.

'Dickensian' is the cliché, but the prisons are worse than Dickensian; at least that is the view of the governor of Brixton, Michael Selby. The people in his prison are technically innocent men, and, he says, 'I really don't see why we should treat them worse than one hundred years ago in terms of the standards of the society outside.'

Walton Prison, which like most of the Victorian prisons is literally falling down, is the largest and one of the worst of the local prisons. Its governor, William Driscoll, wonders: 'How would people like to be confined in the space of a bathroom with two people they don't know for three years?' and, showing me one of the landing recesses which has to do for 90 men, says: 'You've got to smell ninety pots' worth of shit and piss to know what it's like.'

These are not the reactions of a squeamish middle class reporter seeing and smelling prison for the first time. These are the sort of things that experienced prison governors are saying about their own prisons. Enlightened men? Yes, but neither of them wet liberals. One of the first things that strikes you about visiting prisons is how nearly everybody – governors, assistant governors, prison officers, and prisoners is – agreed that their condition is deplorable and well-nigh intolerable for those who have to live or work in them.

Liverpool, with accommodation for about a thousand, is

over-populated to the tune of 1,600. Brixton, designed to hold about 700, is regularly stuffed with 1,000 or more. Out of a total prison population of 44,000, about 11,000 – most of them in local prisons or remand centres – are locked up two or three to a cell. This cell-sharing is the most remarked upon aspect of overcrowding, but not necessarily the most evil. The worst feature of it is the lack of integral toilet facilities; that apart, company for many prisoners is preferable to solitude, especially where staff shortages or difficulties are causing cell doors to be closed for, in some cases, 23 hours a day.

Overcrowding, one soon begins to discover, is a syndrome which aggravates the cruellest and most fundamental aspect of imprisonment, the loss of liberty. Prisoners are powerless and helpless creatures; they can move nowhere, do nothing outside their cells without supervision. Overcrowding exacerbates under-staffing. Because security is nearly always put first, there are not enough officers to ensure the right of daily exercise, to supervise visits to the library or canteen, to enable workshops to function or to enable cell doors to be left open so that prisoners can socialize on the landings. One prisoner at Walton, asked how he was treated by the screws, said simply: 'Some let you out. Some don't.' He meant, to go to the lavatory.

Victims of these conditions at Liverpool include not merely the standard population of a local prison – short sentence prisoners of one kind or another, including those who ought to be in mental institutions or hostels for drunks – but getting on for 600 long-term prisoners (five years of more) who are there for allocation but who for want of places in other institutions may experience Liverpool's crowded conditions for as long as two years.

At Brixton the condition of remand patients, innocent until found guilty, is worse than the condition of convicted men in the training prisons. The condition of the prisoners on 'F' wing of the hospital is especially deplorable. There, through no fault of the doctors or staff, sick men – disturbed and unhappy creatures – have to be treated in crumbling cells. Many of them are there because the hospital unions will not accept them in psychiatric institutions. At exercise in their squalid, overcrowded yard they are as pitiable a sight as in any print of Old Bedlam.

How did these deplorable conditions come about? Through years and years of neglect, often chronicled but never remedied. Society prefers to place its rejects and its enemies out of sight and out of mind, leaving them either, as between the wars, to the reformers or, as since 1966 – the year of the Mountbatten Report – to the security men.

There are two fateful years in post-war penal history. In 1963 the Great Train Robberi took place; in 1966 the master spy George Blake escaped from Wormwood Scrubs. The train robbers were given sentences ranging up to 30 years. Until then 14 years was enough to catch the breath; before the war, three years was sufficient to make a headline. The train robbers' case set off a monstrous escalation of sentences, dragging all the others up. The Blake escape, which led to the Mountbatten Report, shifted the whole emphasis of the prison system in the direction of security, pre-empting resources both of money and men.

The modern crisis of the British prisons can be conveniently dated from those two developments. That crisis consists in more and more people being sentenced to serve longer and longer in prisons, the over-riding purpose of which has become simply to contain them. Escapes are now minimal – of dangerous Category A prisoners are virtually non-existent – but the cost has been prodigious and not just in barbed wire, dogs and men; it has meant that every institution containing Category A prisoners has had to revolve around the need for their elaborate incarceration. For all the others, humanity has been made the victim of security.

Meanwhile, the police and the courts – the inputs of the system – have poured more and more of humanity into the social dustbins of the prisons. When the Government has dared to devalue the currency of the prison sentence, as with the introduction of suspended sentences in 1968, the judiciary has before long inflated it once more. In the present atmosphere of Mrs Thatcher's Britain, with the crime rates still rising, the combined rhetoric of law-and-order and taxpayers' revolt ensures that the demand for retribution exceeds the supply of humane and civilized prison accommodation.

If the prisons explode this summer or autumn – at the Home Office they worry about a 'dark November' – the most likely trigger will be the discontent of the prison officers. Industrial action, if it involves putting prisons on virtual lock-up for days or weeks at a time, can make the condition of the prisons finally intolerable. Mutiny can lead to riot.

The unhappiness of the prison staff is a complicated subject. The first thing to remember is that prison officers are also inhabitants of prisons; they work long hours, and often they live in ghettos of tied housing beneath the prison walls. When everything is reckoned in, they are not so badly paid – gross earnings below £7,000 a year are rare – but their financial position depends upon long hours of overtime. These long working hours – 50 a week is about the average – are undesirable in themselves but result also in overtime being a valuable and barterable commodity; at that point it becomes hard to distinguish a security precaution from a restrictive practice.

Working conditions in the prisons – lavatories, the absence of showers or recreational facilities – are scarcely better for the officers than for the prisoners. The environment is brutalizing for everyone. Recruitment these days is largely from industry, from the shop floor, or the growing ranks of the redundant; today's prison officer tends to be imbued with the spirit of modern Britain, that is to say he is simultaneously conservative and militant.

Proverbially he is the authoritarian personality, but whether or not that is the case he is liable to be someone conscious of his own limited attainments and opportunities – perhaps he would have liked to have been a teacher – and inclined to be resentful of the welfare attention he believes to be lavished on the prisoners. Fathers of kids dropped out of tough comprehensive schools where the teachers won't or can't teach are not always enthusiastic about Open University courses for bank robbers.

However, the prison officers do not deserve much of the blame for what's wrong with the prisons. They are a part of what's wrong. Judging from my first impressions, they are also still a large part of what is humanly right about it. They, too, for the most part, find no vocational satisfaction in acting as the turnkeys of an uncaring and thankless society.

Before long Mr Whitelaw will be forced to emergency action to relieve the prison population. Measures to shorten sentences already being served, or to limit future ones, will ease the pressure for a while. Until the law and order industry fills them up again, the prisons will become slightly more humane places.

Emergency measures of that kind, however, can do little to remedy the fundamental wrong. That is that far too many people are in prison who should not be there at all, while of those who should, many are serving sentences of quite excessive severity.

It is a difficult point to drive home in the face of the crime statistics and in the face of a fear of violence which is growing in the country. The harsh penal attitudes of the public – 'serve the bastards right!' – are perhaps part, and an understandable part, of a more general brutalization in a world in which torture, terrorism, and gratuitous violence have become commonplace, brought nearer to home by television but at the same time made less real. Nevertheless, the punishment inflicted in our prisons, day after monotonous day, is too cruel to be condoned. No cheap or easy reform is available. We need fewer prisoners in better prisons, serving shorter sentences. We cannot continue as a society to degrade ourselves in this way.

21 May 1980   **Peter Jenkins**

The game of the name

Mr Anthony Wedgwood Benn, repenting of his Wedgwood, shed it; and then, as if anxious not to give compositors unnecessary labour, truncated himself still further, becoming plain Mr Tony Benn. Mr Mostyn Evans, general secretary of the Transport and General Workers, prefers the shorter form of Moss; a wish generally respected by those who write about him, save only for the editor of *The Times*, who insists on having him called Mr Mostyn (Moss) Evans. Mr Evans is not the only man whom *The Times* thus forbids to mutilate his name. Mr Joe Ashton, Labour MP for Bassetlaw, frequently appears disguised as a Joseph. Mr Bill Sirs is William to *The Times*, though Mr Lionel Murray, who was pictured in *The Times* the other day sharing a rostrum with William and Mostyn (Moss), was allowed to get away with a simple Len. It is time that a delegation, preferably consisting of the managing director, Mr Duke (Marmaduke) Hussey, the paper's political editor Mr Fred (Frederick) Emery and the correspondent in Zimbsbwe, Mr Dan (Daniel) van der Vat, lobbied editor Mr William Rees-Mogg (Bill Mogg) in favour of a man's right to self determination.

Over at the *Daily Telegraph*, meanwhile, they habitually put the Primate of Ireland, Cardinal O' Fiaich, in his place by calling him Cardinal Fee. Why do they not also call the Italian composer Giuseppe Verdi by his anglicized name, which is Joseph Green? We tell the *Telegraph* editor: come off it, Mr Diaichdes.

12 March 1980   **Leader**

The oil and the isles

Our home in the Shetlands was long and yellow and wooden and constructed by my father out of an old Admiralty hut he picked up for £250. He sawed it in half and carried it to the top of a hill where nobody else would build because it was supposed to be haunted by the ghost of a leper woman who had been turned out of the community 200 years before.

We had two rowing boats, a Shetland pony, and a lot of draughts. A cheery man from Edinburgh once came with a television set and an extremely long aerial. We were to be 'an experiment'. The BBC in Scotland wanted to test the range of their transmitters. We never got any pictures but the wind, annoyed by the aerial, threatened to tear the chimney-stack out by the roots. A week later my father wrote to Edinburgh asking them to take the contraption away as quickly as possible.

I used to lie awake at night watching the rain seep through the ex-Admiralty fittings. On a clear day we could see 20 miles through these windows out to the three peaks of Foula, which may explain why someone wanted to convert Admiralty war surplus into a swell hotel.

But one of the worst experiences a man can have is to return home and find the garage converted into a Bar-B-Q pit. And not an ordinary Bar-B-Q pit. This one was a gleaming steel 'n' charcoal monster, a grillers' paradise, tended by a king griller with a wispy beard. When the chef poked at his little charcoal pile I couldn't help wondering if the wind still blew all the smoke back down the chimney.

Now, of course, the house has a television and piped music, and Chateau Death wrought metal, and (until they get cold and go back to Aberdeen) little Filipino waitresses whose job is to flip the carp out of the pool at the front and, giggling, drop them on your plate. It is also crammed full of guests paying £15.50 a night for bed and breakfast. They sign in at the natural pine reception desk, which stands almost exactly where the old diesel generator blew up in 1954.

Not all the changes that have overtaken Shetland recently strike one as forcibly as this. In truth, away from the technology circus at Sullom Voe and the odd service company installation, the island will still satisfy the casual seeker after ethnic purity.

There are still peat banks, crofters, fiddlers, ponies, fishing boats, and red-faced fishermen who will fall off piers when they're consuming vodka, the islands' favourite drink. Not so long ago local businessmen used to send to Aberdeen for records that taught them to talk properly; but now everyone shows off his Shetland patois, which comes out a cross between Chicago Black and Portuguese. (Anti-litter sticker: Bruk An Muk, Redd It Up.)

The weird sense of dislocation is still restricted to those who remember it as it was. Shetlanders were stubbornly isolated. This was part tradition, part latitude; when King William IV died, Lerwick was still doggedly praying for his recovery three weeks later.

In the fifties the newspapers arrived a day late, and it was easier to pick up Radio Luxemburg than the Light Programme. Boys' ambitions were to sign on with the Salveson whaling fleet. The airport was so unused gentlemen practised mashie shots between the runways. Moors were things you left to the sheep. Foreigners were any strangers with binoculars and thin legs who came to look at the birds. Charlie Smith's bus, which rumbled into Lerwick every Saturday at ten, was a hen house on wheels.

Now the cars are all T-registered. The airport employs 700 men, not seven, and a new golf course has been laid down over a swamp. The chip shop has become The Camera Shop. The minister has become a silversmith. The moor below the Admiralty hut has become a mink farm, and the one behind another airstrip.

When things were bad, they used to fly up Lancasters from Lossiemouth to drop food parcels. Now they have supermarkets.

The rapidity of the changes can be measured by what still remains of the past. Maggie Thompson personifies an older form of the pioneering spirit. She is around 50 years old and has lived alone, apart from her sheep and goats and dog, for the past 30 years on a croft at Cott on the west side of Mainland. I had been asked to see if she needed anything.

'Just tar,' she admitted, 'but I can get that from the P & O.' She wanted to repair her roof, though her fingers were badly swollen with arthritis. Inside her house the wood smoke hung so thick you could barely see a face six feet away.

One of her goats, Sweet William, was said to have had the gift of bestowing good fortune. People 'laid him on an aamos' (alms) if he'd pull strings for them. More often than not he did, and would be rewarded with biscuits.

'One woman took first place in the Highlands and Islands Crafts because of William,' said Maggie with some pride. 'And she was from Yorkshire.'

The cultural mix seems fused in A. I. Tulloch. He is a dynamic little man who wears a bow tie and sits behind a large

43

wooden desk in a tiny Lerwick office whose principal decoration is an illustrated version of Rudyard Kipling's poem 'If' . . . In the right light he looks uncannily like a hybrid of Tintin and Harry S. Truman.

AI, as he is universally known, is County Convenor. He has been for five years. This often means, as he puts it, 'making the oil people understand that what is good for them is not necessarily good for Shetland.' It was AI who got the oil people to agree that any tanker caught discharging polluted ballast water would be fined £50,000.

In his spare time he tends to the family knitwear business. Tullochs of Shetland created a world fashion almost single-handedly. At one point they were sending out a million mail order coupons each year for Shetland woollens. In the process he created something of a reputation for himself as a smart dresser. For a long time it was asserted that he was the only man between Edinburgh and the North Pole to wear whites for tennis.

He is also a disburser of charity, a spiritualist, and an earnest defender of Shetland ritual. 'I wouldn't lay an aamos on anyone myself,' he says gravely, 'but I don't dismiss it. I remember my grandmother laying one on me, that she'd sell a hat to Anderson and Co.' True to the pioneering spirit, he plunges into the Atlantic each morning. 'Sixteen strokes out, and 70 back, with the winds and tides.'

But the contemporary pioneers are the workers. For perhaps the first time in history, they've got their fingers in the jam pot. At the high-rate Sullom Voe site the average annual wage is £12,000. Off it, with the service companies, you can still make a killing: carpenters are on £1,000 a month, a welding overseer picks up £400 a week, a driver on £200 a week can double his wage with a weekend's overtime.

No one in his right mind would begrudge it. In two years' time there will be no work left for the 6,400 construction workers – 650 of them Shetlanders. With agriculture and fishing going to the wall, oil represents a colossal reprieve for the islanders.

Extraordinarily, some of the service companies are still short handed. 'We hold interviews all over the country,' one manager said, 'and we get the most awful types in. They're often more concerned about getting the cost of a meal off us than considering a career in Shetland.' And this company offers inflation-proof living. All wages are reviewed every three months.

Some would-be employees are infinitely more adventurous. I had met Rab and Donald on the boat sailing north from Aberdeen. Rab had hair like mangled seaweed and Donald a tartan waistcoat nailed down by Jethro Tull badges. Wild, likeable Glasgow men, with eyes like tar puddles, they were after some of the jam.

'We've a freend wha wuz a plummer on £40 a wik, and noo he's just labourin' fer £240. He'll fix us up nae bother.' Donald wanted the money to go and hear Jethro Tull in America. Rab was thinking of opening a hair-dressing saloon.

On our return sailing south, they told us how they had fared. They hadn't got a job but they were all right. A Shetland burrd was fixing them up. The Jobcentre would ring the burrd and the burrd would ring Glasgow and they would fly north and maybe stay with the burrd.

As things stood, they'd almost managed without her. Sullom Voe terminal, £1,000 million investment, deliverer of 900,000 barrels of daily crude, national lifeline, is guarded night and day by legions of BP stormtroopers. Rab and Donald got through them all, smuggled in on a workers' bus.

The first Irish contractor they approached actually thought they were part of the new shift and nodded them through. 'We couldnae believe it! We wuz sent on tae this line where there wuz a' these geezers with fancy parkas and helmets and that. So me and Donald stand there pretending to be hot stuff like, till this other geezer comes along and looks at wir shoes sharpish and says "Where's yer wellies, boys?" ' Seconds later they were out on their ears.

But not out of the terminal. The rest of the morning they knocked on doors. All morning aghast executives threw them out. Giving up, they actually hitched a lift through the wire. 'He wuz a heid yin, so we gie'd him the patter. We said wir mithers were ill in the Western Infirmary.'

They still managed two illegal nights in the workers' camps.

There are two of these, vast Portakabin Hiltons, where the food and lodgings are so good (and free) that men called Cruelty Officers are employed to winkle idlers out of broom cupboards and toilets. 'It wuz unreal. You've never seen sae much food in yir life. We could have had breakfast six times over.' Nobody is too worried about burrds. 'The lads are all either knackered or doped or in the gym or on the booze.'

Booze is a problem. It always has been. Skid marks on every corner were Shetland's living art form till the council took the roads in hand. "It's the only place I've seen where they actually order pints of whisky,' said a white-faced barman. The Jubilee 77, Lerwick's raunchiest drinking den, took £2,700 one night. The rigs and platforms are supposed to be dry, but there are ways and means. One favourite means is to fly out with a crate of oranges under your arm, all injected with vodka.

It's not just the money or the boredom that makes them do it. The Shetland landscape is a total mind-bender. The colours are brown and dark brown and a yellow that turns to green three days a year. The land forms are long, listless, and empty; the houses are small, the animals smaller, the trees virtually non-existent. On a clear day it has a stupendous purity. The rest of the year it's like the set from After The Bomb Has Dropped.

The women are usually the first to go. The local doctors all cite a condition known as Shetland Depression. 'I'm afraid one treats Shetland as an overseas posting,' an oil man confided late one night in the Jubilee. 'One dines in a lot.'

It depends what you're used to, though. 'Shetland's great,' insisted Margaret, an oil wife. She lives in one of the oil colonies that have nicknames like Alcatraz and Toytown. 'Everybody's got their hi-fis an' that blarin' out the windaes. To me that's more of a social life than being flung aboot by a bouncer.'

That's the spirit. But heaven help her if she goes under. The *Shetland Times* soothes: 'Suicide? Despair? Your problems are ours. Write to the Samaritans, PO Box 9, Stirling.'

2 April 1980   **Erland Clouston**

46

Locked up in velvet boxes

This is a letter from the new purdah. In this protected eyrie, heavily scented with Preen floorwax and Chloe, time and space intrude only through other people. Mrs Fleetwood brings news of arson on 135th Street. The dancer across the hall whispers of Baryshnikov making Makarova offers she can only refuse. The banker next door tells of falling interest rates and four day breaks in Bermuda.

The streets are dirty. The rain pours. Spring teases and then disappears. And all over Manhattan women are locked up in velveted boxes. Some are called 'homes', others 'offices.' The effect is the same. Freedom is a dream, a soaring seagull swooping over Central Park, glimpsed through sooty glass.

What is there to do out there for those women who have no offices to go to? No one needs to meet and make new friends. Everyone's lists are full; no one has any openings. 'Call again in a year or so. Someone may have moved to Minnesota.' Women no longer lunch together. They stay home and, while munching through a can of tuna packed in spring water and examining their faces in the looking glass, chatter down the telephone wire to those whom once they sat across from.

There are no choices left in life that necessitate going out to meet its challenge. The book-of-the-month-club has replaced the library. The cheque book has supplanted charity. Charity is now the rationale for not passing on the dirtiest of the gossip. No one gives to it or works for it in these dutiless days since one is instead into Causes and then only when tax deductible, preferably with Sinatra closing the bill.

The poor are no longer with us, only with them, i.e., the Federal government. To be accepted as a Cause the poor should be no older than 8 and artistically gifted, preferably in dance, which means a good chance of their growing up to be blessedly inarticulate.

Going out to shop is, of course, a charming old-fashioned custom still practised, it is reported, in the suburbs. The idea of having to push a cart up and down jostling aisles is as distasteful as that of running on the streets – another quaint ritual still practised where estate cars run. Mingling is out; privacy is in. Body contact with strangers is to be had only with the battery of doctors or nurses to whom one turns over the machine for its biannual check-up. All must be perfection within the new purdah, in direct relation to the chaos feared without.

It is no longer necessary to retreat into psychological symptoms. There is no agoraphobia any more, there is, simply, no reason to go out. The video tape collection makes nonsense of sitting in a darkened cinema at the mercy of sleepers, snorers, chatterers, and flashers on the loose. Seven television channels are seven windows through the lace curtains of which the women peep.

Of course there is a fad for filming programmes about what are implausibly called 'real people' committing independent and outrageous acts like farming or being a grandmother. It is not in order to make of these nonentities a momentary star. It is to replace the memory of the street, bustling with everyday life, to be snooped on and clucked over from the safety of the parlour. And again on television everyone wins. Out there, beyond the world of the box, and the security of the hermit's shell, is sensed a gallery of losers.

There is no sense of missing anything through this restricted life. It is, after all, a condition of extraordinary privilege. To be able to telephone in shopping lists for delivery suggests charge cards, a background of respectable credit rating. Even sales have been reduced to the level of a gentle living room distraction – bargain hunting as Mah Jong.

There are those in the new purdah who can price to the cent every item that has been on offer in every major department store in Manhattan over the last year, such is the efficacy of the colour catalogue. Over on East 86th Street is a beautiful and legendary woman who has not been glimpsed outdoors for years. Nevertheless no one buys so much as a love seat or air conditioner without checking in with her first. She is a computer of store catalogues.

But loneliness, a scratching desire to belong, intrudes eventually. Those who have been working at home (photographing, putting together the novel, getting into futures or yen) start to crave an office. The world has been withdrawn from, rejected, studied and now is the moment for non-involvement. It is no longer enough to have two telephone lines and one answer phone. There is a longing for a switchboard, a secretary, major medical insurance, withholding tax and above all, a sense of being part of the game.

All that changes is the costume, the decoration and the tone of voice. The velour lounging suit with scarlet racing trim gives way to the austere tan two piece with matching brief case. The bed of cushions gives way to one of thorns. Voices go up an octave. Six months' work with moisture penetrating, anti wrinkle eye cream is put aside under one week's neon. And since everything must be embraced wholeheartedly on Manhattan, office hours start in darkness and end in darkness.

She who was fluid and graceful with time now boasts of being a workaholic, unable to sleep until 200 telephone calls have been made or returned.

Sometimes it escapes notice that she is carried unseeing by metal tube from her old quarters to the new which are no less of an enclosure. Papers are sent in. Lunches are sent out for. Communication is a telephone wire.

And all this was brought to mind by the ever fascinating incarnations of Marilyn Haft. Regular readers might remember that we last left her living peaceably in Greenwich Village, sleeping late, writing the big books and recuperating from three years in the White House. Nights that were once interrupted by calls from Air Force Two somewhere over the Pacific have been transmuted into timeless extensions of formless days.

One morning Mrs Haft woke up on Madison Avenue running the Carter Mondale campaign for Manhattan and Brooklyn, 19 hours a day. That she is already back again in the Village sleeping, reading and nibbling fettucine alfredo will last only as long as it takes for her next security clearance to come through.

Mrs Haft, former Civil Rights activist, 35, one time drop-out, will shortly become 'Senior Adviser on Economic and Social Affairs to the US Mission to the UN.' It will be long hours in the glass house by East River. And yet one senses that nothing changes but the quality of the wall to wall carpet and the colour of the telephone that conjures the world outside into existence.

Liberation is today's hypocrisy; welcome to the new purdah.

2 May 1980   **Linda Blandford**

A country diary: Keswick

I have lately received a number of old stereoscopic glass slides and their elegant French viewer. These slides were taken by my family mainly between 1890 and 1902 and most of them are of rock climbing in Britain, the Alps and the Dolomites, especially around Arolla. The ones of snow and ice have an almost uncanny reality and though the gear of those early climbers was very different the mountains have changed only in varying degrees. The local valley views are perhaps unremarkable but some of the high, mountain ones have surprises – for instance, Napes Needle with a figure suitably on top has a thick, shrubby growth near its base. There is nothing like that now. My father, in old age, used to complain that a lot of interest had gone from the more popular routes with ledges and holds cleared of debris and the rocks near-polished by nailed boots. He should see, say, the ground above Ashness Bridge (a too popular beauty spot) now for not only is the grass gone but the earth itself is going fast and the rocks are bare. It is, it seems, the actual skin of the land which suffers worst, and while the National Trust does its best to nurture the land it holds it must be a discouraging battle at times. Not only are there more people; there are more animals too. Yesterday a neighbouring farmer told me, as we talked over his yard gate, pushed and rattled by young cows, that there are four times as many animals on that farm as there were in his

50

fore-elders' time. That afternoon I met another farmer on the hill road, a small ageing man in an elderly car carrying fodder for his beasts in the valley. The car boot was open and piled high with blocks of hay until it seemed astonishing that the front wheels of the car were still on the road at all, and as I got home in the gathering dusk a helicopter crossed High-Lodore, its lights winking, to leave more blocks for the sheep on the fell tops before the real winter sets in – as it will.

21 January 1980   **Enid J. Wilson**

Beer and skittles now

It's no wonder that Chancellors of the Exchequer, holed up in Number 11 Downing Street in the Kanzlerbunker, get worried about what is going on in the real world. For a start, there is nobody to tell them. Treasury civil servants, who spend their daytimes compiling misleading statistics and their evenings singing madrigals in Croydon, certainly don't let on. Now and again an MP with more courage than sense might try to bring intelligence from the outside, but that doesn't happen very often.

Sir Geoffrey Howe has adopted the tactic of asking people he meets by chance in his constituency. Recently he was driving his car along a lane in East Surrey when he was stopped by local authority workers engaged in some task in the public service. After a moment they recognized him and offered messages of support, e.g. 'Keep up the good work, Sir Geoffrey' and 'Stick at it, Chancellor' and the like.

Sir Geoffrey was heartened by this and has been describing the incident to friends and colleagues as evidence of the way in which ordinary working folk appreciate what he is trying to do.

As indeed they may well do. Recent surveys, including one which has just appeared in the new journal *Fiscal Studies,* show that it is the middle classes which have proportionately lost most through the tax changes. They will be hit even harder by the rise in the mortgage rate. In the meantime, there are large parts of the working classes who are freed from wage restraint, don't own houses, spend a higher proportion of their money on VAT-free goods, and are afloat on a sea of phoney money.

It can't go on for long. But in Manton, a mining village in the South Yorks and Nottinghamshire coalfield, last Friday they were celebrating the 20 per cent pay rise agreed with the NCB. The pit itself voted against, but no one seemed remotely bitter about the result. Certainly there were the routine cracks about Mrs Thatcher ('I'll tell you what I think about her,' said one miner, who then blew a loud and lengthy raspberry), but there's little edge to it; no tales of children going hungry or struggles to afford clothing.

Did they think that Sir Geoffrey's policy would hold down inflation? 'Don't make me laugh!' But inflation is something people have learned to live with now; keeping one jump ahead of it is simply another of life's routine problems.

There is a curious affection for Ted Heath, who is seen as the first Prime Minister to recognize the miners as a special group of workers, set apart and above from the rest. They mention Fleet Street printers frequently: 'They complain about miners wanting £145 and them printers earn £238 a week. They wouldn't come down a bloody pit, would they?' It's status as much as cash which the miners are looking for.

Pensioners are of course more worried than those still working. 'We got a rise, and six months later it's all gone with prices going up,' they say. One couple who admitted with a blend of bravado and embarrassment that they voted Tory in May, said the only way to keep down prices was to hold down wages. But how could that be done? 'Make it the law, you can't give them everything they ask for.' Might there be any other causes? 'The Common Market. The sooner we get out the better, it's just giving money to the French and the Germans.' In that case, weren't their political views closer to Mr Callaghan than Mrs Thatcher? 'We've always voted Conservative.'

For some working people voting Tory is a badge of respectability, a sign that they are able to look beyond mere

'*I do feel sorry for Peter and Harriet. They got so fed up with all this talk about the Day of Action they nipped off to Madeira for a few days and who should suddenly turn up at their hotel . . .*
13 May 1980

money to some assumed national interest. Like beleaguered members of an obscure religious sect, they sit through the joshing and banter with some dignity.

A nearby pit village is called Rhodesia. The original owner was called Rhodes and thought that if it could be done in Africa it could be done in Yorkshire. He named the streets in the village after his daughters, Margery Street, Mabel Street, and so on. Here most of the miners are buying their houses, even though the mortgages will cost twice as much as their present rent, and they will have to pay for the repairs. 'It's a good buy, isn't it?' one of them says. 'Mine'll cost £4,000, and it'll cost me £3,000 getting it right. Not bad, is it, seven thousand quid for a house?'

Everybody in the miners' institute dislikes the Government, no one here admits to having voted for it, although few have serious complaints about events since last May. But they do complain often about the rise in television licences. Another point about working class people is that they still tend to live from Friday to Friday, from pay packet to pay packet. This means that burdens such as VAT which appear piecemeal and only on certain goods are accepted, whereas costs such as licences, which have to be paid all at once, are the cause of prolonged grumbling, even though VAT costs any family far more each year than the TV.

Oddly, the same general lack of alarm felt by the miners is also reflected among steel workers, whose problems are far greater. They have been told that they cannot hope for a rise bigger than 2 per cent, and they face huge redundancies. Yet at a working men's club in the heart of the steel area of Sheffield the manager said that takings were as high as ever.

'It won't last. Christmas is coming, and they'll spend a lot then, and those who've got redundancy are spending that. But our takings will go right down in the New Year.' Beer costs 33p a pint here and singles of spirits are 27p. Virtually every one of the three or four hundred people in the club were playing bingo, eyes down reverentially, raised only to admonish people talking too loud at the bar.

What would they do when they lost their jobs? 'Don't

54

know, go on the social security, maybe find some work doing summat else.' Would they move? 'Oh no, we wouldn't move!' You might as well inform people there's work in Patagonia as tell them about jobs in the South-East. For some the idea of abandoning their grandparents, in-laws, aunties and nephews in the city they were born in is as bizarre as the idea of abandoning their children might be to the middle class.

An old lady, a strong Labour supporter, grabbed me in a miners' club and whispered: 'If you're writing about the Tory Government, you couldn't have come at a worse time. The miners are getting their rise, and the pensioners have just got the £10 bonus. They've nowt to complain about. They'll learn soon enough.' No doubt they will.

12 December 1979   **Simon Hoggart**

Chilling tendency raises blood pressure

In response to market forces and the battle against inflation, Mr David Howell announced yesterday that he is forcing up gas prices by 29 per cent. As if to reinforce the essentially religious nature of the Monetarist Tendency, it transpired that the decision was dictated jointly by the Holy Cities of Qom and Chicago.

All the same, to heathens still languishing in outer darkness, it seemed puzzling. Was it a sporting gesture to our industrial competitors? Or a kind of CAP in fuel, with Britain's energy resources (what a curse it is to be blessed with so many) tied to the world price or the least efficient alternative, whichever is the highest?

The Energy Secretary had several good reasons for his conduct, all of which pointed to some kind of increase, but not this one. This turned out to be the Gas Corporation's view, too, but they had probably forgotten Mr Howell's need to keep down public borrowing. It is a gas tax, as countless Labour MPs complained.

It was, as usual, a strikingly efficient Despatch Box performance from the tallest micro-chip in Britain. Having voiced the conventional wisdom about the need to conserve energy 'for future generations', Mr Howell even coped with Enoch Powell's trick question ('Why?') by emphasizing the strategic need not to depend on 'politically sensitive' regions – a reference, so Labour's John McWilliam assumed, to the nation's coal-fields.

And yet, as so often with the Tendency, it sounded all wrong psychologically, and Labour MPs railed against the inhumanity of such a steep increase before a proper fuel rebate scheme had been organized to protect the poor and old.

Mr Howell made all the right noises about this, as he seems programmed to, but one senses that his own advice would be to wear an extra shirt next winter.

Tory backbenchers initially reacted to the statement as if the Minister had just turned off their central heating. Thawed out, they divided into two camps, those who sounded suicidally depressed by the news and those supporters of the Tendency who were delighted. Every time some Labour MP, such as little Leslie Spriggs from St Helens, complained that it was 'rationing by price', they fell about laughing. Did not the naïve fools know that everything is rationed by price unless, of course, you can afford it?

A few minutes later Labour backbencher Andrew Bennett was introducing a bill designed, among other things, to stop sheep worrying. After a statement like Mr Howell's you could hardly blame them.

17 January 1980   **Michael White**

The Keynes we need now?

Is it possible that the 'new Keynes' we have all been waiting for is Mr Wynne Godley? If so it couldn't have happened to a nicer man. Mr Godley, who is a Fellow of King's College and the director of the Department of Applied Economics at Cambridge University, has since the early seventies been predicting that the British economy will degenerate into permanent recession. His remedy for decline is trade protection and as his gloomy forecasts have been increasingly vindicated there is growing political support for his economic prescriptions.

Mr Godley would make a splendid 'new Keynes'. He is that rare creature, a gentleman among economists – indeed the son of a peer: he came late to the dismal science from the orchestra pit where he played the oboe professionally. Now he is a virtuoso of the computer, but although a highly professional econometrician he maintains the air of an amateur. Like Keynes his interests range from the arts to the casino (he is the croupier at the King's summer feast) and he has been known to speculate on the exchanges. He is married to a famous beauty but, unlike Keynes, is not known to possess tendencies which would explain to the editor of *The Times* his distaste for money aggregates as instruments of economic discipline.

Keynes, as Mr Robert Skidelsky has pointed out in a stimulating essay (*Encounter*, April 1979), performed a unique political service to his generation. He postponed the class war and, for the time being at least, saved liberal capitalism. By discovering a technical device for preventing mass unemployment he spared the liberal intelligentsia the unpleasant choice between Soviet Russia and Nazi Germany. He offered the intellectual ground on which the centre could regroup. Skidelsky discusses the need for a repeat performance:

'Keynesian economics made possible the reconstruction of liberal politics. Today the decline in Keynesian economics endangers that political achievement. After 30 years or so of Keynesianism we return to the original question. Can we look once more to an improvement in economic technique to solve the political problem? Or must we rely on political and social change to solve the economic problem?'

It is an excellent question. Godley's scheme for a general tariff is essentially a Keynesian device. That is to say it is a macro-economic measure. Its prime purpose is to permit a sustained economic expansion.

If he is right it would be possible once more to manage the economy at a level of demand which did not pose questions about the governability of society: there would be no need either to entertain the delusions of the monetarists or suffer the interventions of the left-wing Socialists.

A colloquial statement of Godley's case, which anybody ought to be able to understand, has just been published in the book *Slow Growth in Britain* (Oxford, £3.50). It is edited by Mr Wilfred Beckerman, who recently declared himself an Oxford convert to Cambridge protectionism.

Godley diagnoses a deepening recession. He attributes the constraint which the balance of payments places upon a policy of sustained expansion to the economy's propensity to import. This was all the while growing during the stop-go cycles of the late fifties and the sixties. In the early seventies came a marked structural deterioration in the import-export ratio. The result, he argues, is that devaluation is no longer feasible on a scale large enough to match the problem.

His reasoning leads him to protection as the only remaining means of maintaining an adequate level of demand. He is opposed totally to 'creeping protectionism', although he experiences difficulty in getting people to grasp this. He is against the kind of selective protection of declining industries which the TUC favours. He advocates a wholly non-discriminatory system of import controls, the simplest form of which would be, 'a high tariff applied uniformly on all imports'.

He would accompany this with a general tax cut in order to ensure that the total volume of imports would remain as high as it would otherwise have been. The chief purpose of this would be to remove valid cause for trade retaliation.

'The control of imports,' he explains, 'would not be used to make our balance of payments any better than it otherwise would have been: the whole of the adjustment would be to make domestic output higher than it would otherwise have been.' Britain would buy less manufactured goods but more raw materials: thus the primary producers would be able to buy more manufactures from the countries who would be selling Britain less. 'Therefore,' contends Godley, 'the net effect is to increase, not to diminish, world trade and output.'

Godley's proposal has an elegant simplicity, which may be

'*And the next competitor to jump is Captain Mark Phillips who
is sponsored by Range Rover, 2p on a pint of beer, 5p on a packet
of 20, road tax up to £60, child benefit with inflation . . .*'
28 March 1980

one reason why it is of growing political attraction. I took note the other day when a *Guardian* colleague of sectarian bent referred casually to 'Godleyism'. To become an 'ism' in one's own lifetime is the mark of a cult figure. 'Godleyism' has cult potential because it is at once simple and complex: everyone can grasp its essence, few can master or refute its detailed implications.

There are two kinds of objections – substantial and operational. The first argues that a general tariff, even if feasible, is inappropriate for dealing with the problems of Britain's uncompetitiveness. The second argues that even if appropriate, Godley's proposals are not feasible.

The feasibility issue turns on the question of retaliation. Here it seems to me that Godley is winning the argument in a technical sense but not yet in a political one. If the measures he proposes did not reduce the volume of trade and might even, perhaps, increase it, why should other nations retaliate? Countries do not usually act in these matters on grounds of principle or out of spite and, if it is in their interest to trade, they will trade.

Politically it is more difficult. This is partly because other countries, the United States for example, might use Britain's behaviour as an excuse to protect on a discriminatory basis and thereby spark a trade war. But a more formidable difficulty is that a strategy of general protectionism over a long period, say at least a decade, is incompatible with Britain's membership of the European Economic Community. That would suit Godley well enough but it has politico-strategic implications which go far beyond questions of economic management.

Let us assume, however, if only for the sake of argument, that the Godley strategy is feasible. Is it appropriate? Computer can be set against computer, quarrelling about the macro-economic quantities which might be involved, but the question turns fundamentally on two other questions. How important do you think inflation is? And do you think that the human and institutional causes of British uncompetitiveness are susceptible any longer to the management of demand? It is on these two related scores that some people instead of regarding Godley as the 'new Keynes' regard him as the old Keynes thinly disguised.

It is true that he has little to say about inflation. He can show that his protectionist strategy is less inflationary than a devaluation strategy, but that is scarcely the point. Comparing it with deflation he lapses into a somewhat agnostic Keynesianism, observing, in this newly published essay, that there are no conclusive correlations between the level of demand and the rate of inflation in post-war Britain. Elsewhere he has remarked that 'incomes policy is a weak instrument for reducing inflation in the long term'. That may be so, but if institutionally generated, or cost-push, inflation is one of the prime causes of British uncompetitiveness it is not plain what remedy 'Godleyism' can provide for that.

The same kind of objections can be made on the supply side. How would protection help to change attitudes deeply rooted in class and history, how would it make it easier to reform institutions? Would British Leyland or British Steel have done better behind a tariff wall? The national newspaper industry is scarcely an advertisement for technological progress in the absence of foreign competition. Would the workers work harder and the managers manage better under Godley's strategy than under all the others which have been tried?

However, Godley's views are gaining political ground. The Left has incorporated import controls into its 'alternative' socialist strategy. Protectionism in some form or another is almost bound to conquer the Labour Party before the next election, although not necessarily in the 'wholly non-discriminatory' form upon which Godley himself insists. Meanwhile, the Conservative Party is being reminded of its protectionist past and when the time comes for a U-turn it could find itself heading in the direction of Cambridge.

It may be said that the political choice today is in no way as stark as it was in the thirties. A polarization between Bennery and Thatcherism is not comparable with a choice between Communism and Fascism. Even if there is the need for a 'new Keynes' to save liberal capitalism it is not clear whether there is any economic technique capable of solving what have become in essence sociological and political problems.

Nevertheless, Godley's is the only brand of economics which addresses itself to the problem of Britain's decline and proposes a strategy acceptable to all classes and interests. It seems to me that the underlying social and cultural causes of that decline are more likely to be tackled in an atmosphere of economic expansion than they are (*pace* Sir Geoffrey Howe) if the economy is squeezed to monetary death. If I remain as yet unpersuaded, however, it is because of my doubt whether a Britain isolated from the European Community and partially cut off from the international trading system would face any the better the challenge of her decline. The social and political response, I fear, might be the opposite.

5 December 1979   **Peter Jenkins**

Budget night at the opera

Straight after the Budget came Charity Gala Night at the Royal Opera House, with the premiere of a new production of Donizetti's *Lucrezia Borgia*. The foyer was buzzing with speculation before the curtain went up. After 92 years would the piece appear foolishly melodramatic? Would the principal singer's voice remain pure and clear throughout the evening? Would the tax on company perks mean that the Jaguar would be replaced by a Granada?

Happily Sir Geoffrey doesn't yet seem to have hit the opera-going public too hard. These people manage to beat the Budget every year – by being incredibly rich. They were the kind of hard-faced men who have done well out of inflation. There wasn't much compensating female beauty either, since, with it being a Gala Night, they had to bring their wives rather than their mistresses.

The extra 8p on a bottle of wine didn't seem to have much effect on business at the Champagne Bar. To give you some idea of how rich they were, some of them brought the stuff at £11 a bottle, scoffed what they could, then, when the bell went, trooped off into the stalls leaving the rest behind.

The place was full of the kind of people who look as if they ought to be famous, but aren't. Could that be Sir Michael Edwardes? No, it is someone even tinier. Surely that must be Roy Jenkins climbing the stairs? No, it is another portly person, his head gleaming under the chandeliers. But then it *must* be Lord Lever next to the Royal Box. Surprisingly enough it is, next to his beautiful wife, of whom he once famously replied, when asked if he would have married her if she didn't have £2,000,000, 'I would have married her even if she had only £1,000,000.'

And then just before the curtain went up, the star guest of the evening arrived. This time there could be no mistake. That tall, slightly stooped and distinguished bearing. The radiant smile. the glistening teeth, the faultlessly elegant dinner jacket; it had to be the Minister for the Arts, the Rt Hon Norman St John-Stevas. But even here our hopes were dashed. It was only the Minister's look-alike, the Prince of Wales.

The souvenir programme (with it being a Gala Night, the programme cost more than a seat in some other theatres) promised 'knights, esquires, ladies, ruffians, pages, maskers, soldiers, ushers, halberdiers, cupbearers and gondoliers.' How true, and that was only the audience. You should have seen the stage.

On to it walked Joan Sutherland. She was wearing even more jewels than the Queen Mother. If their tiaras had met they would have fused all the lights. Her voice was superlative, soaring above even the rustle of chocolate wrappers and the rumbling of tummies waiting for the first batch of smoked salmon sandwiches. You could tell it was Gala Night, because the intervals were almost as long as the acts.

Covent Garden was built on sound commercial principles, that is, on the general lines of a slave ship. Instead of being able to wander round inspecting each other, the upper classes are obliged to elbow each other viciously aside as they fight through the hell that is the Crush Bar. Here at last were famous people. Lord Gladwyn, one of our less interesting former ambassadors. Sir Charles Villiers, chairman of the

British Steel Corporation, glugging hock with surprising good cheer. In keeping with the government policy of non-intervention in the strike, the youthful Lord Gowrie, Minister of State at the Department of Employment, was drinking at the far end of the bar.

We had to get into our seats 15 minutes before the Royal party. This was presumably so the Queen Mother would not have her toes trodden on by late-comers. In fact most people managed to get there half an hour in advance so they could have a good gander at each other.

You can tell the very rich by their evening dress: the more they earn, the sillier it is. One man wore something that looked like a pair of paisley pyjamas with a black tie on top. Some wore quilted affairs like sawn-off dressing gowns. Others had yards of ruffling on their shirts, so their chests were puffed out like swans on heat.

I had to scurry away early in the pouring rain. Outside in the seedy streets of Covent Garden, you could still hear the music and the singing. It would be fitting to report that on the evening of this harsh Budget a few impoverished music-loving students were huddled near the stage door listening to that thrilling voice. But there weren't, just a few drunks beating the next Budget by getting stoned now.

28 March 1980   **Simon Hoggart**

Keeping the chaps happy

It could be the answer that Britain's troubled car industry has been seeking – a little white tablet that keeps production workers happy. The Japanese motor industry believes it is an important aid to its productivity, and now workers at a British car plant are being invited to take a daily dose of ginseng. Doctors who are hoping to start clinical tests next month are anxious to cast aside ginseng's reputation as a Chinese aphrodisiac, claiming that its true effect is to reduce stress and act as a tonic.

'It is of the greatest help to people who are under pressure or who have monotonous jobs,' said Mr Hamilton Cooper, managing director of English Grains, manufacturing chemists of Burton-on-Trent, which is providing ginseng tablets for the test.

Volunteers on the production line and in the administrative offices will get daily ginseng tablets, the others fake tablets. Their feelings and job performance will then be compared with those of workers who have received nothing.

And the firm involved? 'Well, it's not British Leyland although I'm certain they will be keen to see the published results,' said Mr Cooper. 'At the moment the doctors who will be running the tests are talking to union representatives about the scheme. Results in other countries are impressive. Two of the big Japanese car makers give free ginseng to their workers and what's their productivity – about three times ours? And workers at the great new Lada car plant in Russia receive it.'

After 40 years specializing in the manufacture of malt-based pharmaceutical products, English Grain has now opened a factory in Ebbw Vale, South Wales where 40 people prepare the ginseng tablets. Ginseng is a white root, rather like a multi-legged carrot, which takes seven years to grow to a length of about 8 in. and will only do so satisfactorily within about 25 miles of the 38th parallel. Not unnaturally, one of the chief sources is Korea, where English Grain's subsidiary, Red Kooga, gets its root at £50,000 a ton. In tablet form a 36-day supply costs £3.39. If the results of the proposed tests should interest British Leyland, supplying ginseng to the company's work force would cost about £4.5 million a year – the equivalent of half a day's lost production.

But what about those aphrodisiac rumours? 'We certainly make no claims about this,' said Mr Cooper. 'But it is common sense that if you feel good and are not shattered after a day's work then you are probably going to have a better sex life. It is significant that many car workers complain about this so I imagine the doctors will be interested in this aspect. The fact is that a happy person makes a better worker.'

10 January 1980   **Malcolm Stuart**

Hull down

In the middle of Hull stands a splendid Victorian building, triangular in shape, with a dome at each corner. It is cocky as an alderman's hat, confident as a bank. Most of the ground floor is taken up by the skeleton of a gigantic whale. But the former Docks Board office is not only a monument to the spent prosperity of the whaling era; it faces on to three redundant docks as well.

From its shabby office on the edge of the fish dock, the Hull Vessel Owners Association announces that it can no longer provide facilities for ships to discharge their catches. Falling revenue from users and the high cost of leasing from the British Transport Docks Board are blamed. The port managed to survive the end of whaling in the 1860s, but now there is grave doubt if it can struggle through the latest disaster: the voluntary liquidation of the company which provides the operating base for trawlers.

The prospective closure is another aspect of shrinking, sinking Britain. Fishing has been a profitable basic industry for centuries; now it is almost severed. The signs which once combined to profile Hull as Europe's premier port are still there, though much changed. Placid sheets of water, but few masts; the early-morning auctions, but much of the fish sold is freighted overland from Scotland, or else is packed in containers from the Continent. The smells and the skills are receding too. Hull has been living with the unthinkable for seven or eight years now: the dismantling of an economic mainstay was signalled by the Cod Wars with Iceland, by the restrictions imposed by the EEC and by Britain's failure so far to negotiate a Community fishing policy which will increase quotas and open up trawling grounds.

The port is still handling general cargo in a biggish way, but fishing symbolizes a vanishing activity. There still is a whiff of the Baltic about Hull. But it is as though in turning the handsome old Docks into a museum, the drive and the daring which took crews into Arctic waters had been laid up as well as the showcases of whalebone artefacts. Even an official whose job it is to promote the area says: 'People here are rather self-effacing; they're surprised if anything good happens to them.'

Nothing much does. In the fishing business at least. If the operating company withdraws from the dock, 113 bobbers who unload fish will be on the dole. Last year, they handled 50,000 tons. But for every two landings by British vessels, there were three by foreigners. Yet 25 years ago, 650 bobbers were unloading 250,000 tons annually. Even two years ago, there were 130 local trawlers. That has dwindled to about 30. Only the distant-waters 'freezers' are active. Ten days ago, most of them pulled out of Cornish waters at the end of the mackerel season. There isn't much to look forward to. Robert Dalton, Secretary of the Association says: 'The quotas mean only one trip per vessel to the North East Arctic this year.'

If the trawlers make that trip and come back at the end of April, it could be that they won't be able to land their catches at the home port. The handful of big companies who own the freezer ships and mutually form the association to run the fish dock have a creditors' meeting fixed for two weeks' time. Mr Dalton thinks it will be wound up; talks in London last week produced no hint of a government subsidy; the association cannot pay the monthly dues of £120,000.

So the Albert Dock will be back in the lap of its owners, the British Transport Docks Board who only four years ago spent £1 million refurbishing it specially for fishing vessels. And the dwindling Hull fleet will put in elsewhere. Since the fishing industry is so gloomy about the dead hand of the EEC, and the weight the Government is giving to Britain's reduced contribution to finance the CAP to the detriment of supply for fisheries, the dock closure will be an expected epitaph.

'Selt out, love, after the bloody Cod War. Selt out, that's what,' says a woman in the Subway Club. There is nothing new in the fact that Hull feels betrayed by what EEC membership has done; but the men are weary of episode after episode, such anger as is left resides with their wives and mothers. This woman is proud to have had a son on one of the Navy frigates in the last skirmish with Iceland.

Many of those whose livelihoods were lost are doing other jobs, or no jobs – the unemployment rate is eight per cent. 'I'm down at Lowestoft with a standby vessel for an oilrig,' says a middle-aged man. Made redundant in Hull? Partly yes, partly because he was a boozer. Another club member, a deckhand for 30 years, is transferring to a line which does the West Africa run. But they detest the thought of living elsewhere and keep their homes here.

When you see those homes where people tenaciously hold on to unmarketable skills, you realize what the sea has done to Hull. For the Subway Club is three tiny houses knocked into one at the end of a terrace opposite the fish dock. There are endless parallel terraces, and off these glum streets yet tinier courts of two-up two-down houses. Hessle Road runs through it; a town within a town they used to call it. But for all the clearance programmes and the new flats, cramped lives are shackled to dead-end streets.

And what larger forces are doing to a rather enclosed and perhaps neglected part of the country is something else. For unlike other big Yorkshire cities, Hull's problems are not primarily to do with the decline of the manufacturing sector. There is scarcely an immigrant presence: its poor are white and local. There are 13,000 idle in a workforce of 170,000; and there is a pervasive feeling that we as a country did not have to give the fishing industry away, even allowing for the shrinkage following rationalization and a bit of bloody-mindedness.

George Andrews, regional officer of the Transport and General Workers, is thinking of the future of the 113 bobbers who belong to his union. Most are in their fifties, so he is not optimistic. 'Only the fish merchants say it's still boisterous here. And they get their supplies overland. The biggest threat after the fish dock is the vast import of processed fish, coming in through the commercial docks.' As if to prove him right, Findus announced next day that it will be making 250 workers redundant at its processing plant next year.

'As a union, we've fought the trawler owners in the past.

But now we agree that the blame for this situation lies solely with the government of the day,' he says. 'If we do get a common fisheries policy, we shan't have the vessels to go fishing anyway.' The owners confirm that many of the wet fish vessels have been sold or scrapped; they were the first to be laid up.

The future is not bright. There is just no possibility of jobs being created on the scale and with the speed needed. Dr Eric Evans of Hull University's economics department reckons that the splurge of spending on regional incentives worked against North Humberside; other depressed areas got full development status, whereas until 1977 Hull was zoned as an intermediate area.

The lack of skills, the dependence on only a few industries, the emigration and the low profile of the area all militate against its revival. With so much economic buffeting, Hull needs an emblem of success. The Humber bridge, due to open at the end of the year, is already taking on that disputed role. The planners say it will bring in jobs and trade, just as the motorway across the Pennines has helped. Dr Evans does not agree.

The Bridge lies beyond the docks, to the west of the conurbation: two tall piers, narrow as needles, and slung between them, a thread of a catwalk, which is actually a two-lane roadway. From below, it is as though the inhabitants of a besieged town were planning a spectacular escape across a high wire.

Indeed, emigration is a problem: Hull's population has fallen by some 20,000 to 270,000 since the 1950s. Some of it has simply moved outside the city limits, of course. But whatever has happened, the city centre has been left with a feeling that it is too large for the use of those who remain. The Co-op has shrunk and shares its premises with another store. Sainsbury's recently decided not to open in the city.

A place where only salesmen and relations come, Philip Larkin once wrote. Hull is still a good place for poets. It has lots. Most famously Larkin and Douglas Dunn, who describes one tight little enclave, Terry Street:

Here they come, the agents of rot.
The street tarts and their celebrating trawlermen,
Singing or smoking, carrying bottles,
In a staggered group ten minutes before snow.

Terry Street was demolished a few years ago. Now they are demolishing trawlermen.

26 February 1980   **John Cunningham**

No Suzukis please, we're British

The BSA Golden Flash lay on its side in the gutter. Its rider, shaken but unhurt, had his helmeted head wedged beneath the bumper of a parked car. As the pedestrian whose fault it had been writhed in pain at his grazed knee, a motorcycle policeman sauntered over to the fallen rider.

'Don't worry, son,' he said, pulling him out by the legs. 'Your bike's hardly scratched. Tell me, do you have much trouble getting spares?'

The policeman had his priorities right. For the owners of British motor-cycles, the machine comes first. They are the sons of a forgotten empire, the heirs to Panther, Matchless and Brough. Their goggles misty, their great-coats flapping round their ankles, they ride proud and alone. The bulldog breed on wheels.

To bike British is to belong to an exclusive club. Like Freemasons, they reserve for fellow cultists the friendly wave on the road, help at a breakdown. For the uninitiated, for the uncaring, there is only disdain.

They stand apart . . . in lay-bys, on pavements, in garages and backyards. Could it be the carb, or the rings? The mag seems fine; have you checked the leads? The helpful inquiries of fallen brethren aboard gleaming Hondas or Suzukis pass unacknowledged. They are glorious in their isolation and semi-permanent immobility.

The art of British motor-cycle maintenance would try the philosophy of Zen itself. Yet the owner's faith is as strong and mysterious as any Oriental creed. In hidden worlds, back street surgeons flourish, breaking bikes and storing spares with the infinite care and wisdom of museum archivists. In these dingy strip joints, cannibalism raises no eyebrows. Leathery individuals in pudding bowl helmets talk in learned jargon of the search for cams and conrods.

An AY387569S for an A7,1951 may seem obscure but in parts of Clapham they talk of little else.

Love of the Beezer or Bonny knows no bounds. Beautiful women languish and grow old while sweet nothings are whispered to a crankcase.

Modern girls with their flashy paintwork and plastic components are no competition for the tactile appeal of a Vincent. Beware the man who speaks softly of slipping clutches; he keeps a mistress.

For their pains, the British diehards are repaid. Now and then, at the appointed hour, the cognoscenti come together. The pack hits the road.

Engines growling, pistons thudding, exhausts spitting, they take to the tarmac. Bonnevilles, a Velocette, A10s, a Gold Star, shrouded in a pall of black smoke. They storm the motorway, five or six abreast, sweeping the carriageways amid Doomsday clamour. For fleeting moments, their vanished supremacy returns; angry, immortal, they make the running once more. True Brit.

British bikers hold firm the last frontier of a once-great industry, guardians of pleasures known only to the Few. But for unbelievers, there is occasionally a glimpse of paradise lost.

As an ageing BSA roared into a country car park recently two smartly-dressed motorcyclists left their large BMWs and wandered over for a closer look.

'What about the vibration?' they asked dubiously.

'It's lovely,' the Beezer man replied. 'Just lovely.'

28 January 1980   **Simon Tisdall**

Civilization men

Sunningdale is where the British Establishment lives at peace with itself, plays golf and organizes conferences. On Friday May 13, 1977, Tony Benn and his party, of which I was one, drove to the Civil Service College, set in 63 acres of beautiful countryside at Sunningdale Park, Ascot, to meet top boffins from Britain's scientific Establishment. They were very grave and led us gravely one step further towards the plutonium economy. But who were they, these men whom ministers consult when the future of the planet is in jeopardy?

Well, there was Lord Todd, President of the Royal Society. He wanted to keep the human race alive and not be foolish. That meant keeping options open. 'Keeping options open' was a phrase that was to recur again and again. It is clearly very important to the British Establishment that options should be so kept.

Modern civilization, said Lord Todd in the conference room, depends on carbon. Later, over drinks, he discussed plants and carbon with Sir Herman Bondi, the chief scientist at the Ministry of Defence, later to become chief scientist at the Department of Energy. Lord Todd looked to me a very large anachronism, far from young, speaking and moving with the tiredness of a dinosaur which has woken up only to find itself in the wrong age.

But I warmed to him in the bar when he said, 'Sir Kenneth Berrill is not a scientist, he's an economist.' 'What's the difference?' I asked. 'Scientists sometimes get it right,' he replied. And, commenting on David Owen's view that Peter Jay, the son-in-law of the then Prime Minister and British Ambassador in Washington, was the most brilliant man of his generation (i.e. the best of his chums at Oxford in that year) he said succinctly: 'I would not have thought that David Owen had much occasion to meet brilliant people or recognize them if he did.'

72

Then there was Sir Kenneth Berrill, head of the Central Policy Review Staff. Sir Kenneth did a very good doodle on the Friday evening which I purloined after he left the room. In between myriad lines one could pick out the letters AGR. Was it a sign? Was the Advanced Gas-cooled Reactor his choice? Was I meant to pick up the doodle?

Sir Kenneth distinguished himself with the conceptually bankrupt remark, 'One can only plan on certainties.' This was his way of saying that Sir George Porter might develop solar power but all he, Sir Kenneth, could tell the Cabinet was: 'With nuclear power we can beat the energy gap, without it there will be catastrophe. It's your choice.' Sir Kenneth's main strength lies in his ability to keep options open at the same time as rendering all options meaningless.

Sir George Porter, Fellow of the Royal Society and Director of the Royal Institution, decreed that Britain could not opt out of the development of civil nuclear power precisely because proliferation was such an immense problem. If we did we would lose our seat at the conference table and all conference tables need the morality and wisdom of figures from the British Establishment.

More alarmingly, Sir George proceeded to upset Sir Kenneth and the tidiness of the whole seminar, which had been organized to enable us all to sit humbly at the feet of the great and good God called 'nuclear power', by suggesting that solar energy was not peripheral to the problem and that the development of the photochemical manufacture of fuel by sunlight would occur much faster than people think and would be commercially viable costing £2-£3 per square metre, which is £7-£8 per square metre less than all existing systems. It was this piece of encouraging news which brought a rebuke from Sir Kenneth and his comment that one can only plan on certainties.

Sir John Hill, chairman of the Atomic Energy Authority, is a cultivated mannerly man with a soft, rich voice – just the kind of salesman that the AEA needs. Up at Windscale, when dealing with a strike that had threatened the nuclear explosion that one day will engulf us all, he had looked desperately unhappy. Problems that involved human beings were outside his compass. Now he was completely at home, thoroughly assured in this rarified atmosphere of science. I was rather glad to see him smiling once again because he had seemed so wretched, so miserable at Windscale. I think he is a nice man.

But it was he who let the side down and revealed, after ingeniously successful attampts to hide the truth from us, that mad boffins were at large. We could, he said, re-process fuel from Japan and send it back in ships, each armed with a thousand men for protection. He omitted to say whether these men would be waving spears or carrying rifles as they surround the deck. Even Sir John's blunders – most of which stem from his belief that there is a scientific fix for everything – contain a certain charm.

If there were any doubt that science has created a world which is both vulnerable and mad, Dr Walter Marshall, chief scientific adviser to Tony Benn, removed it. Any nation that has one physicist, one chemist and one metallurgist can produce a bomb within three months if they have one stored spent fuel element ' – and there is nothing anyone can do about it.'

Paradoxically, he went on to say that proliferation, and here he seemed to be agreeing with Sir Kenneth, had gone too far. Everyone seemed agreed on that, but the logic of most of what they said pointed to further proliferation. Although Dr Marshall never quite said so, I suspected that the fast-breeder reactor, breeding as well as using plutonium, could not come fast enough for him. The march of science is a challenge for some and what better challenge than handling the most dangerous substance known to man ?

Sir Alan Cottrell, Master of Jesus College, Cambridge, sees no alternative to going down the nuclear road. In answer to Sir George Porter he emphasizes the need to distinguish between 'alternative' sources and 'assured' sources. Sir Alan is however against the Light Water Reactor (usually referred to as the Pressure Water Reactor) and argues that although in theory it can be made safe, in practice the specifications required to ensure this make unreasonable demands on human beings.

Sir Brian Flowers, FRS, Rector of Imperial College,

London, is seen as a sort of umpire in this field, not terribly committed to the development of nuclear power yet not hostile; rather a bit worried about the environment. Someone at the conference commented that Sir Brian changes his mind every day. I should say that this was unfair. If Sir Brian were the umpire and I were the batsman for the anti-nuclear lobby, I would be very worried indeed.

Sir Brian began by saying that the nuclear industry could not be judge and jury to its own cause and then went on to argue that re-processing was not necessary, but carefully balanced this by calling for options to be kept open. He kept up his balancing act by making it clear that his position as regards the Flowers Report had been misunderstood because he was manifestly not against the plutonium economy; he merely wanted it to hasten slowly, like Sir John Hill. This statement was a classic illustration of the unity of the British Establishment. Even when they seem to be disagreeing they are really united. Umpires, batsmen and bowlers are really all on the same side, as in the great game of cricket.

Sir Herman Bondi injected small doses of sanity and wondered whether it might be less expensive to stockpile uranium rather than rush into fast breeders and the plutonium age. No one bothered to answer. All that was part of the trouble, as I told him afterwards. We were talking to scientists about resources in seemingly absolute terms. Whether something cost £1 billion or £1,000 billion hardly seemed relevant in the world to which we had transported ourselves.

Sir Kelvin Spencer, the former chief scientist at the Ministry of Power, upset some of the others present with prickly references to the wishes of voters. Science proceeds not through the wishes of voters, Members of Parliament, or even governments, but through peer group assessment. This means scientists judging scientists with research programmes, and projects being pushed forward through the corporate scientific institutions which most of those at the conference represented. This was no seminar to discuss the needs of voters. Sir Kelvin was out of order. Not even the presence of Walt Patterson, a Friend of the Earth (at the conference in much the same way that statutory blacks and statutory women are invited to sit on important committees) could put him in order. Walt was the statutory human being.

The only other human touch was provided by Jack – Sir Jack Rampton, Tony's Permanent Secretary – who had threatened not to come at all because of the demands of family life. In the end Jack turned up for the Friday evening session and left after breakfast on Saturday morning. Jack's contribution to the seminar had been to tell it straight, tell it true. 'By keeping our options open, I mean keeping our options open,' he had told the assembled multitude before departing for bed.

Tommy Balogh, one of the few sane and likeable lords I have ever met, summed up Sunningdale, as we traversed the manicured lawns and rounded the silent lake, as Armstrong's Folly, Armstrong being the head of the Civil Service from 1968 to 1974. The atmosphere of the college, he said, was both seductive and irrelevant to the modern world. One could understand what he meant. It was good to be alive. The rhododendrons and azaleas were beautiful. One could do a bit of work in these surroundings.

I wonder how the scientists saw it. Each had been provided with a study bedroom (containing a wash-basin, an electric shaver point, a wardrobe, a table and chair and a Bible) in halls of residence built in red brick and named after dead civil servants who had received great honours from their country for their services. Come to think of it, most of the scientists had received honours for their services too. What, I wondered, did they make of the presence of the Bible, whose metaphysical mysteries were some way from their accursed certainties?

Or have I got it wrong? Is it their plutonium-processed world that is real and the rhododendrons and the azaleas that are the illusion? Or are they both part of a dream?

10 March 1980   **Brian Sedgemore**

Windscale caught off guard

Consciously or not, the Nuclear Inspectorate's report on a large leak of radioactivity at Windscale (discovered more or less by accident) treats the works as though it were a old-established family brewery of interest to local historians. 'Records of liquor levels ... have not been found prior to 1967 although earlier operational log books which occasionally mention the plant are in existence.' A new instrument panel was installed in 1977 'using renovated and re-calibrated gauges from the old panel (which had deteriorated badly with time and weather)'. 'Examination of old operating logs has revealed an entry in the shift foreman's log for July 1, 1964, which refers to splashover from the 8-way diverter into the ageing tank.' But these agreeable memoirs of an antiquary amount to so severe a criticism of the Windscale management that prosecution was considered for breach of its licensing conditions. British Nuclear Fuels has accepted the censure. It had no choice. But it looks as though the bad housekeeping of which the Flowers Report wrote in 1976 has not improved much. Windscale is not like any other factory. It is potentially one of the most dangerous places in Europe. On the whole its record is good, but 'on the whole' is too low a criterion. By good fortune the leak has done no damage – yet – to life. Now that it is known about it can be contained. But there are too many loose ends at Windscale, too little safety consciousness.

In the film *The China Syndrome* the panic was caused by a gauge which stuck, giving a wrong reading. At Windscale the rise in the level of radioactive liquor in the tank which overflowed was not detected because the circular gauge measuring from 0 to 50 cm was on its second journey round. It measured 30 when it should have measured 80. But worse, it appears that the management did not know whether the stuff in the tank was radioactive or not. It rather thought not, which is why the old plans and old logs of the plant were scoured.

This was an old part of the works. Nothing much was happening there at the time. But radioactivity can outlive many generations of management and the sins of the 1950s intake can be visited upon the 1980s. British Nuclear Fuels is not going to discipline anybody, presumably because the old-timers have retired. Nor will there be prosecutions of the company: to what end, since the fine would be a transfer of public funds from one account to another? But after this sharp rap from the inspectorate BNFL should expect an even sharper public eye on its workings. It has unlimited funds only because the public needs maximum safety. That has not been provided.

1 August 1980   **Leader**

Bertie's booster

Now that most of the clotted cream and treacle has dripped off the eulogies to the Queen Mother for her 80th birthday, I feel able at last to reveal the story of my brief association with the gracious lady many years ago. The indiscretion is unlikely to figure greatly in the official royal biographies, so it might as well figure momentarily in mine.

At the time the lady was on the throne, and I was in Sussex. Very late at night, I got a phone call from the foreign desk of a newspaper, which was not *The Guardian*. It was to this effect: would I go to India, and there was a plane booked at six next morning. Reasonably enough, it seemed to me, I asked why. The man on the phone said he had no idea; the foreign editor had gone home, leaving this urgent requirement.

Had it occurred to the foreign editor, I asked, that I had only that very morning got *back* from India, and I knew damn well there was no story? The hireling replied: 'All I know is it says here, "Get the six a.m. tomorrow." '

So, obedient to a fault, as I always am, I got it. In those days there was no question of 747s and soft seats; you travelled on horrible converted Yorks or Lancaster bombers; it was hell, and it took forever. A lifetime later I decanted at Karachi and

78

found a feeder to Delhi. I cabled back asking, with respect, what the hell I was supposed to do?

To which, in the fullness of time, my master gave reply. (He is still a friend of mine, or I would tell you his name.) 'Most sorriest,' he said. 'Didn't mean India, meant South Africa stop proceed Capetown soonest accompany royal tour.'

Anyhow, that is how I came for the first time and last time to be part of a Royal Party. Never having been what you might call an over-enthusiastic monarchist, such a thing had not occurred to me. In the event, it turned out to be rather fun.

We travelled in what was called the White Train, and in a style to which I have always vainly hoped to become accustomed. We went all over the place. South Africa is, mostly unfairly, a vividly beautiful country, and we were fed and watered profusely. There was practically nothing to do.

No two personalities could have been more different than those of the King and the Queen. She was, then as now, composed, eager, on top of every situation; he was tense, unbearably nervous, alternating diffidence with bursts of temper. At the time there was a frightful cold spell in Britain; the papers were full of snowdrifts and power failures and freezeups; he kept saying he should be at home and not lolling about in the summer sun; never was a man so jumpy. The Queen kept smiling through.

Three or four times a day the White Train stopped at some wayside halt, where everyone was formally lined up. The King would stand shaking at the door of the train, dreading the inevitable encounters. The Queen would appear beside him, looking (the word is inescapable) radiant, or at any rate full of beans.

'Oh, Bertie, do you see, this is Hicksdorp! You know we've always so wanted to see Hicksdorp! Those people there with the bouquets – they must be the local councillors. *How* kind! And those people at the far, far end of the platform, behind that little fence – I expect they are the Bantu choir. How kind! We must wave, Bertie.'

And with a little nudge, the King found himself on terra

firma, clearly wishing he were anywhere else on earth, with his wife as clearly having waited all her life to see Hicksdorp.

One evening he called some of us press people along to his dining-car, ostensibly because he had a communication to make, but more probably to relieve the deadly boredom of the Hicksdorps and the Bantu choirs. I believe it to have been the only Royal Press Conference ever. We found him behind a table covered with bottles of all sorts of things, with which it would seem he had been experimenting, with some dedication.

'We must not f-forget the purpose of this t-tour,' he said, bravely, because his stammer was troublesome for him, 'trade and so on. Empire co-operation, for example, South African b-brandy. I have been trying it. It is of course m-magnificent, except that it is not very nice.' (It was in those days quite dreadful.) 'But,' he said triumphantly, 'there is this South African liqueur called V-Van der Humm. Perhaps a little sweet for most. *But*, now, if you mix half of brandy with half of Van der Humm . . . Please try.'

The South African journalists were ecstatic. They, and their fathers before them, had used this brandy-Humm mix for generations; nevertheless they applauded the King for having stumbled on something as familiar to them as gin-and-tonic. Their stories could have done the South African liquor trade no harm.

We arrived one day at a place called Outshoorn. This was a centre of the ostrich-feather trade, and ostrich-feathers had suffered a sad decline since, I imagine, the days of Queen Alexandra. Our passage through this empty place was supposed to stimulate it – to which end the King was detailed to nip a tail-feather off a sacrificial ostrich for the cameras, presumably to create a renaissance of feather-boas.

The King was understandably more nervous than usual – the ostrich even more so, its head and neck buried in a long stocking-like thing as if it were for an execution. The King fumbled the operation, and his tweezers nicked a quarter-inch off the ostrich's backside, at which the unlucky bird made a fearsome screeching hullabaloo, from which we all retreated in terror.

Enter the Queen, stage right, as usual in total smiling command. She took the clippers from her husband, and there and then did an absolutely expert featherectomy – snip. She spoke to the nearest bystander, who happened by chance to be me. 'We do a lot of gardening at home in the Palace,' said the Queen. 'The King is good at the digging and the weeding. It is I who concentrate on the secateurs.'

Here endeth the first and last of my Monarchical Memoirs. Let me be the last to wish the old lady a happy birthday. The ostrich can look after itself.

5 August 1980   **James Cameron**

Cultivating their garden

Whatever you may think of Transcendental Meditation, its promoters are undoubtedly livening up the long-isolated pile of Mentmore Towers. The ancient Rosebery estate, now the headquarters of meditation in Britain, is going to be opened to the public on Sunday afternoons (1–4 p.m.) from next weekend.

Entry will be free but a small price will be exacted in the form of polite attempts to interest the visitor in the meditators' activities as well as their historic surroundings. Anyone who goes merely to examine the grand architecture and vaulting rooms will probably find themselves paying a courtesy call on the TM 'laboratories' and 'research centres' while they are there.

As they tour the estate, they might also keep an eye open for a party of Buckinghamshire planning staff marching round the gardens with worried frowns. Any day now, the local authority is going to receive an outline planning application for a thousand-room extension to the Grade One listed building.

This will not take the form of a jarring office block, according to the meditators' leader Mr Peter Warburton, as the planners would clearly not contemplate that. Instead the building plans to conform to the original but unrealized designs for a Mentmore landscape as ornate as the house in the middle of it.

Like hobbits, the meditators living in the extension (which would act as a centre for transmitting peaceful thoughts to Northern Ireland and the trade unions), would be housed in a sort of burrow. The original garden plans, which the meditators got from Sotheby's at the time of the notorious Mentmore contents' auction, show a series of steps and banks adorned with fountains, sweeping down from the house.

By building these, Mr Warburton explained, the meditation rooms would be created inside the slopes with their residents peeping out through windows in the lawns, well screened, presumably, by shrubs. Whether the famous 'flying' of TM experts, which has earned Mentmore the local nickname of 'London's third airport,' could go on under such cramped circumstances is not clear. But if Buckinghamshire approves the scheme, we may find out. . .

The commonest cry of London at the moment is 'Ouch!' as something quite heavy and frequently sharp-ended falls on the passer-by's head. On examination, it probably turns out to be a piece of plane tree bark, dislodged in daggers of anything up to three feet long.

This is quite normal, as you will read shortly, but the public's growing interest in trees has led to an outbreak of concern. The gusty winds of the last few weeks have made the tree-peeling much more spectacular than usual and people have been worriedly phoning and writing in to Kew.

'Is there a Dutch plane disease?' is the commonest query, as the capital's inhabitants tramp through little piles of splintered treetrunk in the parks. 'Are the planes dying?' the amateur ecologists want to know, 'and is there anything we can do about it?'

The answer is No, unless you are commercially-minded, in which case you could bag up as much of the bark as you can and market it as compost or kindling. All trees do a sort of arboreal moult every year and the plane is just a lot more showy in doing it all at once than the rest.

'It was one of the things that made them particularly suitable for London,' explained Dr David Cutler, who has been fielding inquiries at Kew. A tree's bark protects it from disease but also needs to be relatively free from dirt and smut to allow the necessary oxygen and carbon dioxide to be exchanged.

In Victorian London the gently peeling type of tree was suffocated by filth and pollution before it ever had a chance. The planes, on the other hand, put up with the blanketing, held their breath until September and then shrugged off the whole of their dust-choked and soot-blackened skins with one great tree-y sigh of relief.

5 September 1979   **Martin Wainwright**

A bishop's market

You might well be suspicious, in this evil world, if a man came up to you and introduced himself as the Bishop of Ysabel or Aipo Rongo. Yet such dignitories do exist, along with My Lords of the Arctic, Pa-An, Qu'Appelle and many other strangely-named places in the far-flung kingdom of the Church of England.

Search as you will in Crockford's Clerical Directory, though, you will not find any bishops of more familiar places like Paris, Madrid or Bonn. The Church's tendency to send missionaries out to the Empire and beyond, and to leave the Continent to the Roman Catholics and Lutherans, has left the familiar names of Europe unrepresented.

Next week, if the General Synod of the Church of England votes as expected, this will change. A Bishop of Europe with a diocese stretching from Helsinki (where the Anglican chaplain looks after the small congregations in the Soviet Union) to the Costa Brava (where expatriates are improving attendance figures) will take his place in Congregation.

The Synod is likely to be pleased about this, but interesting speculations are prompted by the next legal step. The measure will have to go to the Houses of Parliament for formal approval, thanks to the position of the Anglicans as a State Church.

The possible obstacle lies in certain quarters of the Lower House where, as you know, the very word 'Europe' is enough to cause angry growls. The time may be coming for Mrs Thatcher & Co to redeem themselves over the Budget Day gaffe by squashing any Little Englander attempts to keep the European chaplains (who include the pleasantly titled Archdeacon of the Riviera) under their present masters – the diocese of Gibraltar and London.

6 *February 1980*   **Martin Wainwright**

A country diary: Lake District

Good weather recently for breaking in new boots – streaming fells, deep, squelchy bogs and flooded becks. If boots are still painful after a day or two in these conditions they'll never be right. My initial breaking-in was on Wetherlam with pouring rain and thick cloud to complete the cure. Nothing and nobody to be seen, but at least it was comfortable to have dry feet. My old, discarded boots had been letting in water on even moderately damp ground. Before the baptism of the new pair I had soaked them, inside and out, with vegetable oil. In the old days we always used goose grease – carefully saved after Christmas by wives or mothers. Dubbin or mineral oil, we were told, rotted the stitches. Once I broke in a new pair of very stiff, steel-shanked climbing boots by an extremely painful round of the Fairfield Horseshoe. About a mile from the end of the walk I stood knee-deep in Rydal Beck for several minutes until the boots were filled with water, and then fastened the laces as tightly as possible. It was a completely crippling last mile but the boots never gave me the slightest trouble afterwards – once my feet had recovered. The recent floods in the fell country finally put the seal on a disappointing summer and autumn; even the cows, still scratching at the last of the grass, look miserable, although the Herdwicks, long accustomed to hard lying, seem more stoically resignred to their fate. Lawns have never been so matted with moss and everywhere hedges remain uncut. Workers say it has always rained on their precious weekends and several recent glorious Mondays, sandwiched between bad days, can only have added to their desolation.

3 December 1979   **A. Harry Griffin**

The Leavin' of Liverpool

> *So fare thee well to Upper*
>   *Duke Street*
> *To something or other and*
>   *Park Lane,*
> *So fare thee well to Back*
>   *Canning Street*
> *I'll be glad to see the back*
>   *of you.*
> *So fare thee well to Sugar*
>   *Lane, Bull Lane,*
> *Dee Lane, Lark Lane,*
>   *Green Lane, Leather Lane*
> *And Little Katherine Street*
> *It's not the leavin' of*
>   *Liverpool*
> *That grieves me.*

Is Phil the Glass Morgan the only man alive who knows all the words to *It's Not The Leavin' of Liverpool*? And then Phil the Glass only knows them after 10 o'clock at night. It is perhaps significant of something that I called round to a dozen places to get the proper words to this famous tune, a tune which Bob Dylan lifted for his *Fare Thee Well My Darling True,* and all I got was a lot of humming. Tony Davis, of the Spinners, probably the only man in the Pool of Life who actually can sing the song all the way through before 10 o'clock of a night, was among the missing. Phil the Glass was probably sober somewhere.

How significant that the two big music shops in the Pool of

Life referred me to Manchester. They may eat thick seamed tripe and cow heel and not have much of a winning football team – or, at least, as winning a football team –but in Manchester, at the Music Exchange, they possessed the sheet music for *It's Not The Leavin' of Liverpool*. But not, I fear, the grand old lyrics that Phil the Glass knows, those lyrics which are a sort of A to Z of Liverpool Streets, cul-de-sacs, back alleys, and jiggers.

More than that, this Ten O'Clocker – that is a song which is sung at 10 o'clock, the old traditional closing time in the North – was a tribute to, a reminder of the lost streets the planners have done away with.

Looking around London I think maybe it is not Liverpool I miss but England itself. Perhaps I am too recently arrived in London to know what it is about the leavin' of Liverpool that grieves me.

Sherlock Holmes came to Liverpool. Well, recently we learned that Adolf Hitler did as well. And Ho Chi Minh, also the Emperor of China (in disguise), Daniel Defoe, Charles Dickens, de Quincey, Herman Melville, Nathaniel Hawthorne, Eugene O'Neill. Only the other week the local newspaper ran a feature on the day Butch Cassidy came to Liverpool.

'And what was he doing here?' I asked.

'Visiting his auntie, just like Hitler, just like everybody else,' a fellow said. Liverpool is a city of aunties. Malcolm Lowry and Wilfred Owen, although they were only from 'Over the Water', meaning across the river in the Wirral, the Cheshire peninsula which protects the Pool of Life from the full blasts of the Irish Sea, Lowry and Owen had aunties in Liverpool.

Armed with a rucksack full of Liverpool reference books I went into the heart of calendar art England, somewhere in deepest Somerset. Sprawled on the grass by a private swimming pool, with the sound of leather on willow somewhere off in the distance, with a good glimpse, stage left, through the fleshy O of my left armpit, of some maniac castle built in 1850 when the English, like the Californians of today, had more money than sense, and with, stage right, through the fleshy O, a pool full of giggling Lolitas who would get me 20 years for just what I was thinking, I asked my hostess, a Liverpool girl, a former head girl of Blackburn House when Blackburn House was Blackburn House, if there was anything in the leavin' of Liverpool that grieved her.

'Good God, no!' she cried. Well, more than 20 years, St Hilda's, long years living abroad, ski-ing in all the right places, and two horseback ridin', public school educated daughters, all stood between her and the Magic Mersey. She had become a genteel country woman, looking like a cross between Jane Austen and Qui Monsieur, who I had hopes for in the 4.30 at Newbury in the White Horse Handicap.

'Oh yes,' she said, 'there is. People talking about things you never hear people talking about anywhere else. People talking not exactly about anything, in fact.'

She had it there all right. Those endless monologues of Merseyside which bring fists flying or agonizing cries of 'For the love of God, shoot first and ramble later!'

Liverpool may not master Dublin for chat, but it talks in the same league. And hard pressed anyone connected at all with the arts is to get any work done in either city.

The street life of the city has changed drastically in recent years. The planners saw to that. For a spell it looked like they might have killed off the chat.   Those fantastic pubs with the long, real marble bars, full of the gorgeous stink first thing in the morning of stale ale, then filling up with smoke, draught Bass and Guinness, and talk, and sea food, too, all vanished.

There was a void. Then the wine bar bistro replaced them. They have sprung up everywhere in Liverpool and they never close, so the chat goes on all day and night. The evening newspaper, the *Liverpool Echo*, even carries a column about them, a patchwork of the super-real, the surreal and nonsense. Allegedly written by Our Man Among The Trendy Riff-Raff, it is the nearest thing to the great days of Myles na Gopaleen in the *Irish Times*.

Last winter *The Guardian* carried a full page by Mr James Fenton on the weird new café life of West Berlin, like a reconstruction of Herr Ishywood's Berlin. It was like reading about Liverpool. The point about Liverpool's Trendy Riff-

Raff, all dressed up with no place to go, is that they are unemployed or half employed, and rather than sit at home and moan they get all dressed up and go out and moan.

Liverpool is a lotus land; even when someone tries to do something it all seems to go wrong. After the success of *Illuminatus!* which Ken Campbell opened at Peter O'Halligan's Liverpool School of Language, Music, Dream and Pun, in Mathew Street, of Cavern and Beatles fame, they tried to get a real fringe theatre going there.

All went well until Campbell put on a science fiction opera and, being Campbell, he had to have the Hell Fires or something and a fire broke out. The fire inspectors did not truly believe it was the best place in the world for extravagant theatrics. The theatre was closed.

The Liverpool Everyman closed for modernization – when it reopened, all new and very Odeon 6, the customers didn't seem to like it because the seats did not collapse any more. Plus it was warm now and the bogs worked some of the time. A contrary race the Liverpudlians. Liverpool is not a piece of England, not even proper Lancashire nor a new county called Merseyside, it is instead a city state.

I've always been a Manchester United fan, but I will miss Liverpool F.C., and the poor, contrary Everton fans like Mr Mike Williams, who is a famous cartoonist – Liverpool breeds cartoonists and comedians – who once went into the Spion Kop with me. There he stood, dressed head to socks in blue, the offending colour of Everton, sketching unflattering pictures of the assembled divs, 22,000 Liverpool supporters.

And why, I asked, was he an Everton supporter? He was not Roman Catholic, the old dividing line. 'I'm a younger brother,' he said, 'I stick up for the Germans and the Red Indians as well.'

I shall miss the divs, and the civic leaders, the good burghers of Liverpool. Where else would you get a city engineer like Mr Jack Bennet, president of the Liverpool Cricket Club, a tall, silver-haired, elegant figure, who explained to me in great technical detail the revamping of the Kop, which in the interest of safety and hygiene had its intake cut from 24,000 to 22,000. 'But it's best,' he added, 'to wear your wellies.' And why was that? He looked at me. I was a true innocent. 'To cut down,' he said, 'on instances of the hot leg.'

I shall miss sitting down before the telly of an evening watching yet another documentary about Liverpool featuring the slate roofed rows of broken down houses, with that three-legged dog hobbling down the cobble-stoned streets. Who is this three-legged Rin Tin Tin without whom no realistic, hard-hitting, in-depth, searing, block-busting look at Liverpool would be complete? That dog's a ringer. That three-legged dog must be Esther Rantzen's dog.

I shall see the documentaries, of course, but I shall not see them from Liverpool.

On a clear day you can see the Welsh hills across the Mersey, with the Mersey wide, wider than a mile, wide as the Mississippi, and carrying with it the smell of the sea which tickles the nose and creates that most curious accent. And out of the Wirral too, from over that water, come those glorious girls, all blue eyes and blonde. It's the Cheshire cheese, they say, that does it.

In a book I read when my aim was serious research I came upon a po-faced, earnest Victorian report on the sordid night life of the Pool of Life, full of frowning sentences about gin palaces and sporting gals with the stern author then ending it all, this sordid picture, with a puzzled note saying that sailors seemed for some reason or other to like the place.

Brian Patten, the Liverpool poet who, with Roger McGough and Adrian Henri, revitalized poetry in England in the 1960s, writes some lovely stuff about the beauty of the Liverpool girls. But he lives in Holland Park. He cannot work in Liverpool.

McGough, who lives in a splendid white elephant of a white wedding cake of a house, on the edge of Sefton Park where strange mushrooms grow, got into an anthology of erotic verse, with an erotic poem set on the top of a Liverpool bus. But Roger is preparing to leave Liverpool.

Only Adrian, who is on so many committees he could not leave without the city collapsing, seems firmly rooted.

But there are more serious matters afoot than poetry and

pretty girls and the assorted trendy trash who fill the wine bars and bistros of the Weimar Republic on the Mersey.

I have seen the militant bishops, Anglican and Papist, and the Methodist too, linking arms and marching at the head of a winding dragon of red banners, down to the Pier Head where angry men cursed a Labour Government for failing to remember that England did not stop at Watford Gap. And now Sir Keith Joseph has, at his mistress's bidding, gone to the economic moors for a day's rough shooting of industrial lame ducks.

Employment figures for Liverpool are not level mirrors. They do not give a true reflection. The city's population is in decline. Once it was 800,000. Now is is 600,000. And the city planners, I have it on very good authority, scheme for a city of a mere 450,000 souls.

Liverpool is shrinking. Back in the Sixties when Atilla the Hun came to Merseyside with a slide rule, they cleared the city of people, moved them to the new towns. In all this movement of people somehow 60,000 people went missing. There is no accounting for them. Nowhere have I seen any serious mention of this. I came upon it through Mr Arthur Dooley, the sculptor. He had bothered to go down to the Town Hall and get the book and then he had sat down and done his sums.

And of all the questioning journalists, all the architectural writers, city planners, civic leaders, experts on New Jerusalem, none of them raised a voice against the relocation of the people, the depopulation of the city centre. Only Arthur Dooley raised a rumpus. And who was he? A local character. Former tugboatman. Former welder at the shipyards. Ex-heavyweight champion of the Irish Guards. A Protestant, born in an area where they are so Orange they used the Union Jack for bedspreads, turned Catholic. A Catholic turned Communist.

The local press actually laughed at Arthur because he said the way they rebuilt the Pier Head spoiled the people's view of the river, that the sight of the river and the notion that it led to the sea and away from it all was what kept the people going. Now everyone agrees with him. The in-depth reporters, city planners, civic leaders, and the leader writers have at long last figured out with their slide rules what the human heart could tell in an instant, at a glance.

Like a wounded animal the city draws in upon itself. The horns are pulled in. The new towns are ghost towns. The middle class are busy leaving the sinking ship. The skilled workers and craftsmen, too.

What is it to me? I only came to Liverpool by accident. And then stayed on out of absent-mindedness. My own home town is thousands of miles away, and if I never see that again it will be too soon. But the North of England is the heart of England. In the North they make things, in London they only make money. If Britain, in Sir Harold Wilson's words, can no longer be the workshop of the world, what then can it become? The world's supplier of waiters? The purveyor of the bizarre in the arts? The inventor of a new, unwashed, State-fed, leisure class like the Trendy Riff-Raff of Liverpool?

'I am amazed,' a German girl said to me, seated in Streets, which is across the alley from Kirkland's and round the corner from the Everyman Bistro, 'I am amazed at the beauty of the people.'

'You thought this was the City of the Three Legged Dog?'

'I would not have put it so. But yes.'

The poor little rich work-orientated German girl could not comprehend the jobless all around her who had nothing to do all day but make themselves beautiful in preparation for stepping on to the stage of Liverpool's new and amazing street theatre. Only in Chelsea and Kensington had she seen such people. But there it is expensive. In Liverpool it is more continental. At Keith's in Lark Lane, Sefton Park, that beautiful park which warms the heart of George Melly and Alun Owen, the kids come in from the chip shop next door. Keith does not seem to mind them bringing food into his bistro.

There are places like Street's, Kirkland's, Indulgence, Keith's in London, but in Liverpool they are low priced.

And in London none of the new beautiful poor will make a sudden, startling entrance like Annalisia, the dusky maiden, sashaying into Street's in her Cleopatra rig-out, a diamond in her nose, little Sasha, her son, at her feet. Annalisia screaming at me, 'You called me a mere star, you . . . you! I am a goddess, you remember that, you . . .'

Annalisia found it psychologically impossible to work behind a bar in a bistro. Others found it an in sort of job. Long tall Brenda, a former model, thinks it is like being a star or top model. Even Lola E. Grace, the world welterweight vanity champion, went behind a bistro bar and saw herself as being on stage.

Allen Ginsberg claimed Liverpool was 'the centre of consciousness of the human universe'. Dr Jung dreamed dreams of Liverpool and called it the Pool of Life. Those magic mushrooms must grow in other places outside Sefton Park.

Let other pens dwell in guilt and misery, as Jane Austen, who had an auntie in Liverpool, said; I feel no guilt at scurrying off the sinking ship. It was never my home. I have no aunties there.

All I ever wanted to be was a prairie Lorca, a sideburned hero of the snowy West, but love brought me to Liverpool and inertia kept me there. 'Come to the Smoke,' Brian Patten told me, 'and pull your finger out.' 'Now that you are in London,' said Little Lynda Marchal, actress, writer, and true daughter of the Mersey, with half a dozen aunties to prove it, 'now you can pull your finger out.'

Packing up to make my getaway I filled two and one half tea chests with the unpublished works attempted in Liverpool these past 20 years, man and boy. 'Unpublished Works' looked rather defeatist for the new life of the finger out. I crossed out 'Unpublished' and made it 'Works in the Works'.

So fare thee well to the rambling chat and the easy living that kept the finger in, I shall not return unless paid to do so.

It's not the leavin' of Liverpool that grieves me.

And Lola has my London number. She had my number anywhere all the time, anyway.

28 July 1979 **Stanley Reynolds**

What a way to spend a weekend

I face the weekend with the resignation of a soul bound for limbo, destined to spend two days in the clutter of an untidy past, my mistakes and my failure to be a Christian. It began years ago. An only child in a house of adults of ill-assorted temperaments which clashed like out-of-tune cymbals from Friday night to Monday morning, I soon tumbled to the fact that my weekends were atypical.

Other fathers, who mostly worked in the City. donned sleeveless V-necked pullovers, mowed lawns, mulched straw-berries, played cricket and puffed pipes. Mine, who worked hard at a job he loathed, indulged heavily in conversation, drink and a love affair with horses that was somewhat greater than his ability to predict which of them would beat the other over five furlongs.

From him I learned mood-swing: optimism (before the 2.30 at Epsom), resignation (after the aforementioned had been run), rage and remorse. On Sunday mornings he was often so full of the latter (a devout Anglican at heart) that he would slip off to Holy Communion and thence, by way of an expedition to pick field mushrooms, wet walnuts or whatever was in season, to the pub. He returned home several hours later partially absolved and fully refreshed to tell, like Hare, of his great adventure and to torment us with any handle he fancied, be it our lack of piety or the fact that the joint was overcooked.

Throughout, his use of the English language was agile and inventive, but since my mother was also a verbal athlete, Manichee and a teetotaller there followed a cacophonous marathon which lasted through *Family Favourites*, lunch itself, the washing up and stopped only, so far as I know, when I went to Sunday school because Jesus wanted me for a sunbeam and they presumably wanted a rest. In the evening the combatants sewed, sipped and sniped and we all listened to the *Palm Court Orchestra* and *These You Have Loved*.

Thus conditioned I went to my first marriage accepting the self-fulfilling prophecy of the weekend: drink, dissent and a good deal of slaughtered lamb to be cooked. I inherited six step-children but only the two youngest were regular visitors on Saturday and Sunday. I did my best. I played with the children, took them out, made them dresses and tried to keep them out of Daddy's way whilst he was working or drinking (which to be fair he did in moderation) or thinking (which was most of the time). I monitored the meat with cordon-bleu precision to avert any row and was occasionally successful; and listened to Mozart instead of Jean Metcalfe. About four hundred weekends passed in this way before, for other reasons as well, I quit.

For a brief year I was free of the two days of the week I disliked the most. I was invited and went to live in the house of two generous, welcoming friends whose own marriage was however at a watershed. Liberated from the constricting ritual of my own roasts, rows and sense of duty I could do what I wanted and mostly did.

Occasionally I spent the weekend 'at home' with my friends and felt nostalgic, like a redundant au pair – wanting to baste the beef, have the children make demands of me, but instead a bystander at the hollow feast of a family which no longer wished to be one.

I moved alone into my own flat and fell in love. My lover moved in too. For a couple of months weekends were bliss. We talked, we cooked and ate and drank and made love and we didn't row. Then I conceived and experienced the inevitable chastisements of pregnancy – in my case a loathing for the smell of dead flesh cooking, alcohol and most forms of conversation. I also acquired a passion for counter-tenors singing of loss. One weekend when I was near my time, my lover went on a trip in a Thames sailing barge. A force nine gale whipped up and they played 'O Hear Us When We Cry To Thee' during a church service on television and I wept because my child would be fatherless and I inconsolable.

He came home safe and sound. Shortly afterwards my son was born, and entered, unknowing, the Roman Catholic

Church to which his father and forbears belonged. I felt somehow that he would be safer there and that later his father would take him by the hand to Mass, leaving me peacefully at home on a Sunday and that we would then all play happy families.

His father continued to sleep in until noon, repairing thence to the pub round the corner leaving me holding the baby and cooking a huge Sunday lunch for him and for all the friends he would bring back. In the afternoon everybody except me slept. Three years later, trundling the pushchair alone in the nearby park, past flower beds and romping families with dogs and couples walking hand in hand in childless harmony, I vowed through tears of gross self-pity to change it all again . . .

There is no fool like an old fool; unless it is one who thinks he can eradicate the past and all the grievances and conditioned responses it created. Now each weekend my small London flat bursts at the seams as children run whooping through it, commandeering every precious inch of space as beds become battlefields and the stairs to the front door more lethal than the Cresta run. Calls for drinks, calls for food, calls for baths to be run, clothes to be found, phone calls to be blocked, children to be silenced. Plans for the weekend are made; nobody agrees.

The man of the house remembers he has a drawing to finish and disappears to the office 'for an hour'. He is gone for three and we row. I am asked out for drinks. I say I have the children. Ah, well, one evening perhaps?

I start lunch and sing the last aria from *Aida* to myself, very loud. I recite the Confession, relic of my semi-Christian childhood, filling in the gaps left for the responses like a practised dentist: I have left undone those things which I ought to have done (taken the veil at seventeen) . . . and done those things which I ought not to have done (this takes longer but includes references to ill-advised alliances and my stubbornness in refusing to accept that history repeats itself).

And then, because it helps me, I recite the Litany of Solidarity for those of my friends – almost all – who abhor the weekend as much as I do, though for different reasons.

There is W whose lover returns to his wife every Friday leaving her 'like the little match girl, staring through windows at families'; X, whose husband comes home bringing his washing with him – 'underpants, socks and shirts which smell of someone else's scent'; Y, whose husband died four years ago but who still cannot give up his ghost and seek a replacement; and Z, whose children go off with a father who traded her in for a younger, prettier version, leaving her desolate with only 'the bottle or other bitter wives' as weekend companions. 'None of us,' said one of my friends recently, 'seems to have got it right. You have kids and a bloke around, you go out in the car, you have someone to shop for, you can do things together, you're needed. I envy you. Who do you envy?'

All I could tell her was of a constantly recurring memory of one Sunday afternoon a few years ago. The clock stood at half past three. Food and drink had been consumed in plenty; newspapers lay spent upon the floor. My infant for once lay quiet in his cot; and the sun flirted with his father's features as he lay supine on the couch, arms folded, and snored his way to eternity.

19 October 1979   **Judy Froshaug**

Carry on caring

Patrick Campbell wrote a piece about Nurse Foley of Tralee, the tireless talker with the sky blue bloomers, who burst into the cloistered life of Paul and Primula Gossett. Remembering this disaster at a distance, I now feel sure that Foley was sent by a social worker. They appear to have a natural or carefully coached aptitude for pushing square Foleys into round Gossetts.

In both programmes I have seen in the *Decision* series (BBC-1) some social worker has struggled, like a demented dating computer, to fit together people who have nothing to say to each other but goodbye. I have struggled like that to stick together disparate materials with unsuitable glue. It always ends with my falling on the foul object with clenched and gummed up fists while the budgie tries to hide bodily under his sandpaper.

I am, therefore, the more moved by the patience shown by social workers, who could model for patience on a monument just by shinning up the plinth and looking natural. This week's *Decision* in two parts records the best endeavours of Coventry social workers to foster Janice, a speechless black 16-year-old, with the Joneses, as nice a pair of enlightened liberals as ever had it coming to them.

Some will have enjoyed most the ominous drive to the Joneses' home in leafy Coventry.

Social worker with a stirring of unease: 'How do you *know* you can drive?'

Janice: 'I drove Stoke Houses's minibus, didn't I? I banged it into one of them things.'

Or tea chez the Joneses.

'Something to drink?'

'No.'

'A sandwich then?'

'Nothing.'

'How about having a cake instead?'

'No.'

Or the Someone Somewhere Wants a Phone Call From You scene:

Social worker: 'I was wondering why you hadn't come in?'

Janice: 'I didn't want to.'

'Can you tell me why?'

'No.'

'Are you worried?'

'No.'

With a ringing or, rather, ringing-off remark: 'I don't want nothing to do with social workers or jobs.'

Janice hung up. Twice.

The social worker searched her soul. 'I just don't know what she's saying.'

I do. She's saying she doesn't want nothing to do with social workers or jobs or nothing.

The little Jones boys were perfectly at ease in this fraught affair. 'They've been waiting with guns and everything to shoot you when you came,' said Mrs Jones in Joyce Grenfell's hostess-in-heavy-weather voice. 'We've been waiting a long time for Janice, haven't we?' The child addressed shook his head firmly.

Do not miss next week's *Collision Corner* in which I confidently predict Janice and the Joneses will come unstuck at the top of their voices to the astonished distress of the social workers.

6 February 1980   **Nancy Banks-Smith**

Making a meal of it

It's nice coming to Dublin because you realize there is always someone worse off than yourself. As the heads of government jetted in for the latest EEC summit meeting, the city was facing a coal strike and a dustmen's strike. The banks had been shut for several days because a rumour that they were going to shut had caused a run during which the three-million population drew out £100 million in a single day. So they had to shut. Worst of all, the barmen were threatening to strike. This would not only have deprived Dublin of drink, but also of its secondary banking system, the pubs.

Not that this can have much affected the Prime Ministers who assembled at Dublin Castle. Ferried from one state building to another in a fleet of monstrous, stretched vehicles – a cross between a limousine and a charabanc, each big enough to hold the conference in – they can hardly be aware of the city they are visiting.

The Dublin police have got those special American sirens which instead of going 'Ow-wow' go 'Whoop-whoop' like electronic banshees. They spent most of the morning playing with them, so that the city centre sounded as if it was on a nuclear alert.

In the afternoon a great cavalcade swept dramatically into the castle courtyard. Was it the BBC crew? No, only the heads of government. Clearly national virility is somehow tied up with the speed at which each car storms the gateway, and the suddenness with which it pulls up to disgorge a shaken premier. Mrs Thatcher looked distinctly wobbly, though this could have had something to do with the sense of anger and outrage we are encouraged to believe she is suffering.

As the cars arrived, the police motorcycle escorts had to peel off and swarm round the courtyard. Since they too did this at top speed, they kept just missing each other, as if at a military tattoo where all the soldiers were drunk.

Naturally, just as important as what happens at the talks is what the voters think happened at the talks. So officials from the various national delegations spend a great deal of time briefing the 800 or so journalists. The British line was that the Prime Minister was 'buoyant and ready for it'. No one explained what 'it' was, though it emerged that she was also ready for the talks.

Officials announced what she was going to say before she said it. After she'd said it, there were informal briefings about what she had said. Next Lord Carrington turned up and thoughtfully read out a text of what she had said. Then an official sat in the chair where Lord Carrington had sat and repeated what she had said, only in more deatil. Later we received further general résumés of what Mrs Thatcher had said. We began to get the gist of her remarks. Her negotiating technique seems to be the one perfected by the Kray twins: 'Nice little Common Market you got here. Wouldn't want anyfink nasty to happen to it. Now would we?'

Meanwhile all the other national delegations are also briefing like mad. But they have a sneaky advantage. They do it in foreign languages, so the British cannot understand. No wonder our people are suspicious of Europe.

All the national briefings, naturally, contradict each other. The Irish briefings are, however, unique. They contradict themselves. As for the participants, it all sounds rather boring, if the briefings are any guide. This is not surprising. Prime ministers have a rum idea of what constitutes good conversation. Your correspondent once eavesdropped on a chat between Mr Callaghan and Chancellor Schmidt. It went roughly: 'You're looking very well, Helmut.' 'And you're looking very well, Jim.' 'I saw Henry Kissinger last night.' 'How was he?' 'Looking very well.'

It only gets half-interesting at dinner time. This is when the prime ministers are on their own. Even the foreign secretaries are banished to another room, where they sit around getting agitated. Prime ministers are (a) notoriously ignorant about foreign affairs and (b) convinced they can manage them much better than foreign secretaries.

What is more, everybody says, dinner time is when the real negotiating starts. As the prime ministers sit around swilling claret and brandy, they tend to cook up all sorts of pally little deals, without even mentioning them to their foreign secretaries. So the latter and the civil servants then have to spend all next morning getting the deals reversed. At this time the prime ministers quite often have hangovers, so it is not too hard to persuade them. In any case, nobody takes any notes at these dinners, except on the back of a menu, so nobody can remember what was agreed in the first place. This enables all nine countries to claim victory at the end of the summit.

1 December 1979   **Simon Hoggart**

La fume de ma tante

The following is the text of a draft document found in Downing Street late last night. It is thought likely to be connected with the Prime Minister's broadcast on French television on Monday night.

'Je viens auprès de vous comme le commis-voyageur d'une campagne qui a été vissé quelque chose de putréfié par ses huit soi-disants amis dans l'EEC, et particulièrement par votre propre tête de condition, President Giscard d'Estaing.

'Je sais que les papiers français ont été genou-profond en

rapports que mon gouvernement a été conduisant la mère et le père d'un brouhaha politique ce dernier peu de semaines. Un de mes pasteurs, M. Jacques Antérieur, est allé si loin au desus du sommet qu'il est aujourd'hui très très triste en effet pour ayant été si trompé. Des autres, comme M. Pierre Promeneur, devenons si fromagés avec votre comportement au sujet des mouton-viandes qu'ils commencent à dire qu'ils ont une demi-pensée à jeter la chose entière dans, jolie tot.

'Je veux dire ici et maintenant que quelconque nous pensons d'un l'autre sur plusieurs sujets, nous sommes unifiés en étant alimenté jusqu'aux notres dents arrières avec votre libertés diaboliques et de visage nu, et nous allons vous arrêter de plumer votres nids propres aux debours de pauvre ancien Grand Bretagne.

'Regardez: c'est assez mal ayant à visage trois années d'un austérité sans parallèle, comme mon ami M. Jean Souffleten l'a placé – cependant j'ai lui dit qu'il a fait meilleur à tenir fermé son cabriolet. Je veux vous aviser que, si vous ne tousserez pas debout en Bruxelles, donc, comme un autre de mes pasteurs a dit au journal *Le Gardien* jeudi, "il va être absolument sanglant. Nous serons sanglants, ils seront sanglants à dos, et puis nous serons justement régulièrement plus sanglants."

'Je suis triste, j'ai à cesser là. Je puis voir le Seigneur Autobaguetonne a l'autre côté de l'autocue, et il me semble qu'il'y a quelque chose qu'il est pénible à obtenir au dessus à moi . . .'

8 March 1980   **Leader**

Man for the Paris fashions

The Gare du Nord in the early morning rain. Cobb gets down from the night train from London, scuffed leather holdall and check cap in one hand. Past the barrier, he makes straight for the only cafe open. He can be seen through its long windows: red face, red pate with wispy hair; he could be taken for a farmer, or maybe a butcher, were he not so slim.

A second pousse café. Then a third. Thus fortified, Cobb emerges, turning up the collar of his black overcoat. He makes for the teeming Metro, abruptly changes his mind, and is swallowed up by the crowd. An hour later, the doors of number 36 Quai des Orfevres swing open at his approach. The vigilant commissionaire has spotted the tiny rosette in his left lapel. The *Legion d'Honneur* is a passport through the portals of the *Police Judiciaire* – the French Scotland Yard.

Cobb passes along the corridors with their green plush benches and their trawl of night people, handcuffed, some of them to pairs of huge detectives. He does not pause for breath until he reaches the top floor – the fifth – where, in rows of green boxes, are the records of crimes remaining only as skeletal memories in the families of those who committed them long ago, but which Cobb will painstakingly flush out.

An English Maigret? Not exactly, though Richard Cobb admires Simenon enough to be embarking on a book about him. It is an unexpected occupation for the Professor of Modern History at Oxford, but then Cobb's interests and instincts are those of an historical detective; someone who is as intimate with the Paris of Maigret as with the Paris of the Revolution and who reconstructs in his books the details of unimportant lives lived in the *quartiers* of the city.

Cobb's latest case is an examination of the deaths of 404 Parisians who came to violent ends in the years after the Revolution, mostly suicides, accidents and murder. Their bodies were brought to a building which was the forerunner of the city morgue – the Basse-Greole de la Seine – and from the archives there he has reassembled in minute detail an account of low life in the capital from 1795 to 1801.

Cobb ties it up in 100 pages of narrative and the book, *Death in Paris* (published by Oxford University Press) has just won the Wolfson Literary Award, worth £5,000. His *métier* is different from Maigret's, but the manner is the same. He once wrote that Simenon's view of history was that it should 'be walked, seen, smelt and eavesdropped as well as read.'

For an historian cocooned in Oxford, that could be a dangerous premise. But Cobb lives the life he writes about; maybe not so much now that he is 62, but especially in his unattached decade when he was researching in Paris. When you meet him, it is difficult to see where the professional historian ends, and the raconteur, who likes a glass or two, takes over. He is strongly anti-academic; he can probably pick up as much from the patron or the concierge as from the municipal archives: he is addicted to both because they offer the same type of information – only the historical period is different.

The people he writes about in *Death in Paris* – the marginals, he calls them – are the very ones he met in his earliest days in Paris. He was first sent there, rather against his will, by his family. He went back, to do research, in 1946. 'I've always been an extremely lonely historian, listening to extremely lonely people. My sort of history is to do with lack of success, and much of it is to do with the art of survival.'

Surviving in garrets at the top of tall houses in Paris, a fantasy at Shrewsbury and the foreboding of parents in Tunbridge Wells, was bearable because he was smitten by the French. 'I got myself demobilized to go back to France. I spent my war gratuities on drink and women. I always liked women, not quite like Simenon' (who claims to have screwed 10,000). 'They were a relief from loneliness. I met quite a few prostitutes in Paris. They were quite amusing as people. I didn't regard them as machines *à plaisir* or as *bêtes de plaisir*. I was quite a Puritan.

'They did not see themselves as victims in the Marxist

sense. Nor were they dejected about it. If they had been dejected, they wouldn't have been very good at their job. They were like the other marginals I met. I'm a drinking man really. I like it because it opens people up. I had the old problem of being a bachelor living in a very small room, and wanting to go to bed as late as possible.'

Loneliness figures quite a lot in Cobb's conversation and his writing. He himself has the compulsive garrulousness of a basically shy man who has always felt uneasy in England and who, by inserting himself in France, has been accepted by a less deferential, more talkative race. He gets on well there, and in Wales where he was for six years a lecturer at Aberystwyth. 'The Welsh remind me of the French. They have this close observation of each other, slightly malicious and gossipy.'

Isn't he a bit of a gossip himself? He doesn't disagree. 'I don't want to know what someone's salary is or what his promotion prospects are. It's private lives which interest me. As an historian, I can't imagine anything worse than writing the life of Lord Beveridge. Or that man Mr Macmillan mentioned' (Macmillan presented the Award to Cobb, and made a speech) – 'Louis Namier – that Central European snob. I suppose one can't blame him for being an Anglophile, but he really believed that England in the 18th century revolved round the boring manipulation of Shropshire MPs.'

Richard Cobb plays fair: he is, after all, willing to reveal as much about himself as he gleans from others. But somewhere at the back of it all is a sort of uncertainty or fear. The only English city he enjoyed working in was Manchester where 'you had an almost French accessibility.' 'I've always been afraid of the country.' Why? 'Oh . . . wolves and peasants.' Why peasants? 'I've never actually met a peasant in my life. I wouldn't know how to behave.'

And yet, in his writing, he can bridge with empathy the distance between himself and some country girl, below stairs in Paris two centuries ago, who jumps into the Seine when her lover deserts her. For *Death in Paris* recreates the last days and last hours of scores of people at the margins of life, and details the moral loneliness they felt. It is a technique that goes way beyond what historians usually offer. Cobb says 'I take very considerable jumps with historical evidence. I think history is as much a work of imagination as a novel.'

There is no dryness here. But still, he is thankful for the survival of official archives, at central and local level. 'France is a suspicious country, and so it has always multiplied its paper checks. The sort of people I work on, you wouldn't find a thing on them in England. A suspicious state is a joy to the historian.'

But Cobb doesn't agree that a suspicious regime and a population with great curiosity are part of the same thing. 'They feed on each other, but authority in France comes from above. I am English but I don't know England at all well. I don't understand the unofficial authority of the squire . . . this unstated authority, deference. That is the difference. France is not a deferential country.'

The French take historians at face value: the man in the check cloth cap, having a drink in the cafe. Who would believe that he is really an Oxford professor? Well, he managed to convince Simenon, who was rather flattered that an English academic should be planning a book about him. But then Simenon approves of anonymity. Cobb has just been to see him in Lausanne. 'He said he's got an anonymous face. He could sit in a second class carriage reading a local newspaper and nobody would notice him. He'd just listen.' It makes you wonder what they said to each other.

8 December 1979   **John Cunningham**

The Exodus allegory

As written by Frances Yates, intellectual history is thrillingly seditious. She deals in prohibited knowledge, subversive sects, and dark, riddling conceits. *The Occult Philosophy* (Routledge, 1979) *in the Elizabethan Age* is another of her narratives of intellectual conspiracy, tracing the transmission of Jewish mystical lore through the Renaissance and

Reformation and its illicit contribution to the official ideology of Elizabethan literature and statecraft.

Not only is Frances Yates expert at deciphering the cabbalistic codes of her historical subjects –the numerology of Dürer. the astrology of Spenser – she is also in her own way something of a cabbalist. *The Occult Philosophy* can be read, like the texts it treats, as a shadowy allegory, discreetly concealing its actual import. For it seems to me that this new book refers not only to the Renaissance but to Frances Yates's own intellectual background and her apprenticeship to the great scholars of the Warburg Institute.

The Occult Philosophy is about exile, diaspora, the harbouring of an endangered knowledge. Expelled from Spain in 1492, the Jews, Frances Yates argues, fled to Italy where they made propaganda for the esoteric traditions of The Cabala, which eventually infected neo-Platonic philosophy. Preserved by being safely Christianized, the Cabala even penetrated Elizabethan England, which supposedly had been long since cleansed of Jews. But this invasion provoked a reaction in the epidemic of anti-semitic witch-hunting summed up, for Frances Yates, in Marlowe's *Jew of Malta* and the low, fraudulent conjurors of Jonson's *Alchemist*.

Decoded, this is nothing less than an account of the intellectual calamities of the 1930s, which convened the school of intellectual history to which Frances Yates is now contributing. Her mentors were all Jewish scholars forced to decamp by Hitler, as the Jews of the Iberian peninsula, in the present book, were ousted by Catholic bigotry in 1492. And like the magical wisdom of the mystagogues studied in this book – Reuchlin, Agrippa, Giorgi –the scholarship of that generation of Jewish intellectuals was conditioned by dispersal and fragmentation, driven by the need to preserve the threatened continuity of European culture by smuggling it underground.

Hence *The Heritage of Images* by Fritz Saxl, with whom Frances Yates worked: those enduring icons are for Saxl sacred talismans, bridges to a past which the Nazis were obliterating. Similarly the *topoi* in E. R. Curtius's *European*

Literature and the Latin Middle Ages are conservative ballasts, an insurance against change and the erasure of memory. In *Mimesis*, Erich Auerbach, writing in exile and without a library, was able to reconstruct the span of Western literature from a few isolated, excerpted texts, as if he were piecing it together from the wreckage which had survived the apocalypse.

The persecution of these men is even represented, for Frances Yates, in the Jew-baiting which accompanied the witch craze of the sixteenth century. In her book, Marlowe becomes a reactionary fascist, inciting racial hatred and viciously relishing the execution of Elizabeth's Jewish physician Lopez. But just as the victimized Germans found a refuge at the Warburg or in American universities, so *The Occult Philosophy* concludes with conciliation and home-coming: the outlawed Jews return to England under Cromwell's regime.

This migration of oppressed ideas is an adventure for Frances Yates, and she narrates it lucidly but also suspense-fully, hazarding Le Carré–like guesses about Marlowe's espionage: 'Could Marlowe, in his capacity of political agent, have known something about Dee's second period abroad?' But because for her the allegory I've expounded is so clear in its structure, she does tend to manoeuvre literary evidence into agreement with it.

Her habit is to begin with an archetype (in this case the inspired melancholic, described by the Cabala and illustrated by Dürer); then to find a historical character who fits the type (the disappointed magus John Dee) and after that, ever more audaciously, to discover literary refractions of that character (Lear, Prospero and Marlowe's Faustus are all, with varying degrees of implausibility, said to be avatars of Dee).

Though she begins by declaring herself unqualified to undertake 'an enquiry into "the occult" in general', Frances Yates does occasionally write like a genteel maven practis-ing necromancy in the suburbs: 'On the whole, one is inclined to the conclusion that Giorgi *is* a kind of magician, though a very, very white one, very ascetic and holy.' Sometimes the occult lapses into the idiom of the detergent ads: '*The Faerie Queene* is . . . infused with the whitest of white magic.'

But *The Occult Philosophy* is an exciting book, which changes the way we look at the intellectual history both of the Renaissance and our own time – for Frances Yates's devious, ingenious achievement is to have established an allegorical analogy between those two periods.

6 December 1979   **Peter Conrad**

Just about everything

We turn increasingly to the novel to find out what's going on, listening for a still small voice in the racket of modern consciousness. And however falsely confident the bulletins of our elected representatives, what the unacknowledged legislators keep on giving us is bad news – worse than the morning's front page, worse than the bedtime picture stories of famine, riot and murder. Worse, because they seem to be insisting that these multiplying horrors – today's race riot or 'fail-safe' failure, next week's leaky power station – will add up to something. Worse, because their intimations serve literally to confirm our own worst fears, 'Coming events cast their shadows before . . .'

From William Golding to Kurt Vonnegut, from J. G. Ballard to V. S. Naipaul, one picks up the apocalyptic note fairly steadily now, more mediated by form or fantasy in some cases than in others. In the case of Doris Lessing, at least since *The Four-Gated City*, the message is direct and unambiguous. She is read quite widely, I think, as a seer, and seems to write more and more like one, in spite of a Hitchcockian appearance in this new novel in a more modest role, glimpsed as if through a window – 'a woman at work on a tale that may help others to see a situation or a passion more clearly'.

Shikasta is the first in an announced 'visionary novel-sequence', drawn, says the title page, from the archives of the planet Canopus in Argos, though earthlings, which is to say Shikastans, might see it more as an extraordinary collage of von Däniken and the Old Testament, Sufism and sf, Blake with UFOs and Dante plus ESP.

At any rate one can see the need for a fair range of archival material, since Doris Lessing's subject now is Everything – from the giants and ancients of Genesis to the fires of the Revelation, or at least to our own imminent little local apocalypse and its meagre aftermath on the margins of a fused and smoking planet. (She writes rather disarmingly in a foreword about 'the exhilaration that comes from being set free into a larger scope'.)

In a sense, even all this is familiar territory to readers of her recent novels. The form of *Shikasta* comes from the Appendix to *The Four-Gated City*, with its file of letters and official reports, while nearly all the themes are rehearsed by Charles Watkins on his amnesiac trip into inner space in the novel that followed, *Briefing For a Descent Into Hell*. Earth/Shikasta is in trouble, thrown into turmoil by an unfortunate shift in the cosmic pattern, and its Godlike tutelary planet Canopus (in *Briefing*, Jupiter) must once more send down angelic spacemen to succour a saving remnant, reminding them yet again of their 'human duty as part of the Harmony', and endeavouring to compensate 'their most powerful defect, the inability to see things except as facets and one at a time'.

Some of the story's elaboration in this longer novel is fairly impressive: the Blake-inspired vision of Shikasta's Eden age, with its geometric cities built by the Giants as transmitters in a kind of cosmic bio-feedback system; the Dantean shades lingering in the purgatory of Zone Six: also parts at least of the show trial of the White Race staged by delegates of the world's youth armies in the Last Days.

Otherwise, the montage might have been managed more adroitly by some of the better old sf hands. But enough of the design is accomplished to give resonance to what we mostly read her for: the painful integrity of her personality and the quality of her insights, won by working special gifts to the limit.

At the simpler level there are details of the serious game she plays of a sort of psychic futurology. How long, for example, before committees start talking about work camps or some sort of conscripted service for unemployed youth (the growing army of the unemployed, as newspeak has it)? What matters more, however, is her burning focus on what we have already done for our children; on ' . . . that generation – part of a generation – who could not see a newspaper except as a screen for lies, automatically translated any television newscast or documentary into what the truth probably was . . . knew that at no time, anywhere, was the population of a country told the truth: full facts about events trickled into general consciousness much later . . .' (The morning after I read that, I woke up to discover that what was currently trickling into general consciousness was that 22 years ago East Anglia came within a hosepipe's length of being made a desert by plutonium radiation from a fire at an American nuclear bomber base.)

What she is really telling us, though, is not that The Wrath to Come will be here tomorrow or next year, but that we are not living well; that it's not surprising that the human cortex looks like a mushroom cloud; that we may actually, clever monkeys, have managed to poison the springs of Nature's own well.

That's her most devastating insight, a piercing diagnosis of the unease spreading through our civilization like the latest 57 varieties of 'flu: that lodged in the gut of those whose sensibility led them to seek comfort and solace in the natural, in 'Everything that lives is holy', there is now the knowledge that 'nature' itself can be poisoned, corrupted, disintegrated.

What Doris Lessing offers for our comfort is mainly an increasingly burdened and ironized faith in the necessity of harmony, a gnostic version of 'Only connect', hence all the celestial paraphernalia and the obsession with ESP and the desperate gifts of madness, of which she sketches a sort of rudimentary physics.

Quietism, those readers will say who react most predictably to her quarrel with a narrowly framed version of politics (here rather glibly opposed to good works and 'making things work'). And some of the sisters will not fail to note that the superior visitants treated so deferentially are all *men*, Wise Men. But if one is uneasy with some of the apparent results of her preoccupation with Sufism, there is a further insight from a notion central to that tradition which is both a clever fictional device and a strong charm against despair.

It is to do with belief, in spite of so much dark history, in the human capacity for transcendence, not least as it might be achieved by being most truly and responsibly oneself. What is suggested, fascinatingly, through one of the characters in this novel is that failure, through greed or faintheartedness, to perform one's essential task, whatever it may be, is damaging not only to the unfulfilled individual soul but in quite concrete ways to other, unknown people who needed him to be in his proper place at the right time. It is a thought which sends ripples through the mind, touching half the ideas and beliefs by which men and women have lived or might live.

Lewis Mumford says somewhere that to overcome the distortions of 'technics' '. . . we must cultivate the inner and subjective as our ancestors during the last three centuries cultivated the outer and objective.' In this powerful though vulnerable fable, Doris Lessing is saying once more what many of our best artists seem to be saying now: that we had really better get down to it: that time is running out.

15 November 1979   **W. L. Webb**

Shared laughter

'Alas! poor Shelley! – how he would have laughed – had he lived, and how we used to laugh now and then – at various things – which are grave in the Suburbs. – You are all mistaken about Shelley – you do not know – how mild – how tolerant – how good he was in Society – and as perfect a Gentleman as ever crossed a drawing room.'

Thus, Byron to his publisher John Murray. The notion of Shelley the Perfect Gentleman is perhaps a bit overdone, though a useful corrective to that view of him which chooses to dwell on his appearing naked from the sea and walking across drawing rooms without a thought for those unfortunate enough to be clothed and breakfasting. I put the quote at the head of this review of the latest instalment of Byron's letters and journals for the other quality. The shared laughter – 'at various things which are grave in the Suburbs'. It is the nearest I have ever reached at understanding the Shelley-Byron friendship. Worth noticing that when Byron addresses himself to Mary Shelley he is much more guarded in tone.

*A Heart for Every Fate** (dreadful title) is the penultimate volume in Marchand's marvellous series, which has done so much to restore Byron to his rightful place as one of the world's greatest letter writers. Like the others it is brimful of slangy, dashed-off, vivid things. Byron is at Genoa. Teresa Guiccioli is installed with her father and her brother in an apartment in his Casa Saluzzo. Mary Shelley and Leigh Hunt are a safe distance away. 'As to any community of feeling – thought – or opinion between L (eigh) H (unt) & me – there is little or none – we meet rarely – hardly ever – but I think him a good principled & able man.'

However, Hunt (and Mary?) were strictly for the suburbs, in Byron's view. 'I do not know what world he has lived in – but I have lived in three or four – and none of them like his Keats and Kangaroo terra incognita.' Minor point of criticism: this reference to Keats goes unrecorded in the usually able index, and Marchand does not explain the Kangaroo.

This particular volume is not rich in remarks on Byron's own verse, but he does speak clearly enough (to Bryan Waller Procter, alias Barry Cornwall) on his aims in *Don Juan*: 'Nothing but a satire on affectations of all kinds, mixed with some relief of serious feelings and description.' Interesting that the seriousness was intended as *relief*. Byron's self-awareness regarding his work was never negligible, and about *Don Juan* he is spot on.

What a feast of a life actually in process of being lived these letters have provided, though. We read them as he wrote them, on the run. They breathe the very spirit of the man, and they bring Byron and his circle of friends before our eyes as no biography has ever done or can ever hope to do. From April 1823 on, they are full of Greek stuff, most of it a moving mixture of idealism and shrewd assessment of his own financial resources which he intended to use to provide arms and food for the Greek forces. 'Privations – I can – or at least could once bear – abstinence I am accustomed to – and as to fatigue – I was once a tolerable traveller – what I may be now – I cannot tell – but I will try.'

He did. Now we must all wait with what patience we can muster for the last volume – the news from Greece. Did he remember Shelley on the road to Missolonghi? Was there time for laughter even then, so far from the Suburbs, at what the Suburbs would have made of it all? I cannot doubt that it will turn out so. If ever there was a mind that could glow in a letter like a 'fiery particle' that mind was Byron's. Expect sparks among the cinders, before the ashes.

*Byron's Letters and Journals, vol 10, *ed. Leslie A. Marchand* (*John Murray*).
20 March 1980   **Robert Nye**

Thompson and Liberty!

The Title* carries a double, a – may I remark? – dialectically opposed image. Thompson quotes a letter to *The Times*, 'Sir, May I, writing by candlelight, express my total support for the Government . . .' (which will never be Edward Thompson's way); but also 'writing by candlelight' is himself, or rather a learned late-eighteenth century re-publican, an early nineteenth-century radical antiquary, reading his 'old books', as he often says, late into the night to find precedents for successful popular protests against the Establishment's encroachments on traditional rights and liberties.

These are socialist essays on liberty, a bird far too rare. When he pours scorn on the official attempt to 'reform' the Official Secrets Act (a classic case of the new bureaucracy's contempt for democracy), he remarks that his comment 'came from a person committed as a historian and a citizen to the libertarian traditions of the radical and working-class movements of this country.'

All these powerful essays remind people of this tradition. He has polemicised (in his recent 'Poverty of Theory') against excessively theoretical and abstract fellow Marxists, both those who reject History as a mode of knowledge and those who discount civil rights as camouflage or mere 'bourgeois liberalism', and he has vindicated his own 'historical materialism'.

But whatever 'materialist' may mean, it does not mean 'determinist'. Marxism to Thompson is an intellectual framework of historical tendencies, it deals with probabilities, sometimes moving its adherents to excessive optimism, sometimes to excessive pessimism, but nothing is determined beyond the capacity of human will and political action. He insists that there is an English working-class tradition of effective activism.

But he also denounces those on the Left who go 'along with a wholesale dismissal of *all* law and order and *all* police, and sometimes with a soppy notion that *all* crime is some kind of displaced revolutionary activity'.

'. . . this rhetoric can be seen to unbend the springs of action, and to discount the importance of any struggle for civil rights. Pessimism is cherished and then it is varnished over with revolutionary adjectives . . . The trouble with all such arguments is that they presume to contrast sordid reality with some pure alternative which exists only in an intellectual's abstracted utopian noddle.'

The book is composed of essays nearly all written over the last ten years. There are some good bits and pieces. 'Yesterday's Mannikin', for instance, analyses the 'compulsive philistinism', the 'celebration of contingency' and the 'resistance of thought' of Harold Wilson's first 800 pages, to warn that the unwary reader may actually come to believe that politics can only be conducted in such a diminished perspective.

But two main themes dominated both concerned with diminished perspectives and pessimism or 'realism' that things must be accepted as they are: the growth of statism in Britain and the threat to civil liberties of the new 'law and order' lobby.

Thompson reminds us that the Whig and Tory gentry of old were hostile to centralized power and rational administration. Though far from a democratic impulse, the Whig tradition 'did afford shelter for libertarian modes of thought', jealous of central power and conscious of the contrast with continental autocracy. Juries were neither fully controllable nor predictable. Local magistrates insisted on local control of the new constabulary.

The growth of large-scale government, of bureaucracy and of the claim that secrecy is necessary both for security and efficiency, these are very recent. Many civil servants are sure that they can govern better than the politicians, and with such weak and conventional governments, both Labour and Conservative (until the blessings of this last year), they may often be right – in the short term. The bureaucracy now, not 'the Crown', has developed a sense of the State, of itself being the permanent embodiment of the national interest: not Parliament, still less Edward Thompson's old friends 'the People'.

A recent essay in six parts, 'The State of the Nation', is a third of the book. It is a great and important piece of sustained polemic against the new vocal law-and-order lobby for being 'the most determined to break up our laws and constitutional proprieties and to provoke disorder or to cover flagrantly disorderly abuses up'.

Nowhere has the constitutional enormity of the growing power and irresponsibility of the Director of Public Prosecutions been better shown, nor the civic apathy as the powers and the independence of juries are attacked (so that the prosecution can make its own rules), nor the danger of the growth of the police lobby such that (shades of tri-partitism and corporatism) their spokesmen begin to talk of themselves as 'an institution of the State'.

Others, of course, have gone for the police. But Edward Thompson is more generous in his anger and more historically minded: policing is very important, most coppers are ordinary blokes, no society could do without them. He denounces specific abuses, not *all* police or *all* lawyers or even *all* politicians. If these abuses threaten to become systematic, it is the political leaders who have given the lead or let out the reins.

Edward Thompson is himself part of the tradition he loves: the learned polemicists of British radicalism. Only occasionally is he too self-conscious and tries, in a heavy, jokey way, to write like a Red Republican circa 1820, and period words creep into his modern vocabulary: 'mountain of official secrets' is good, then and now; but Chapman Pincher as 'common conduit' for official leaks is too antique. Would my sons know what it looked like and smelt like, the open gutter?

None-the-less, one suddenly realizes that Edward Thompson has grown out of his early over-writing and has become, for my money, the best political essayist in the country today in the tradition of Swift, Hazlitt, Cobbett and Orwell.

*Writing by Candlelight, *E. P. Thompson (Merlin Press)*.
1 May 1980   **Bernard Crick**

Officers' mess

Field Marshal Lord Carver, the former Chief of the Defence Staff, has confirmed that 'fairly senior' officers at the army's headquarters were talking about the possibility of a military intervention at the time of the miners' strike in February 1974. He told the Cambridge Union that he personally 'took action to make certain that nobody was so stupid as to go around saying those things'.

Lord Carver's remarks are the first formal admission of what were widely circulating rumours in 1974 of army dismay at the unstable political situation. There were two general elections that year.

There was a good deal of smoke but little sign of fire. Brigadier (now Lieutenant-General) Frank Kitson's book *Low Intensity Operations* had been published. There was unease at the army's insistence on keeping internment in Northern Ireland. And a journalist on a tour of officers' messes in the north reported in July that the main topic of conversation was 'what would the British armed forces do if faced with a stalemate political situation, such as we may well have after the next election, with the extreme Left pushing for power?'

In the Cambridge debate on the motion 'This House would fight for Queen and country' – passed by 185 votes to 74 – Ms Pat Arrowsmith, opposing the motion, asked Lord Carver whether he had played any part in the 1974 discussions. Lord Carver said neither he nor any senior officers had been involved in talk about a coup. 'It was exactly the opposite,' he went on, 'in that a certain interview took place by a young journalist at the army HQ near Salisbury, Wiltshire, in which not very senior, but fairly senior, officers were ill-advised enough to make suggestions that perhaps, if things got terribly bad, the army would have to do something about it.'

5 March 1980   **David Pallister**

'What worries me is that it might be a productivity deal.'

Sir. – Bryan McAllister (*Cartoon, April 30*) is premature in worrying about the Armed Services' productivity deal. He should save himself for the day when, in line with other nationalized industries, they are expected to show a profit. – Yours

Richard Sykes,
527 Finchley Road,
London NW 3.

The last four-minute picture show

Even regarded as TV the Government's four-minute warning
films (pinched by *Panorama*) leave something to be desired. If
these are the last TV films I am ever going to see, they could at
least have used the Muppets. They seem to have been heavily
influenced by Get the Strength of the Insurance Companies
Round You.

Enter the Turnip Tops in their toy house. A little bit has
broken off the left hand corner and outside it is raining
radiation. The Turnip Tops are staying put because Patrick
Allen has told them to or because 'if you leave your home,
your local authority may take it over for homeless families.'
That scares the hell out of them so they stay where they are,
and busy themselves shoving Grandma in a plastic bag.

'If anyone does die label the body with its name and address
and cover it tightly with polythene.'

A Yorkshire family were persuaded by *Panorama* to try the
Government's suggestions for do-it-yourself dugouts. 'Do
you really think it is wise to take the dog into the shelter?'

At Humberside the sub regional control room has the
situation well in hand. 'Have you a bearing on the bomb which
dropped near Hull? Fine. Thank you.' Nothing was ever lost
by cheerfulness and courtesy.

The hour brings forth the man and Keith Bridge, former
accountant and Controller of Humberside, was dealing with
30 starving survivors of the atom bomb which dropped near
Hull. 'Nobody must get in here and make a thundering
nuisance of themselves. This may mean the ultimate sanction
at the end of the day.' Bill and Ben, his right-hand men,
chimed in with 'This is an emergency situation' and 'This
could escalate.' 'We may,' insisted Mr Bridge, somewhat
eerily happy in his work, 'impose the ultimate sanction at the
end of the day.'

I should have mentioned that of the 200 chosen souls who
will staff each control station when the bomb drops many are

civil servants. Lord Belstead, junior minister at the Home Office responsible for civil defence (as of course you know) said shelters would cost 'billions and billions and billions', and said it very well.

Meanwhile, the Yorkshire volunteers were still in there with their dog. 'That's the last of the beans, Trevor.'

11 March 1980   **Nancy Banks-Smith**

An historian leaves his desk

Is CND on the march again? The Campaign for Nuclear Disarmament was founded in 1958 and quickly mushroomed into a mass movement of the middle classes. An article by J. B. Priestley in the *New Statesman* was immensely influential. In 1957 the Soviets had put a sputnik into space which showed what their rockets could do. The Defence White Paper of that year had told the British people straight that there were no defences against nuclear attack. Tests were polluting the atmosphere; there was a fallout scare.

It took two years only for CND to capture the Labour Party. The bomb was banned at Scarborough in 1960 but after Gaitskell had fought, fought and fought again it was unbanned at Blackpool the following year. By the time the Wilson Government came to power in 1964 the CND was over. Atmospheric tests had been banned, the world had survived the Cuba missiles crisis. CND was split, the annual Aldermaston march became a trickle of stragglers.

Canon Collins resigned in 1964. Frank Cousins joined the Government. Among his responsibilities as Minister of Technology was the Atomic Weapons Research Establishment at Aldermaston. Did he have plans for paying a visit there, he was asked at Question Time. Did he propose to go on foot, was the supplementary. CND had become a joke.

Today there is an expectation that history may repeat itself. A pamphlet by E. P. Thompson seems to have caught the conscience of the times in the way that Priestley's article did. World events have reminded of the dangers of war. The plan to deploy cruise missiles in the English countryside has brought the fear of nuclear weapons closer to home. The arms race is resuming on a scale more lunatic than ever. The CND reports reviving membership rolls. The Labour Party conference may go unilateralist again at Blackpool in October.

Thompson is not keen to see history repeat itself too exactly. He doesn't want to see his crusade taken over by the Labour Party, he wants it to be a broadly-based movement and to avoid the fellow-traveller's tag. He declined to speak at the Labour Party rally in Hyde Park last month.

In 1960 the Labour Movement was taken by coup d'état; Cousins turned the T & G against the Establishment and the AEU, in a classic balls up, voted both ways. Under Moss Evans the TGWU is ready to ban-the-bomb again. What happens in Blackpool will depend largely upon the AUEW once more. In 1960, however, there were 50,000–100,000 Aldermaston marchers to give popular legitimacy to the Labour Party's unilateralist lurch. In 1980 the character and complexion of the CND and its friends are very different, and contrary to E. P. Thompson's fond hopes.

In the 1960s the extra-parliamentary leftists were late entrants to CND and it was they who destroyed it; this time they are its founding hard-core. The Christians and the pacifists, the environmentalists and the ramblers won't have a chance this time; the movement is much more highly politicized and the Labour Party is the first target. The CND of today is predominantly a broad-left front. Note how 27 CLPs have drafted resolutions based on the CND model resolution which appeared in *Sanity* last month. The terms of the resolution are tantamount to a repudiation of NATO, for it opposes 'any defence policy based on the use or threatened use of nuclear weapons' as well as seeking to ban the stationing of all such weapons in Britain.

Last autumn E. P. Thompson 'left his desk' to try his hand at making history from the bottom up. He makes it sound rather as if he was abandoning his nets in order to begin his ministry. There is something messianic as well as apocalyptic about the tone of his writings on the bomb. As essayist and pamphleteer he is compared frequently to Paine, Hazlitt and

Cobbett. His left-wing admirers are more disconcerted when he summons Burke in evidence.

His political writings remind me of those of Jean-Paul Sartre, especially his rambling, egocentric yet splendid 'Open Letter to Leszek Kolakowski' which ranks with Sartre's great polemics against his friends, Camus and Merleau-Ponty. The theme is the same, too – apostasy. E.P.T., like J-P.S., takes his duties as intellectual with extreme moral seriousness.

Yey there is something slightly comical about him, too, in the way that there usually is with people who may suspect themselves of being candidates for sainthood; although frightfully clever, he is naive. On a visit to California he finds 'many evidences of the desire for peace'. From his dialogue with the Soviet historian Roy Medvedev (*Guardian*, June 19) he comes out looking if not exactly an unworldly fool, an innocent.

E. P. Thompson is a fine Englishman for all that. His moral credentials – as he presented them to *Guardian* readers in the first of his influential articles (January 28) – are 'plain to the whole world'. He is a good historian too and a writer who has both elegance and passion at his command. That doesn't make him right about nuclear weapons, however, nor does it mean that his successful pamphlet, Protest and Survive, is above intellectual reproach.

The purpose of *Protest and Survive* is to explode the theory of deterrence. The theory rests upon the proposition that mutually assured destruction makes nuclear war unthinkable. But why then are strategists and scientists thinking about it? Because, Thompson concludes, 'each party is actually preparing for nuclear war, and is ceaselessly searching for some ultimate weapon of tactical/strategic point of advantage which would assure its victory.'

This intent, he asserts, 'has been hidden within the mendacious vocabulary of "deterrence"; and behind these veils of "posture", "credibility" and "bluff" it has waxed fat and now has come of age.'

Thompson quotes Lord Zuckerman and Lord Louis Mountbatten in support of his case. It is true that Lord Zuckerman has frequently drawn attention to the dangers of the seemingly autonomous technological spiral which thrusts upon the world a quantity and quality of nuclear weapons vastly in excess of what is required for the purposes of deterrence. It is true also that Lord Zuckerman, in fact since 1962, together with Lord Mountbatten, has warned against the illusion that tactical nuclear weapons could be used as an extension of conventional warfare in Europe without triggering a full-scale nuclear exchange.

What Thompson does not choose to tell his readers, however, is that Zuckerman, in the lecture from which he several times quotes (*The Times*, January 21), says: 'Given the existence of nuclear weapons – and no one supposes that they are going to be swept away – the concept of mutual deterrence, based upon an appreciation of their enormous destructiveness, is valid and inescapable.' And: 'I do not believe that any of us (the scientists who have pointed to the dangers) is so starry-eyed as to believe in unilateral disarmament.'

E. P. Thompson plainly cannot bear to think about the unthinkable. Why should he? He is a moralist, not a strategist.

A large part of *Protest and Survive* is directed at Professor Michael Howard and the letter he wrote to *The Times* on January 30. The letter argued that civil defence was 'an indispensable element of deterrence'.

Thompson accuses Howard of wishing 'to hurry the British people across a threshold of mental expectation', so that they may be prepared, not for 'deterrence', but for actual nuclear war. The accusation is false and unjust. It flows, I charitably assume, from the mental muddle which Thompson gets himself into on the subject of theatre warfare. He believes that the Pentagon is plotting to wage a limited nuclear war in Europe and that this is the purpose of the cruise and Pershing II missiles which the Americans are forcing (he believes) upon Britain and Europe.

The discovery of conspiracy, and the exposure of mendacity, are a part, perhaps, of the art of the polemicist and pamphleteer. They are a part of E. P. Thompson's art. Facts which are vouchsafed to him (presumably from his reading of the newspapers) are 'concealed' from the public; defence correspondents (he cites *The Guardian*'s David Fairhall) are

'NATO apologists'; the debate about nuclear weapons 'is not permitted to intrude in any sharp way into our major media'. Note the mealy-mouthed qualifications here – 'sharp', 'major'.

Thompson is himself stern on the subject of lying. Deterrence is 'mendacity', all official statements are 'lies' or 'propaganda'. Calling people liars is, perhaps, another part of the polemicist's art, or at least a part of E. P. Thompson's. The moralist's own 'truth', I suppose, transcends ascertainable fact, even the historian's empirical discipline.

Or, perhaps, Thompson is merely muddled. Theatre warfare is a muddling subject. The point which Zuckerman and Mountbatten make, which he seems not quite to grasp, is that NATO's strategy of 'graduated response' envisages an early recourse to *tactical* nuclear weapons. These are regarded in NATO doctrine as, in effect, an extension of conventional war by other means. Their use would be against advancing tanks, etc.; their range falls well short of the Soviet Union.

The cruise, which is what brought Thompson from his desk, is quite another matter. It has no role in the NATO strategy. It does not belong to the concept of tactical nuclear warfare. It is not to be under double-key arrangement but under sole American control. It is in effect part of the forward-based strategic deterrent of the United States. It is a 'modernization' of existing weapons already targeted on the USSR; many of them based in Britain – American Phantoms and British Vulcans.

The new weapons are *theatre*, or regional, weapons only in the sense that they are of equivalent capability to the SS–20s (and earlier SS–4s and SS–5s) which the Soviets have targeted on Western Europe.

Thompson believes (although he produces no evidence for his belief) that the purpose of cruise and Pershing is to enable a theatre nuclear war in Europe which, although it would obliterate the Allies, would – he thinks – allow the US to inflict immense damage on Russia west of the Urals, while the soil of the US remained immune. How he arrives at this improbable scenario I cannot say, for he does not favour us with his reasoning.

What he does not appear to realize (or does not choose to know) is that the cruise and Pershings were not thrust upon Europe by Pentagon warmongers but provided with some misgivings in order to quieten European doubts about the credibility of the US strategic deterrent.

The genesis of the NATO modernization programme is to be found in Helmut Schmidt's lecture to the Institute of Strategic Studies in London in 1977. The history is accurately set out in the ISS's latest strategic survey which comments: 'The European worry over the SS–20 had in reality been a concern over the reliability of the American nuclear commitment to Europe.'

That Thompson's facts are often wrong and his thoughts confused does not mean that his moral insight and imperative are invalid. There has been many a fool in Christ and E. P. Thompson is no fool. He may be right that to think about the unthinkable ought, in itself, to be morally unthinkable, in which case the facts don't matter, nor does the quality of his reasoning. We are bound to listen when he rises to his full literary and moral height and warns us, 'Wars commence in our culture first of all, and we kill each other in euphemisms and abstractions long before the first missiles have been launched.' There is something of majesty in the sheer impracticability of what he recommends, in the simplicity of his faith in men.

And there *is* an issue. There *is* a danger of war and holocaust. The arms race is spiralling once more. Détente between the super-powers has broken down. The risks of miscalculation are greater than they were. Fear breeds misunderstanding and adds to tension. Something *must* be done.

Zuckerman is correct. NATO has to abandon its perilous and no-longer-credible strategy of graduated response. The idea of tactical, or any form of limited war, must be ruled out. Medvedev is correct. The brigades of sanity should be protesting first against the non-ratification of SALT II. That has to be the first priority if disarmament is to get anywhere. Schmidt is correct. Détente in Europe must be kept open. Arms limitation must be extended to the intermediate regional systems not covered by SALT I or II. The deployment of the cruise and Pershing (which I do not myself think is wise) must be linked to this arms control negotiation.

Those should be the three priorities. They are political objectives and achievable, unlike Thompson's moral gesticulations. They are relevant to the imperative to survive. They are causes worth the protest. Yet whoever saw a placard saying 'Sign SALT now'?

I see no prospect of Thompson's 'gum boot' crusade improving the situation in the slightest degree. He may, however, assist in the process by which a small minority of anti-American ideologues capture the Labour Party Conference and commit it once more to an ineffectual neutralism. Then it will have nothing to say about effective arms control, no credentials for protesting the arms race and no influence in reducing the risks of nuclear war. As for E. P Thompson, he – no doubt – will return to his desk where he will protest and survive.

23 July 1980   **Peter Jenkins**

END in view

To receive some 2,500 words of attention from Peter Jenkins (*Guardian*, July 23) is indeed to attain to eminence. I thank him for his attention. It is kind of him to warn me that I cannot walk on water, and I will have to think out some other way of getting across to Europe.

But I don't intend to be put down so easily on questions of fact. Jenkins says that I have got into a 'mental muddle' on the subject of theatre warfare: 'He believes that the Pentagon is plotting to wage a limited nuclear war in Europe.'

I must urge him, and others, to read the account by the Swedish expert, Dr Alva Myrdal, in chapter two of *The Game of Disarmament*. This account, first published in 1976, outlines the history of United States strategic thinking on this subject. It is a long history, which long pre-dates NATO's decision to introduce cruise missiles.

This is not a 'plot' or 'conspiracy' to wage a limited war so much as a contingency plan, with appropriate weapons and dispositions, to ensure that in the event of nuclear war the holocaust will be limited to some 'theatre' remote from the United States. Europe is a likely theatre.

But what appears as a 'theatre' from the other side of the Atlantic does not appear in the same way to the Russians, whose European territory is *within* the theatre, and whose strategists have never been comfortable with such notions of 'limited' nuclear war. As Mr Lawrence Freedman, the director of policy studies at the Royal Institute of International Affairs, has noted (*Times*, March 26):

'Recent moves in NATO have encouraged plans for selective, discrete strikes rather than all-out exchanges . . . Unfortunately, the Soviet Union has shown little interest in Western ideas on limited nuclear war.'

President Carter's national security adviser (the architect of the Iranian helicopter fiasco), Zbigniew Brzezinski, re-stated the United States' strategy in an interview in the *New York Times* (March 30). Speaking of 'our nuclear targeting plans' he said that these were designed to provide a 'wider range of options' than either 'a spasmodic and apocalyptic nuclear exchange' or a limited conventional war. A limited nuclear war in the 'theatre' of Europe is exactly one such option.

Peter Jenkins is wrong to state that 'the genesis of the NATO modernization programme is to be found in Helmut Schmidt's lecture' of 1977. It long precedes that lecture. But he is right to say that Schmidt (and other NATO politicians, including British) eagerly beckoned the cruise missiles on.

West German politicians, denied their own nuclear weapons, were anxious lest Pentagon strategists should fall back on ICBMs and 'decouple' from West Europe. By bringing Pershing IIs and cruises forward into Europe, they hoped to entangle the United States military inextricably in European affairs.

And they have done exactly that. Helmut Schmidt, not for the first time, has been too clever by half. What seemed clever in 1977 now seems exceptionally dangerous in 1980, as the hawks circle over Washington. The cruise and Pershing missiles (Jenkins says) 'were not thrust upon Europe by Pentagon warmongers'. But whatever mixed motives gave rise to the policy, these missiles are very certainly being thrust upon us by the hard men of the Pentagon now.

This month Mr Warren Christopher, the American deputy Secretary of State, hurried over to NATO capitals to strengthen waning European resolve. M. Nothomb, the Belgian Foreign Minister, was dressed down in public because his government, under pressure of public opinion, has postponed agreement to cruise missiles. And American spokesmen made clear their hostility to the new Brezhnev proposals for negotiated European nuclear arms control which Schmidt – in a last-minute attempt to reverse his own clever policies – helped to elicit.

Peter Jenkins complains that I see all this as a 'conspiracy' or a Pentagon 'plot' to make war in Europe. He can then put me down as a fluffy moral crusader. On the contrary, I see it as the classic kind of historical pile-up which takes place when clever amoral politicians team up with 'worst case' military strategists, pushed forward by the avid technological thrust of the armourers – and when, moreover, they confront a similar complex of forces coming, on head-on collision course, towards them on the same lane.

This is not plot or conspiracy but *process*. If not reversed, a European theatre war, which will probably escalate to an intercontinental war, is the probable outcome. That the Pentagon (and Brzezinski) have a fatuous games-plan for 'limited' war adds greatly to the risks.

Jenkins is correct – and, among British commentators, unusually candid – in saying that the new NATO missiles are 'in effect part of the forward-based strategic deterrent of the United States'. This is certainly so in Russian perception. Cruise missiles can reach some 500 miles further into Russian territory than can the Vulcan or the F–111, whereas the SS–20, foul as it is, can reach nowhere near the United States. The Pershing II, based in West Germany, will be able to hit Russian targets in four minutes flat. These missiles creep beneath the thresholds established by SALT II (if that is ever ratified), and, in the disguise of 'theatre' weapons, augment the American strategic forces.

I am glad that Jenkins has said this, because it is not what the British people have been told over the past 10 months by Mr Pym, Mr Rodgers and successive defence experts. But Jenkins is pained with me because I have drawn attention to the lies and propaganda served out to us in the media in the guise of consensual information. How can facts, which I have read in the newspapers, be 'concealed from the public'?

The first answer is that I and many others, in the past few months, have been finding out the basic facts, not from our newspapers, but from such sources as Alva Myrdal, the peace research institutes in Stockholm and Oslo, and little under-funded British research units, such as the Armaments and Disarmament Information Unit at the University of Sussex.

We have also benefited greatly from the candour and courage of American researchers – and from the openness of sections of the American press. This makes a striking contrast with a British press which is hedged around with Official Secrets Acts, 'need-to-know' circulars, and 'D' Notices, and the majority of whose defence experts appear to be self-selected for their servility to Ministry of Defence briefings.

Once one has got hold of certain basic facts, from Swedish or American sources, a certain amount can be garnered from the British press, provided that one holds it at arm's length and reads the interpretations upside-down.

I am astounded to read that Jenkins supposes that there has been a major debate about nuclear weapons in our media. Before the NATO decision on cruise missiles last December there was no debate whatsoever, not even in Parliament. All we got was 'official information', and main-line BBC TV and ITV news programmes have been (and remain) especially discreditable.

In the past few months, by an immense number of hands (within the press and TV as well as without), openings for discussion have been arduously prised (*The Guardian*. with its

Agenda page and correspondence column, has been as generous as any). It has been an astonishing contest between the Established Consensual Opinion of the Realm and many thousands of unrepresented people – individuals, church groups, far leftists, ecologists, Welsh Nationalists, not to mention the NEC of the Labour Party – to obtain some representation for their opinion.

By my reckoning it has been necessary for over 2,000 persons to march in the streets to get one (slanted) TV minute, and an equal number to attend a public meeting to get one column inch in any daily paper.

It has been heavy going, and rather more people have been involved in the work than one E. P. Thompson.

I am wholly unrepentant. There has been a massive attempt to keep the issue closed, under the rubric of loyalty to NATO. (This has even had its moments of high comedy, as when sheets which loathe the Labour Party have tried to serve up Mr William Rodgers as a high thinker and a national saviour.) The media and leading politicians have been kept constantly plugged in to the public relations operations of NATO, the Ministry of Defence, and the armed services (all of them funded out of our taxes). Not only official hand-outs but much official money has been washing through the corridors of power.

Now at last the door is open a crack, and discussion is coming through. One result is that a few independent-minded commentators are telling us, not what they think we ought to be told, but what they actually think themselves. Peter Jenkins is a case in point. His article in criticism of myself is the first sustained discussion of these serious issues from his pen this year. In this he confesses that he does not himself think the deployment of cruise and Pershing II 'was wise'. Professor Michael Howard has also informed me, courteously, that I have misrepresented his views in my pamphlet, and that he does not think that cruise missiles 'will do much good'. But when did Jenkins or Howard say this clearly, and in a public place, before? Is it only the clatter which we have been making off-stage which has forced these whispered confessions out?

One trouble with the means taken to force this discussion open has been the absurd personalization of the issue – E. P. Thompson versus the Rest.

I had a hand in drafting the appeal for European Nuclear Disarmament. It was then knocked about and redrafted by a dozen hands, all over Europe. The final form was agreed at a meeting attended not only by many British, but also by Claude Bourdet, the former French resistance leader, now editor of *Témoignage Chrétien*; Ulrich Albrecht, the professor of Peace Studies in West Berlin; and other European representatives. It has subsequently won the adherence of thousands – and of substantial organizations – across Europe. Yet it has to remain 'E. P. Thompson's Campaign'.

Since E. P. Thompson is shortly off to teach for a term in a hospitable United States university, that is a bad look-out for Europe. But I predict that the movement will survive his temporary absence. In Jenkins's view it will survive in Britain only as a rabble of 'anti-American ideologues' and 'hard-core' far leftists. Two comments on that.

First, in the past month I have spoken at meetings in Oxfordshire, Bradford, Nottingham, Bristol, Birmingham, Reading, Leamington Spa, London and Manchester. Every meeting has been packed; the audiences have been profoundly serious, attentive, and often better informed than (it would appear) a random assembly of MPs and editorialists. The audience, in every case, has represented not only the left but a deep, and articulate, swathe of opinion running right through the middle of society.

Secondly, this 'hard-core' of the far left. True, at most meetings, outside the hall and sometimes in the discussion, there has been a scattering (20 or so) of know-alls (who know, among other things, that Russian missiles are 'purely defensive' and that El Salvador is immensely more important than Afghanistan). But the audience, and organizers of the meetings, have simply turned off those sounds as boring. This is not where opinion is at. It is at greatly more challenging and difficult problems, such as those of building a united movement which no one can nobble, and those of knitting together, in the coming months, East and West European opinion into a common movement. That is the most complex of all.

As for the great majority of that (very numerous) extra-parliamentary left, I do not find a 'hard-core, at all. I find persons profoundly shocked by the arms race, by the wars (China, Vietnam, Cambodia) in the Far East, by Afghanistan, and mobile in every opinion except as to the need to confront the dangers of war. We are in a time of profound re-thinking, in the centre, the left and the far left also.

Peter Jenkins, as an experienced commentator on es-tablished political affairs, sees extra-parliamentary groups as a sort of sub-human phenomenon – a threat to the status quo. And I hope that they are a threat to that kind of status quo. They bring to the common movement a radical scepticism as to the reasons of States and of established politicians which can only do good.

There will be wrinkles, of course, as there are in any popular movement. But I am confident that neither CND, nor its European dimension, END, nor the many anti-cruise missile groups which have been formed, are there for any parasitic sect in search of a new host to feed off. And the best insurance against that is not to stand apart in anxiety lest one should rub shoulders with a 'hard-core' undesirable, but to get in and ensure that one's own position is both represented and regarded.

Give him another hard push, and perhaps Peter Jenkins will come in as well. For his article shows the evidence of his own re-thinking. He appears to be opposed to cruise and Pershing II missiles. He wants SALT II to be ratified. He wants the explicit rejection of notions of limited nuclear war, and the opening of genuine European disarmament nego-tiations.

I – and we – agree with all these demands. Provided (one qualification) it is realized that SALT II is *not* a treaty for any kind of disarmament: that under its terms strategic nuclear weapons will actually *increase* (from some 14,000 to some 24,000): and that the MX missile system (and, no doubt, its Soviet 'answer') are already making nonsense of its terms.

SALT II does not really get us far, although the refusal to ratify even this is menacing.

What is needed is . . . precisely, END – an all-European direct initiative actually to DISARM, and to keep new armaments out. It is simple. The triple-headed monster, the SS–20, must go, and the cruise and Pershing II must never come: and then a lot more, from Back-fires to Phantoms and Tornados, must be pushed back also.

The results of twenty years of 'negotiating from strength' have been very much worse than nil.

Already NATO's American advisers are pussy-footing away from such negotiations, and 'a highly placed negotiator' for NATO told *The Times* (July 18) that any talks on the Brezhnev proposals for all-round 'theatre' nuclear disarmament 'would almost certainly last into 1983' – by which time, of course, the new NATO missiles would be ready to be installed.

Why? Why 1983? Why *three years* of talking? I don't know whether Brezhnev and the Soviet military establishment are sincere or not, but they have made an offer, and that offer must now be called. What Jenkins cannot understand is that the politicians and the military will do nothing, absolutely nothing, unless they are pushed by massive popular pressures – pressures which must ripple across Europe in the next three years from one country to another: now Holland and Belgium, now Poland: now Hungary, and now Britain.

But in such a movement Jenkins – even though he shares its objectives – can only, by habit, see a hideous threat to political propriety: 'ideologues' might 'capture' the Labour Party and reduce it to 'ineffectual neutralism'. That is the real place where we differ. I think that such non-alignment could be highly effective, not only in busting the holy NATO consensus up, but also in pressing a correspondent non-alignment across towards the East. As to the established proprieties, which play echo to each other from the opposing front benches, so far as we are concerned they can go and boil their heads.

28 July 1980   **E. P. Thompson**

Boom!

The countries of the world last year spent the staggering sum of £212,000 millions on various forms of military activity, including £60,000 millions on weapons. On an average they invested £8,000 a year on each of their soldiers compared with £130 a year on education for each school-age child. The spending on armaments has outpaced inflation for the seventh successive year and in constant prices is now running 70 per cent higher than it was in 1960.

These figures have been compiled by Mrs Ruth Leger Sivard, the former chief of the economics division of the US Arms Control and Disarmament Agency. She now works for a private organization and her report has been published by a group of sponsors including the British Council of Churches. The publishers say that her report is the only one produced which compares military and social expenditures.

Mrs Sivard says in her report: 'The most buoyant sector of the world economy is the arms business . . . arms sales are larger than the national incomes of all but ten nations in the world.' In sheer tonnage, for example, there is more explosive material on earth than there is food, and investment in war machinery is running at 2,500 times that of the machinery of peace.

One of the gloomiest statistics is the continued expansion of the military budget in Third World countries. In constant prices, the poor nations have expanded their military spending by 400 per cent since 1960, compared with about 44 per cent among the developed nations. The average figure has tailed off because of the cutback by Egypt and Iran. What this means in Ethiopia, as an example, is that it spent £64 millions for military purposes compared with £35 millions on education and £13 millions on health. In Pakistan the figures are £390 millions on armaments, £141 millions on education. and £40 millions on health. Britain, by comparison, spent £5,537 millions on its military needs, £6,673 millions on education, and £5,720 millions on health.

'The increase in numbers, in addition to the flood of modern arms throughout the world, adds significantly to the power and potential danger of the armed forces in the present situation,' Mrs Sivard writes. 'In the developing nations in particular, the armed forces may represent the largest block of trained manpower. As a result, they have become an increasingly important political force and in many nations they hold the principal seats of power in civil government. In Latin America and among the relatively new nations of Africa, one government in two is now under direct military control.'

The report lists 123 armed conflicts which have taken place in 65 countries since 1955, the overwhelming proportion of them in the developing world. In Africa, for example, there is barely a nation, running alphabetically from Algeria to Zaire, which has not been involved in combat.

'The link between arming and outbreak of war is not a simple one. Conflicts usually develop out of a complex of causes – political, religious, demographic, social and economic among others – but many of the tensions that lead to conflict are exacerbated by military spending that is excessive.'

Military spending, Mrs Sivard notes, is often defended on the grounds that it is a boon to the economy, a means of nation-building, a stimulus to investment, and that it increases employment and brings greater skills.

'No analytical studies, however, have yet established a positive link between military expenditures and economic development in the broad sense. There is, in fact, a growing body of evidence pointing to retarding effects through inflation, diversion of investment, use of scarce materials, and misuse of human capital.'

15 October 1979   **Harold Jackson**

'...The saplings of the third world war'

'A beautiful and wild valley ... sheer mountainsides rise up on either hand,' says the book. And at first glance that is just how the Ratgoed valley, near Machynlleth in Mid-Wales, appears now. But look closer, and the drawn skin of the hills is goosepimpled by millions of tiny conifers. Ratgoed's days as farming country are over. This winter the 600 sheep graze the hill for the last time. Henceforth Ratgoed will be part of the 75,000 acres of new land that the Forestry Commission or the Economic Forestry Group need for planting each year.

First the humans have gone; now the sheep. Soon there will only be 'the cruel victory of the conifers'. The problem, of course, is an old one. There were questions about Thorlmere's 'monotonous and level tones of green' in the 1930s. And more recently there have been Gwenallt Jones's bitter outpourings:

They have planted the saplings of the third world war in the land
of Esgeirceir and the fields of Tir-bach by
    Rhydycwmerau :
and today there is nothing but trees,
their insolent roots sucking the ancient soil.
Trees where fellowship was ; a forest where farms have been.

Poet after poet has slammed the forest. 'Spruce, quietest of the carnivores, have done away with bird, beast, man.' But the march of the trees goes on. Short of land, the Forestry Commission has recently been trying to get hills by barter. Four smallholdings in the Dolgellau area have been offered 'in exchange for rough or poorer farmland suitable for afforestation.' Which points to a usual reason for quitting the hill – the retirement of the farmer. Or an ageing widow may sell up the hill. Much land has gone for a song: £10 an acre has been paid for planting land only a decade ago.

Ratgoed, with its rich social history, defines the problem clearly. The Roman Sarn Helen skirts its hills; one of its farms, Ffynnon Padard, dates back to a medieval healing well.

The level valley floor was host to half a dozen farms, with their byres, hay-sheds, and sheep locks. Then in the mid-nineteenth century, slate was exploited commercially, when the old soft moss slates of the local buildings were replaced by deep quarried blues.

A whole community now arose, with Ratgoed Hall rising in slaty dignity, with stables, bridges, and ornamental walls. Men were housed below the quarries in a barracks block: there was a bay windowed shop and even a chapel with graceful splayed lancets. Dressing sheds for the slate sawing bays, a smithy, and weigh houses were built. A reservoir was made and a tramcar connected the quarries to the Corris railway, and hence the main line. In 1883, just one of the quarries, Cymerau, produced 762 tons of finished slate and employed 29 men. It lasted until 1972.

Today there is no permanent inhabitant in the entire valley. The chapel, now roofless, has a congregation of trees. And the highest of all the farms, the big block of Ceiswyn, proves on approach to be blind, all the windows boarded up. An entire community has come and gone, and all is ready for the conifers.

The new scene is heralded by the recently finished forest road that blasts its way four miles to end just below the cliff of Waun Oer. It crosses the boundary of the Snowdonia National Park without so much as a hiccup, and, new detritus streaming below, can be seen for miles, like something branded on the nakedness of the hills. In due course it will be softened, finally buried, by the trees.

When a local farmer is all but served an enforcement notice for rebuilding a hardstanding for his stock trailer, it calls into question the aims and powers of a national park planning authority. A valley has been changed in all but name: change of use, change of scene, change of communications, change of society. And yet, under existing legislation, the planning authority has done, can do, nothing.

The harsh economics of today also affected the forest. Until a decade ago, the Forestry Commission housed many of its works in forestry holdings. These provided oases of grass amongst the forest, restored the buildings, and gave work to the smallholder, who was able to keep his own stock. At least one young Welshman has worked his way via a forestry holding right to the top – a 220-acre hill farm of his own.

But recent policy has been to sell these holdings off – the holdings now offered for barter. Inevitably, barter apart, they fall to the highest bidder: and inevitably that is a second home owner, the weekender. So in the end the already tenuous human life of the forest disappears altogether.

The march of the conifers is slow and insidious. The goosepimpling of today is the forest of tomorrow. And the forest of tomorrow is a permanency. When farm changes to forest, it can seldom, if ever, go back again.

The last human beings to work on the hill are mossmen like William Pugh. Once the hill is fenced from the 'nibbling and omnivorous sheep', vegetation surges ahead. Soon the wet, northerly slopes cushion out in knee-high sphagnum moss. Self-employed, usually working in pairs, buying the mossing rights by tender, this is when the mossmen move in. It is to be the last natural crop of the mountain.

The mossmen have three brief years to gather their harvest in. It takes a year or two for the sphagnum to grow fully after the sheep; and in another few years, the trees are closing in. Meantime, one cutting, the other bagging, the mossmen scythe or rake the two-thousand-foot hill.

It is hard, lonely work, with only the mist and the dripping trees for company. And of all 'the fine-hewn, strong-armed men who once broke the colt of the weather in, or saw that the mare of the earth was always expecting', there is today only left the figure of William Pugh. That tiny figure on the skyline, his scythe changing the colour of the hill, is to be the hill's last human; final, patient, hardy, historical.

7 November 1979   **Mark Bourne**

A mobilized people

'The world's brow was hot, and we were out to fan it with banners. We suggested a possible definition of Wales as a non-stop protest with mutating consonants. Navels distended by resting banner poles became one of the region's major stigmata.'

Gwyn Thomas, novelist and playwright from the Rhondda, catches a community in revolt. On February 3, 1935, at least 300,000 people took to the streets in South Wales in monster demonstrations against Chamberlain's 'Slave Bill', with its UAB, its Means Test, its onslaught on the family values by which this crippled society had lived.

Bleeding to death from 'social leukaemia' (half a million people had been driven out), battered to its knees by British capitalism in crisis, a people stood up and spat this insult back at the grotesquely misnamed National Government.

This was not 1926 with its urchin jazz bands, not the grim tramp of lock-outs and hunger marches. This was a society which since 1928 had known that it had to live with structural, permanent and monstrous unemployment, and a union which had its Unemployed Lodges and a workless militant like Will Paynter on its executive.

The whole coalfield moved out of doors, miners, un-employed teachers, shopkeepers, chapel ministers, Labour, ILP, Communists. Day after day they marched, day after day their disciplined militants fought their by now traditional battles with Lionel Lindsay and his baton-wielding police, and filed their traditional way into his gaols. Many of their leaders talked of the Chartists of 1839.

And they won. This was one moment in the Thirties when a mobilized people stopped a government in its tracks. That people was mobilized by a trade union which was infinitely more than a trade union. This was a union which since 1917 had written the abolition of capitalism into its rulebook, which in 1921 was struggling to organize 270,000 miners and inevitably a whole human complex in a uniquely export-orientated society dependent on them, a society which until that moment had been a cemtre of immigration second in intensity only to the United States itself. This trade union, in order to be a union, had to represent a community; it had to institutionalize fraternity and win social hegemony for it. The union was the South Wales Miners' Federation, The Fed.

Even today, when there are only 27,000 of them left, when the only seams most South Walians know are stitched, when the Weed kills more Harry Dampers than the Dust, these men move through our society with the moral precedence of princes. When British capitalism first proposed to eliminate us in 1930 (there was actually a proposal to transfer the population out), they saved us. In a South Wales faced with extinction in 1980, they offer a pledge that some at least will not see a world end with a whimper, will not go gently into anybody's good night.

This distinctive people has at last found its remembrancers. The two young authors of this book* come out of its ranks and were prime movers in that remarkable enterprise which rescued what was left of the celebrated Institute Libraries (Tredegar had 58,000 volumes) to erect the Swansea Miners Library with its memorial to the International Brigade, and Llafut, the Welsh Labour History Society, sustained by the miners, which is in fact numerically stronger than the parent British body.

They have written a book which has no parallel that I know of in the English language. It is as good as, often better than, Paolo Spriano's studies of Turin and the occupation of the factories in Italy. It makes disciplined and effective use of the wealth of oral testimony now stored at Swansea, and has been well served by its publishers, not least in its riveting photographs.

It is not perfect: read the introduction and the footnotes, they are essential. The discerning may detect shifts in authorship and occasional failures to integrate. The team is working in abnormal places. But the book's majestic, crisply analytical, colourfully human and occasionally brilliant progress does not falter until the final chapter when the present world of the NUM is too much with it.

Beginnings are always difficult, said Marx; these authors had the earlier volumes of R. Page Arnot to contend with. The consequence, in 'union histories' virtually unique is an opening chapter of quite stunning brilliance, which is the best introduction to modern South Wales history I know.

The authors decisively establish (against the current trend) the central necessity of organization, of institutions, in working class history. They skilfully locate the Fed in that South Wales whose rooted culture and confident respectability were being transformed by immigration, the advance of Combines, and of the English language as a vehicle of liberation; by the revolt of the young and the Marxist in their unofficial Reform Movement and Plebs League which offered an alternative culture.

To this world recruitment of one hundred per cent membership, rank and file leadership and democratic centralization were imperative. The mechanistic language of committees encompasses a vision of social renovation.

In a sense the whole book is a commentary on the programme of The Miners' Next Step of 1912 and its final realization in the face of appalling difficulties in the NUM of 1945. Hence the massive and detailed concentration at its core, on the struggle against non-unionism and the Industrial Union, with its great battles at Nine-Mile Point, Bedwas, and Taff-Merthyr, its unforgettable portraits of communities like the Little Moscow of Mardy, implausible Bedlinog, which at one point had a Communist Chamber of Commerce, and of that stubborn and intensely Welsh Anthracite Region which, less hard hit, blocked victimization with its vital 'seniority rule' to serve as a dynamo and the seedbed of a distinguished communist leadership.

The reorganization of The Fed in 1934 in fact revitalized a society. The consequences in the late Thirties were striking. As the authors say, parts of South Wales then were more like France or Spain than Britain; the commitment to the Spanish Republic was breathtaking as a destitute people gave its money, its clothing, its milk and some of its blood. The

Popular Front was a reality in South Wales long before it was official in Europe.

Through it the qualities of leadership shone, the serried ranks of Labour men, Aneurin Bevan with his workers' militias, Jim Griffiths who stands out here as a giant. Most striking of all, of course, that apostolic succession of Communist leaders, Will Paynter, Dai Dan Evans, Dai Francis (now member of the Order of Bards of the Island of Britain), Lewis Jones the writer (who refused to stand up when Stalin came into a room), and a host of local heroes all captured here in penetrating sketches. Towering over them all, the architect himself, that Arthur Horner who emerges from these pages as a statesman of the European working-class movement.

Small wonder that today, in a South Wales which has generally found *Times* editorials as relevant as the Rosicrucian cabala, the Communist Party finds itself in the simultaneously comforting and uncomfortable position of being almost as respectable as an Eisteddfod.

It is appropriate that the creative tension slackens in the final chapter with its dismal record of short-sighted expertise triumphing over that Welsh miner who asked Alf Robens, 'Do you think Arabs are going to live in tents for ever?' Yet in this shrunken world 1972 was visibly a repeat performance of 1934. It was moreover a time when Welsh miners began consciously to repossess their history, as they did in 1935.

This book will re-engage that past. It is a committed history; its purpose is to 'sustain a collective memory'. It will do more. As an age of iron returns, it makes the past, in the words of the miners' own motto, into an instrument for the future. 'We paid our dues before the rent,' they used to boast. Hywel Francis and David Smith have certainly paid their dues; it is their readers who will have to pay the rent that's due to history.

15 May 1980   **Gwyn A. Williams**
The Fed: A history of the South Wales miners in the twentieth century by Hywel Francis and David Smith (Lawrence & Wishart.)

The drooling class

Twenty years away from home and so, of course, America seemed like a vast, strange land, with me a complete and utter stranger, lost and with that inner compass, the compass rose of the head or the heart or perhaps even of the soul, not showing true north, until I was standing on the White House lawn and saw Dominic 'Mimi' De Pietro grab the President of the United States by the seat of his pants. Then I started feeling more at home.

There they all were on the South Lawn, the White House's back garden, 5,000 of the party faithfuls, Democratic Party committeemen, Democratic committeepersons, Congressmen and Congresspersons, Senators, ward heelers, who had moved heaven and earth to get a ticket to sit under the spreading magnolia trees on this historic occasion when the Pope of Rome blessed the President of the United States and Mimi De Pietro grabbed the President of the United States by the seat of his pants.

After the speeches on that famous back porch the Pope suddenly went walkabout. He came down off the portico and walked among the party faithfuls. The orchestra broke into Jesus movie music, like a Cecil B. De Mille film, and there was the Pope, all dressed in gleaming messiah white, getting gripped by the party faithfuls, who were pushing and shoving each other out of the way in order to kiss the Pope's ring or, at least, get near enough to the Pope so that a photographer could take a picture to send back home to their constituents: Me and the Pope. That's the way you keep the vote. This wasn't C. B. De Mille. It was Monty Python's *Life of Brian*.

And there was Jimmy Carter, with that death defrosted smile of his, walking side by side with the Pope while the party faithful got into this rugger scrum, and the photographers shouted: 'Papa, Papa, over here, Papa!' And then, suddenly, the American genius for politics asserted itself in the form of

Dominic 'Mimi' De Pietro from Baltimore, Maryland's first district.

The White House rose garden was swarming with Secret Servicemen, with their sombre, dark, three piece suits, with the lapel pins of the Secret Service and the earplugs that keep them in touch with each other, and, just in case you have not sussed out the act, the highly uncool bulge in the drape of the coat where the revolver is, and suddenly in the middle of all this high priced security, Mimi grabbed the President, Mimi, all five feet three inches of him, with a gleaming yellow suit and a gleaming white Italian smile, grabbed the President and said:

'Hey, Mister President, you remember me?'

Mimi had Carter held by the back of his trousers, gripping him by the waistband and pulling upwards. This is the old fashioned policeman's grip, used to give drunks and petty malefactors the bum's rush. If you start struggling against that grip you come out a gelding.

President Ford had this way with mechanical objects. They just would not function when Gerald Ford was around. But Carter, he has this beautiful gift for the bizarre encounter. He grinned down at Mimi, who said: 'T'ree years ago you come to Baltimore when you wanted to be President. You promised me money to fix up my streets and alleys an' I'm still waitin', Mister President, I'm still waitin'.'

Click! Click! go the cameras. Mimi has got himself photographed alongside the President. The *Baltimore Sun* newspaper will tell the story the next day.

While all the phonies were trying to kiss the Pope's ring, while the big shot Congressmen and Senators might have private chats with the President about the situation in Iran, the Russian troops in Cuba, Mimi De Pietro wanted to know about the goddamn holes in the roads in Baltimore because there's a man down in Baltimore who votes for Mimi and what does that man care about the Russian troops in Cuba, he's got a hole in his road.

'Listen,' Mimi says, 'I coulda got th' Pope. I was gonna kiss his ring. But there was this crippled, handicapped lady kissin' it. How could I push her outa th' way, I mean I got my health an' she ain't. Naw, I don't mind the Pope bein' only Polish. Listen, I got a lot of, I gotta swell bunch of Polish constituents.'

America the Beautiful, I thought.

But it was nearly 20 years since I was home. Ten years ago I had gone back north of Boston, back to the Robert Frost country where I was born to see my grandmother buried, and I spent two weeks swimming and sailing and drinking beer in New Hampshire. And that was not seeing America at all. This time it was more like it, and it was the Air-Conditioned Nightmare Revisited.

America's just like the 1950s again, looking for a role, looking for a leader, but wanting to be quiet, wanting to be secure, wishing to hell that everything and everybody would conform or get the hell out. All that rebellion of the Sixties is dead, long gone. Walking about you notice something is different, something has been added. Then you see. It is the flag, the flag which hardly anyone flew in the Sixties because it became a sign of being for the Vietnam war. The flag is back. They've got it flying everywhere, and the people are walking about, too, as if they are on parade.

The people are walking about as if they knew where they were going, as if they had some place to go, being very purposeful, businesslike, goose-stepping, striding, walking fast and tall, but there is a nervous look in their eyes. In the fifties they had Eisenhower and John Foster Dulles, the coldest of all the Cold Warriors, and now they've only got Jimmy Who.

In the big hotels and high class restaurants the Lords of the Earth come in. How stiff and uptight those haute bourgeoisie Americans are, but panic stricken, so frightened that you, a stranger, might talk to them that they could almost be . . . Englishmen! The bourgeoisie are the same the world over, but the Lords of the Earth are different.

They come in with that purposeful, slightly swaggering walk, gazing down the menu with their dead eyes, ordering in those flat, dead, robot voices, getting very very fussy and particular about what they want and the way they want it, ordering in that curious 'menu French' with the accent so correct that it doesn't really sound like French at all, but, instead, like a sort of parody of French.

And then the food comes and the sauce isn't right. The goddamned chef has made it too thick, he hasn't stirred in enough stuff or he's beaten it too goddamn much. The Lord of the Earth is really giving the waiter hell.

The waiter is some kind of foreigner, of course. He stands there, slightly bowed at the waist, listening very carefully, practically taking notes on the way the goddamn sauce should be beaten or stirred or whatever they do to sauces. In fact, I think the waiters actually do take notes.

But then the waiter catches my eye. He sees me wearing this sort of bummy tweed suit which is not razor-sharp cut like the American suits but looks instead as if it were cut out with a knife and a fork and he knows I'm European just like himself. He gives me this look which says: 'I'd kill this sonofabitch and get the hell back to Budapest if only the pay wasn't so good, know what I mean?'

Then the too thick sauce or the too thin sauce or whatever the hell was wrong with it comes back to the table and the waiter asks the Lord of the Earth if this is the way he wants it and the Lord of the Earth looks down and smiles and then the waiter smiles and then the Lord of the Earth and the waiter have this big, warm, confidential conversation about sauces of the world, and the woman with the Lord of the Earth keeps looking at the goddamn food saying: 'Bootiful, just bootiful, isn't it bootiful? Doesn't it look marvellous?' All the while making these disgusting drooling type faces with accompanying lip smacks. The goddamn food looks so good she could almost eat it.

I'm sitting at the next table in my bummy suit and I can see the food is getting cold and I keep wondering why, after all that trouble, they have not fallen upon the food. I had forgot; after all these years living in England where you just do not leave a saucy plate I had forgot. Eating out in America has nothing to do with being hungry. It is all about conspicuous consumption.

When the waiter leaves, the Lord of the Earth and his lady

146

pick at the thing and then they leave it, all messed up and not even half eaten. The waiter doesn't ask if it was not right. He knows, eating out in these classy places has nothing at all to do with being hungry.

And then the Lord of the Earth and his lady get up and swagger out, with the lady swaggering in that particularly American Lordperson of the Earth swagger, which is meant to show off the cut of the skirt I guess, but is full of arrogance; a walk like an actor might use to play the Nazi strolling through the occupied town. All the waiters, and the headwaiter especially, are bowing them out; and the funniest thing is that the Lord and the Lordperson of the Earth cannot see that they hate them, that all the waiters and even Mario, the maître d', hate them like poison.

The waiter comes over to me and asks if I am going to have some afters. I cannot move, I've eaten so much. They let me out of the joint to walk around before coming and pigging down some more. 'Sure, dat's awright, I like to see a fella can use a knife 'n' fork, know what I mean?' Sure do.

Brainwashed by the old Hollywood 1930s Clark Gable fast-talking out of the side of the mouth newspaper guy movies, brainwashed by Ben Hecht and Charles MacArthur's *Front Page*, brainwashed by *All The President's Men*, and by the 'new' journalism also, I got to thinking that all American reporters were, at the very least, the sort who could kick down the front door of city hall, stick their foot up on the mayor's desk, whip out the pad and the pencil, and inquire, 'Who you screwing now?'

Here is this vast country of 200 million souls of great diversity, of which all but the stiff and uptight, constipated haute bourgeoisie, the Lords of the Earth, will talk to just anyone and tell everything, spill out a life story to a total stranger, just to pass the time of day, and who, when confronted by a microphone, will wrestle it away from the media person and start performing, and yet here are all the American reporters acting just like bank managers.

All the American reporters look like bank managers these days. Except the White House press corps. The White House

147

press corps have been hanging round presidents so long that they all think they are Senators, and not just any old Senator but . . . Presidential Timber! I guess 20 years of waiting stories that all start 'The President said today that . . .' is enough to do anyone's brain.

Reporting over the telephone, rewriting the handouts, the American reporters never get out to see any people, unless it's a big shot giving a prestige interview, doing some briefing for the press. Ah well, you see, a fellow said, in the old days – in your day! – the newspaper was right smack in the middle of town. Now they are moved out of the cities, out near the freeways, turnpikes, motorways so that the vans can get out and deliver the papers free of city traffic jams. 'Why don't you jump in the car, get into town, see the people?' 'What, with those traffic jams?' Do it all by telephone.

Then, looking round at all these reporters, who are not even just reporters nor even correspondents, but are called editors, no less, a sad, hard truth dawns on me as I realize that these are Harvardmen and Yalemen, Princetonians, and graduates of Columbia School of Journalism. They are, themselves, Lords of the Earth, and I understand that what has killed the old style Clark Gable fast-talking, wisecracking, kick down the city hall door reporter and ask the Mayor just who has been ruined, utterly destroyed by nothing less than . . . education!

My return to the air-conditioned nightmare was not extensive. I travelled less than 3,000 miles, a timid, baby step in the land of giant strides. Out there somewhere I knew there were the real people but I was not getting to them. I saw them only briefly, got only fleeting glimpses of them.

Like the rodeo rider in Iowa with the battered rodeo rider's face but glowing with health and humble pride, like a blond, sunburnt Montgomery Clift, who told me how his bronco busting days were through and then grinned a broken-toothed, face-cracking grin of true pride as he said: 'But m'boy, Scott, though, he's only 10-years-old and he rode his-self two big *Texas* bulls last week down in Amarillo. You bet.'

Or the philosophical barkeep at Penn Station in New York

City who, while I was hymning the marvel of America, where you push a button and something happens, as opposed to England, where you push a button and something *might* happen, said: 'Is that what it's all about, the Freedom to Push?'

'Yeah,' I said, 'but all our telephones are vandalised.'

'Yeah, yeah, yeah,' the philosophical barkeep said, 'over here we just vandalise people.'

'You ever coming back home?' he asked me.

Harvard, I told him, had asked me about teaching some sort of writing course.

'Yeah, yeah, yeah,' he said, 'I heard all about it – they're gettin' all the old beatniks back.'

Or in Chicago, late at night, coming back from the shore of Lake Michigan, walking down State Street, with the giant, broadshouldered buildings, built way out of all proportion to any human scale, dwarfing everything, and the evil noise of that weird overground railway – like a tube train suddenly burst to the surface – hurtling by, and the crazy black man, dressed in US Army surplus, saying: 'Can I walk 'long with you gents because I'm scared, scared to death.'

Great big black man but wobbly on his legs. 'Your legs look a little wobbly,' one of the fellows said. And the black man looked down at his shaking legs and he laughed at us and said: 'Look at them legs! So you think they're my legs! They ain't my legs!' Then he shook his bowed head and laughed at us for thinking such a thing. 'My own legs, gents, they don't wobble. I was in Vietnam, gentlemen, and they never wobbled there.'

And I never saw such food in my life. Or, if I had, I forgot all about it. Behind the big plate glass windows of the delicatessens, under the flickering signs saying 'Deli', it's like all the storehouses, all the larders of the world have been broken into, looted, and spread out here for passersby to gape at.

Inside there is even more. Great wheels of cheese, mountains of salad, running rivers of the fruits of all the world, plus confectionery, enough to rot one hundred thousand sets of teeth. And all that before you turn the corner and get down to the serious business of . . . meat! (Don't eat too much because round the corner is Mac's or Joe's or Jim's, Somebody's Famous Fish Restaurant. How come England, surrounded by sea, has no seafood like this?)

And why weren't the plateglass windows of the deli's smeared with the rubbery, distorted faces of people pressed up just gazing, hypnotized, and sighing over all that grub? Because they're all inside, leaving saucy plates.

'Well, well, well,' a man said to me. A regular Babbitt he was. He even slapped me on the back. 'Twenty years since you bin home, eh? Well, well, well, what do you think of America?'

And I am looking at all those great wheels of cheese, mountains of salads, running rivers of the fruits of all the world – plus oceans of beef, ham, pork, turkey, and chicken – and say: 'If I were America's dad, I'd smack its arse and send it to bed with no supper.'

17 November 1979   **Stanley Reynolds**

Reagan loses his ticket

Ronald Reagan inserted one unscripted item in his speech accepting his party's nomination for the presidential election – a silent prayer for the oppressed people around the world who did not have the fortune to live in the United States. With the hall silent around him, and in a voice broken with emotion, he finished: 'God bless America.'

It was, in all candour, unadulterated ham. But it also summed up the spirit in which the Republican Party is entering the battle to take over the leadership of the Western world. The mood of this week's gathering has been that of superpatriotism, of religiosity, and of a total conviction that only the United States can save its friends from the expanding communist menace and themselves.

The 1980 Republicans are increasingly composed of the growing number of fundamentalists in the country. Their belief in their cause is total and their missionary spirit is awesome. They proselytize in the certain knowledge that the Godlessness of the world is destroying every institution and value they hold dear and that they are surrounded by the malevolent or the misguided, who must be led back to the true path. To this end they need an America which can dominate economically and militarily.

Mr Reagan does not share all these views, but he has shrewdly seen the coalition of them and his own right-wing attitudes as a powerful engine for his drive to the White House. Ignoring the inevitable partisan verbiage of these past days, his campaign is virtually an exact parallel of that run by Jimmy Carter four years ago. Reagan, too, is running against Washington, drawing on the populist fervour against big government, stoking the pervasive American feeling that the world has turned sour on it.

Like Mr Carter, Mr Reagan started running long before most people had given the slightest thought to the 1980 campaign – by some versions in 1964. He nearly made it four years ago and he has patiently continued building up the local organizations that sewed up this year's primaries so tightly that only 55 delegates could be found to vote against him in the convention. He talks in the language of bumper stickers, as Mr Carter did, and his sole experience of administration is as a State Governor.

It is beginning to look as if this is now the standard campaign against an incumbent and that it chimes in with the distrust of established national politicians precipitated by the Vietnam war, Watergate, inflation, and America's tangled role on the international scene. With President Eisenhower's departure in 1960, the US lost the last two-term President it has had. There is a desperate search for another who can bring the tranquillity and prosperity of that age inaugurated 28 years ago – and an apparent readiness to toss out each succeeding failure.

So Mr Reagan is in the business of reassurance, of projecting that same fatherly image as Ike's, of one who recognizes the distress, offers a shoulder, and comes up with the perfect answer. That is partly why the issue of his age has become so ambivalent and it is certainly the underlying reason for the attraction of ex-President Ford as a running mate. But the lesson of that bizarre episode is that Mr Reagan is also a politician and, on the evidence here, not all that astute a practitioner.

The question of whether he fell or whether he was pushed will be discussed and argued for years. There is little love lost between the two – the heritage of the bruising fight in 1976 – but each recognized the other as the key to success. Mr Ford's soundings about a campaign of his own earlier in the year showed plainly that he had not lost the taste for power. He arrived in Detroit only too ready to be wooed. For Mr Reagan, of course, he came as the perfect answer to the dilemma of attracting the floating voter and simultaneously gagging the manic wing of his party.

There is now the inevitable dispute about whether his invitation was the ritual gesture to an old party warrior, designed to be refused, or whether it was serious. Most observers favour the second view. In the event, anyway, Mr Ford not only agreed to consider it but made sure it was leaked to the media. Mr Reagan showed an astonishing naivety about the realities of modern American politics in his apparent failure to grasp that the endless television coverage of the convention, so assiduously courted by the politician, also gives it the power to devour him in its relentless maw.

The most notable quality of a convention is its sheer tedium. Potent evidence of this was the catastrophic slump in the viewing figures of the three networks during their hours of coverage, and the corresponding rise in those of the independent stations which carried on their normal programmes. The only way out for the networks is to try to present the event as live theatre, to attract the viewers back. So they seize on any nugget of drama, magnify it, project it, give it any quality they can to zip up the performance. Gerry Ford may not be all that bright, but he is certainly cunning. He knows well enough when he is God's gift to the cameras.

So his staff fanned out to whisper in each willing ear and, having set the scene, Mr Ford came on stage. His interview with CBS and Walter Cronkite caught the Reagan forces on the hop. They thought it was all being conducted in decent secrecy in the plush wastes of the Detroit Plaza Hotel's top floors and Ronald Reagan was stunned when that slow Michigan drawl boomed out from his screen. It was downhill all the way after that. Nobody really disputes the central points and what they boil down to is that Mr Ford had come to Detroit willing to let Mr Reagan have the party's nomination so long as he could have the job after the inauguration.

The idea was extraordinary enough: even more astonishing was that Mr Reagan was prepared to buy it. The negotiations had apparently reached the point of actually drawing up a written understanding before the sheer unworkable pre-posterousness of the whole thing brought it crashing. And, even then, it was Ford who pulled out, not Reagan. It has inevitably raised the question of why, when he has been struggling for the Presidency all these years, Mr Reagan is apparently willing to give most of it away if he gets it.

It also poses the issue of Mr Reagan's judgement and that of his closest advisers. They got themselves into a position where there was simply no credible way out. Just as the candidate was coming up to the crowning moment of his party's acclamation, they not only distracted attention from it but they also landed him in the position of having to pick a running mate who was publicly acknowledged as the second best. It was a virtual rerun of George McGovern's fiasco with Senator Tom Eagleton in 1972.

The party rallied round him faithfully on the final night and gave the television audience the standard picture of people properly delirious that the saviour had now come among them. But there was a feeling in the air that the delegation chairman had had to put in a lot of elbow work to stage it. And, out in the cities and the farmlands where the real struggle will take place in the coming weeks, they must be wondering if God has postponed salvation for another four years.

19 July 1980 **Harold Jackson**

A great game not worth the candle

Mrs Margaret Thatcher would like a great propaganda crusade to alert the world to the perils of Kabul. Jaw-jaw. Meanwhile, with the Spring, comes a slight diplomatic thaw. Mr Muskie and Mr Gromyko may meet. Other contacts at the Tito funeral cannot be ruled out. America is hedging a little on its grain embargoes. Lord Carrington is at the State Department, shuffling his neutrality permutations. Five-and-a-half months after the Soviet tanks rolled, what are we to make of Afghanistan?

The first essential – great crusades or no – must be to sort the truth from the propaganda. And here, by chance, Mr Richard Nixon proves a considerable help. Mr Nixon (in case you've been in Patagonia for the last three weeks) has written a book called *The Real War* and journeyed relentlessly along Western airwaves to plug it.

'Texas-size Afghanistan,' says the former President, 'is the crossroads for conquerors: Alexander, Genghis Khan, Tamburlaine'. Three years ago a 'bloody Soviet backed coup' ousted President Daoud and installed a 'stridently anti-Western Marxist regime'. Shock waves eddied throughout the region. 'Less than 10 months later, in fact, the Shah's regime had fallen and leftist guerrillas staged their first takeover of the US Embassy in Tehran.' There were, of course, a few problems along the way. Mr Nixon skates briskly through the overthrow of the first 'strident Marxist', Mr Tarakki, by another such, Mr Amin, and Mr Amin's overthrow at the hands of 'a reliably pliant Soviet puppet, Babrak Karmal'. But he does not allow mere detail to interfere with his simple conclusions. 'The proud people of Afghanistan were crushed in the iron fist of the Soviet Union, and Russia came one country closer to achieving its goals – now within tantalizingly short reach – of a warm-water port of the Arabian Sea and control over the oil of the Persian Gulf . . . The Soviet seizure is a continuation of the old Tsarist

'*I suppose it's some consolation to know that the Russians are as frightened of Jimmy Carter as we are.*'

16 May 1980

imperialism – the relentless outward pressure that has continued since the Duchy of Muscovy threw off Mongol rule in 1480.'

Mr Nixon's version of history is worth quoting at length because – iron fists and all – it neatly encapsulates the thoughts of Mr Ronald Reagan, Mr George Bush, Mrs Thatcher and President Carter (with his talk of the 'freedom-loving Afghans', as though they were Swiss mountaineers yodelling off to a referendum). Perhaps some amongst them might balk at the odd cause-and-effect. Did the Shah really fall because of the Tarakki coup? But the perception and the rendition are largely shared. If we are to have an international propaganda drive, then here essentially is the script.

The trouble, alas, is that this version leaves out more than it includes. It forgets the corrupt tyranny of the Daoud years. It conveniently fails to remember (pre and post coup) that Afghanistan is one of the most impoverished nations in the world. It fails to square such neglected poverty with all the old phrases about the crossroads of Asia. (If Kabul were really so vital in an age of jumbo jets, would American aid have been such a derisory trickle?) It fails, too, to make any real sense of the past three years.

Mr Tarakki was a Communist, emerging from Iron Curtain exile. Yet when he took power, the world stayed steady on its axis. Afghanistan had, for decades, fallen naturally within the Russian sphere of influence. The land had a stretching Russian border. Military and civilian advisers were thick on the ground. And the Tarakki coup began amongst air force officers who flew MiGs and had been trained to fly them in Russia.

So in 1978 there was little buzzing alarm. What had happened was both predictable (sooner or later) and no more than a shift of emphasis. Who knows, in a country with 90 per cent illiteracy, a reforming central government might have done some good where (sure as eggs) decades of dilatory Western involvement had made no impact. But Marxism and Islam fit ill together: just as Islam and democracy fit ill. Mr Tarakki had intellectual support in the few cities, but out in his wild and dusty domain the tribesmen were as rebellious as ever. He struggled for control. He called in more Russian advisers. He was too weak and too intellectual. Amin, his brutal deputy, overthrew and murdered him. But Amin was worse than Tarakki, the tide of battle was flowing fast against him, too many Soviet advisers were getting killed. At which point the Russians moved forward rather than back. They sent in the tanks, they murdered the murderous Amin, and they installed the peaceable Mr Karmal, a Communist from a separate Afghan faction, to restore calm. Mr Karmal, in turn, has proved a miserable flop.

There is more butterfingers than iron fist about this fumbling sequence. Tamburlaine stubs toe on Hindu Kush. The Afghan army has dwindled through defection to a disorganized rump. Russian tanks and helicopter gunships have made the few major roads and towns safe, but the rebels still hold vast tracts of wasteland (as they have held them for centuries). They can be napalmed and starved into retreat, but not into submission. Meanwhile in Kabul some 70 odd students lie freshly dead after a campus riot: freedom-loving democrats, as it happens, but followers of the late Mr Tarakki's faction. Strident Marxists shooting down strident Marxists. Mr Karmal will not last long. But it is extra-ordinarily difficult to see who the Russians can choose next, and extraordinarily difficult to see him surviving more than a few months. The enduring Afghan obsession is the constant rubbishing of central authority.

Meanwhile, along Afghanistan's borders, matters are no less confused. Iran is one sensitive border. Pakistan is another, and the perceived target for Finlandization and the push to the warm water. But Pakistan is in a very curious condition. Its unpopular military ruler provides some respite for hundreds of thousands of Afghan refugees cum guerrillas. But he dares not risk the four-square American backing that (on Nixon reckoning) would make him the front line of liberty. Indeed, liberty is not his area of special expertise. He is beset on every side. By a collapsing economy; by the burden of sustaining the refugees; by brother generals who would like to take every American weapon going; by a bevy of extremely popular politicians who, in the shadow of Mrs

Gandhi, would prefer a Pakistan rapprochement with Kabul rather than messy tangles across a militarily open border.

Here again, then, the simplicities of propaganda come up delusion. The ruthless Russian jackboot has not crushed Afghanistan. It is knee deep in a familiar quagmire. The countries most immediately threatened are not clamouring for Western aid. Tehran is full of hatred for the West. Islamabad shifts querulously between amity and anxiety. We, the allies, cannot draw a line on a map and say to Moscow: thus far and no farther. We draw those lines through sovereign countries touchy about many things besides White House approval.

And so to Lord Carrington and his hopes of Afghan 'neutrality'. If we are to forget talk about 'the cockpit of Asia' then expectations need not be unduly inflated. A neutral and non-aligned Afghanistan, six months ago when rhetoric was cool and Olympic preparations were proceeding on schedule, had a Marxist administration and a medieval taste for assassination. The status quo was not, and never has been, a liberal democracy elected with an attendant UN peacekeeping force and supervised by Lord Soames. Any status quo over the past three decades implies heavy Russian infiltration and orchestration; it tacitly acknowledges Kabul as a Kremlin sphere of influence.

A sensible Western policy, then, would exert all reasonable pressure for a pull-back. It would talk to Mr Brezhnev and Mr Gromyko in the search for ways and means. It would encourage Pakistan to find a settled form of government with a settled policy – and indicate to the Iranians that here at least is one border that co-operation could make quieter. But such an approach matches uneasily with Mrs Thatcher's propaganda crusade. The myths of that crusade – the Duchy of Muscovy and the rest – are simplistic battle cries. They make a Russian retreat less easy; worse, they may delude the propagandists themselves. Afghanistan six months ago was an anarchic tribal land deserted by the West and fitfully manipulated from the East. As long as that is all we expect (and we have no moral right to expect much more) then relentless, unflurried diplomacy has plenty of opportunities.

6 May 1980   **Leader**

After supper in Jalalabad

The only lights were a distant string of bulbs at the hydro-electric project a few miles from the city. A few hours earlier an Afghan electrical linesman trying to repair a sabotaged main pylon had been shot dead by Islamic rebel snipers, and two Soviet army guards had died with him.

Engineer Mahmoud, the commander of a Mojahadin force in the area, was satisfied. 'When the city is dark we can move around easily,' he said. 'That is why we attack the pylons. Tonight we will have dinner with friends in Jalalabad, and then we have something else to attack.'

Mahmoud, five other Islamic fighters and myself moved towards the city through fields and over ditches, past bushes alight with glow-worms and fireflies. I left my pack behind and took only a water bottle. 'Carry little,' Mahmoud advised, 'because we might have to run.'

Our object was the black road – the main highway to the capital, Kabul, and we were to ambush a tank. For this tank, Mahmoud carried an antitank rocket launcher, together with the only missile the group possessed. The others were armed with Kalashnikov assault rifles, captured from Russians or Afghan soldiers. It was clearly to be a one-shot affair, and then run like hell. A Kalashnikov is no match for a tank.

Ahead of us, on the other side of the Jalalabad canal, was an army camp, housing Russians and Afghans. Inside it, something was burning, but no one could tell what. The flames illuminated billows of smoke.

Tracer bullets were being fired from the camp at random, their red firework balls flashing out in all directions in a spectacular display. Occasionally, the bullets passed close enough for us to hear their whine, a few feet away. We assumed that the riflemen were Afghans. It is said that many Afghan soldiers avoid firing directly at Mojahadin, and aim over their heads. This certainly seemed to be the case that night. There were three shots in every volley, the first high, and the others descending to body level, thus giving fair warning to anyone in the way to throw themselves down.

Behind us, and out of sight, was another army camp, housing only Afghans, and throughout the night magnesium flares lit their area.

We walked beside the Jalalabad canal for about a mile, finally crossing a bridge, and moved swiftly in the dark over ploughed fields towards houses on the edge of the city.

We stopped at a big house and waited quietly at the gate while one of the rebels went inside. Whoever owned the house was clearly not expecting us, although his servants were. We were ushered round to a walled orchard where rugs were laid out for us and food was immediately produced – large oval-shaped nan, the dry unleavened bread which is the Afghan staple diet, and bowls of gravy with a little meat. We ate hurriedly, while, on the edge of the light of a single paraffin lamp, ancient faces watched impassively beneath twisted white turbans.

Immediately the meal was over it was time for prayer and the Muslims kneeled, foreheads touching the rugs, chanting in low voices 'Allah Akbar' (God is Great). The armed rocket launcher had been propped against the orchard wall in front of them, almost as if it were a symbol of their salvation.

Then out into the night, still walking quickly. There was no light, just the shadow of the man in front who had to be followed closely if you wanted to avoid being left behind, while at the same time you had to stay clear of the darker shadows on the ground which were usually drops of two or three feet, or ditches of water.

In the city dogs began to bark as if aware of our approach. Soon we were walking through deserted streets in the blackness, with houses on both sides. Suddenly, there were other shapes ahead, and Mahmoud had stopped. There was a low murmur of conversation, while the rest of us pressed flat against the walls.

We were picking up a couple of dozen other armed Mojahadin from the city and there were to be two attacks that night: the ambush on the black road, and also a raid on a city police station to capture a particular policeman.

We walked swiftly through a city which showed no sign of anything else living, although it could not have been later than 10 o'clock. We climbed walls, tramped through gardens, and finally split up. The bulk of the group went off to the police station, while four Mojahadin and myself headed for the ambush point.

Several times we heard the rumble of tank engines and saw the approach of headlights, while the rebels tensed themselves for action and myself for flight. Each time, the tanks turned off before reaching the ambush point.

In the distance, automatic rifles began blasting off and there were yells of 'Allah Akbar!' as the other group attacked their target. The dogs of Jalalabad yapped furiously. There is something spine-tingling about men screaming 'Allah Akbar!' as they open fire on others. It is part Red Indian war cry, part a warning that they believe implicitly in their cause.

After 10 or 15 minutes, the attack faded away. Whether it was successful or unsuccessful, I never found out. Information exchange between Mojahadin in different areas is often a slow business.

Through the night there were other explosions of rifle fire and machinegun fire in various parts of the city, but still no tank for Mahmoud to use his one rocket on.

I found myself falling asleep. At last Mahmoud gave up. As we walked back out of the city he said quietly: 'It doesn't matter. There will be other nights. I have already shot 12 tanks. Soon I will make it 13.'

13 June 1980   **Peter Niesewand**

A job for Mada Khan

A mile from the gloomy mud-walled prison in which Islamic rebel fighters are holding Mada Khan is his first chance of death – an unexploded Russian bomb.

It has been impacted into the bank of the Agam River for more than a fortnight, its light grey tailfins protruding and being given a wide berth by the stream of refugees trudging up the ravine towards Pakistan.

Inside the bomb is the orange explosive which the Mojahadin need for their own homemade devices. When they are satisfied that Mada Khan, aged 23, has told them all he knows about the spies, Russians and Khalqis, they will give him a hacksaw and an armed guard, and send him to cut out the explosive.

While he saws at the metal casing, the guards will sit on the opposite side of the ravine, covering him with their Kalashnikovs. Dozens of Mojahadin have died trying to remove the explosives from bombs in this way, so now the job is given to condemned prisoners. Although he does not yet know it, Mada Khan is a condemned man.

He was kidnapped by the Mojahadin just over a month ago, when he went from Jalalabad, where he was a member of the Afghan militia, to his home village of Bachir. A government-issue rifle was found at his house.

Like the other eight prisoners in the gaol at the Torabora Rebel Centre, Mada Khan's case is being dealt with by a mullah in accordance with Islamic law.

Theoretically, after questioning by the mullah, further inquiries and researches are carried out in the prisoners' home villages before a decision is reached and sentence passed. In fact, in Mada Khan's case, he is being played like a fish on a line.

Engineer Mahmoud, one of the senior rebel commanders in the 'liberated area' of Nangahar province, said: 'He is very important to us, because he can give us the names of other spies and people in the militia, and we can then go and capture them.'

And then what will happen to him? Mahmoud shrugged: 'His life is finished,' he said simply. One day Mada Khan will be taken from prison for his date with the unexploded bomb. 'We will not tell him of the danger,' Mahmoud said. 'We say to prisoners that the Mojahadin are very busy, so they have to do this work.'

If Mada is careful, and the explosive packed into the 5ft-high bomb is sufficiently stable, there will be no reward for him, beyond a few extra hours of life. At night he will once again be taken from his gaol and led into the mountains far from the centre, where a firing squad will shoot him down.

Executions are carried out in the dark, at remote locations, by order of the centre's chief, Mahboubi Elahi.

'If his family know where he is,' Mahmoud explained, 'they will try to carry the body away.' In this *Jihad* against the Russians and their allies, there is no sentiment and no forgiveness, even in death.

Mada Khan, who tried to disguise his terror as he stood before us, is to be denied all Muslim rites. The rules of the *Jihad* are clear. Every Mojahid who dies is blessed by Allah and goes straight to Paradise as a shaheed – a martyr – while every dead enemy is cursed and his soul descends into hell, where it remains in torment for eternity.

Mada Khan will not be the only man to face death by firing squad. Of the nine men and boys who shuffle from the gloom of their cell into the afternoon sunshine, perhaps another three or four will be condemned. Most have been kidnapped on information received. One of them is Mr Mir Gholam, a pathetic grey-bearded old man, wearing broken black lace-up shoes. With him stand his two sons, Mohammed, aged 30, and Isatullah aged 15. Mir Gholam said: 'It was 11 o'clock at night when about 16 Mojahadin came to my house at Jalalabad. They asked us to come out from the house, and then they took us here.'

18 June 1980   **Peter Niesewand**

Red tape instead of red carpets

The Soviet Union is so eager to impress but does so much to depress foreigners. If any Western visitors have illusions that their reward for defying the Olympic boycott will be a red-carpet welcome in Moscow, they should prepare to shed them now. Unless the authorities change things in the next few days, absurd security hassles and poor planning are more likely to be the norm.

Take the new airport terminal at Sheremetyevo, the gateway to Moscow. It was built by a West German firm, and opened only three weeks ago. 'An exact replica of Hamburg airport,' they told me as we waited by the conveyor belts for our luggage. Not having been to the Hamburg airport, I cannot vouch for the comparison, but what was immediately apparent was an absence of luggage trolleys. The only one in sight was being pushed by the only porter. 'Any more of those?' I asked a policeman. 'No,' he said.

After staggering to the customs desk, one is asked to put one's baggage into a brand-new (and again Western) X-ray machine. The customs man asked if I had any foreign newspapers, looked through them, and gave them back. Next comes the search for a place to change money. There were signs for telephones and toilets, but nothing for a bank. Ask at the Intourist desk and a woman says upstairs. Still lugging the cases, I went upstairs, found a bank where three people were chatting behind a sign saying 'Closed'. They directed me 50 yards to another bank which was open but which could only change roubles into hard currency, and not vice versa. Fortunately a clerk was kind enough to accompany me downstairs again and show me a third bank a few yards from the Intourist desk where I had originally inquired.

The Hotel Rossiya, the main press hotel, was bristling with half a dozen policemen at every entrance while more patrolled on the pavements. They would not accept my temporary accreditation papers, and it took another half an hour of discussions at the Office of Permits to find an official prepared to escort me past the police. The luggage was put into X-ray machines and opened again. My washkit caused great fascination. 'What is this?' said a policeman, holding up a canister of shaving cream. 'And this?' – shampoo. 'And this?' – toothpaste. Three empty notebooks were closely scrutinized. Newspapers and books were discussed before being returned.

The next day I tried to bring an English friend into the hotel. We had arranged to meet in the street outside. It was a sensible precaution, because she could not get in without a permit. At the Office of Permits she showed her British

'*If Russia invades Iran and releases the American hostages,
will we all be able to go to the Olympic Games?*'
17 April 1980

passport and was issued with a permit. But even with this, the police at the door would not let her in. Back to the Office of Permits. After a short wait, a plain-clothes official said that the permit would only get her in at the west entrance of the hotel, and not the east where we were. Now the Hotel Rossiya is one of the world's largest hotels, a concrete and glass version of a four-sided medieval keep. It took a brisk walk to get to the west entrance where another policeman said she could come in but I could not. Olympic accreditation was only valid for the east entrance.

Incredulously we asked whether we would be able to meet inside the hotel once we got in through our separate entrances. 'Of course,' he replied as though we were daft. Was it not rather absurd that we had to use separate doors, we suggested. Reluctantly he agreed, and hastily let us both through. As we went in, we wondered how first-time visitors to the Soviet Union, who speak no Russian and who are less trained to be tolerant, will fare, especially when more people arrive and the hotels get fuller. Last night I heard some extraordinary oaths emanating from a German, who was objecting to having his credentials scrutinized as he tried to walk out of, not into, his hotel.

If the police go on like this, they will pick up a rich, if lop-sided, smattering of foreign languages by the time the Olympics are over.

One area where the Soviet authorities have done well, though, is in blocking out the West's explanations for the Olympic boycott. My first few encounters could be un-representative but they certainly did not suggest that President Carter's and Mrs Thatcher's hopes of provoking an internal debate over Afghanistan are going to be realized.

I asked the taxi-driver from the airport what people thought of the boycott. 'Unpleasant and offensive,' he said. What did they think the reason was? 'Carter's policies. For a long time he's been trying to put pressure on us.' What about Afghanistan? Did he believe the boycott was linked to that? 'Yes, we've heard that explanation, but we went in there to help the Afghans. There was a counter-revolution and now they're killing our soldiers. For nothing. For nothing.'

A student at the Foreign Languages Institute in Moscow took a similar view. Why was there an Olympic boycott? 'It's a question of politics.' What did he think? 'Well, Carter has decided on a boycott and he has influence on other Western leaders. I don't know why he has done it.' Did he think it was connected with Afghanistan?

'I don't see why it should be,' he answered. 'We went into Afghanistan legally at the request of the Afghan government. We violated no laws.'

In the courtyard of a block of flats children were clearing an area of hardpacked earth for a small football pitch. The grown-ups are not too happy with the plan because of the noise. A tenants' meeting this weekend will decide whether to let the children have the pitch. What did the kids think of the Olympic boycott? 'The Americans are afraid to be beaten,' came the confident reply.

1 July 1980   **Jonathan Steele**

A bronze that glister'd

For the purists it was Gary Oakes who made the Olympic adrenalin flow on Saturday. Two gold medals were handsomely won for Britain by Steve Ovett and Daley Thompson, but the bronze for Oakes was the day's stunningly unexpected event.

It was the performance of an opportunist, for he was only in the final by the whim of President Carter. Somewhere in Europe is Ed Moses, the champion of Montreal, waiting to get at any Moscow Olympic medal winners and ram his world record down their throats.

But that is for the aftermath: put the blinkers back and take a look at Oakes, whose international intermediate hurdling days put him in a kindergarten compared to his famous British predecessors, Hemery, Sherwood, Cooper and Pascoe. He got into the British team in 1978 and only this summer managed to dip under 50 seconds for the first time. Therefore to reach the Olympic final was almost an intrusion, but to match the heavies of Europe, Volker Beck and Vasily Archipenko of the Soviet Union, looked like folly.

He had the inside lane, hurtled off and was up on Beck and Vassilev, another Russian, for five flights. Archipenko then got an edge but coming into the straight for the ninth Oakes rose with Beck and at the tenth his leading foot touched down first. Here the fairy story looked like ending, for his body seemed to shiver, the Russian went by him and Vassilev looked as though he would snatch out and get the bronze. But Oakes, realizing the sensation he was causing, pulled his concentration together, shut out the pain and dug hard into each stride to hold third position in 49.11 seconds.

It was a fighting performance that Lord Exeter, who presented the medals for this event – probably for the last time – must have understood, since he won the gold at Amsterdam in 1928.

28 July 1980 **John Rodda**

The shadow boxer

The pile is full of noises still or rather waffle. Right up to the closing ceremony, the last Olympic day is usually full of sport for the British. Our horsey hyphens and Harveys were always up and over with a last day chance in the show ring.

They stayed away this year, so we had a day off and were able to catch up on our postcards and attend in our hotel the odd little farewell functions offered by various sporting bodies. And I do mean odd. I went to the 'banquet' where the Amateur International Boxing Association announces its choice of the best boxer in the tournament. Each of the 27 association members vote.

Preening pomposity sits formally down to lunch in blazers bearing the most outrageous badges in the name of their sport. We stand around the table, flunkeys with pencils, and after an intensely long preamble, each sentence translated into three languages, the president Donald Hull tells us they have chosen the Italian light welterweight Patrizio Oliva to follow such illustrious names as Dick McTaggart, Benvenuti, Teofilo Stevenson, and Howard Davis.

There is an intake of breath and some of us look at each other and start to giggle. The handkerchiefs are to our mouths in no time. No offence to the pleasant young Neapolitan bank clerk but he was certainly the least technically proficient of all the 22 finalists on Saturday. As my neighbour Hugh McIlvanney aptly put it, 'He might fight like a bank clerk but he sure doesn't fight like a Neapolitan.'

Anyway, in comes Patrizio – wearing two lovely black eyes – to receive his whopping silver cup. He has no accreditation pass, so how did he fight his way past the hotel security guards, asks the president by way of a joke. How the blazes, I want to know, did he fight his way past the quarterfinals? He is all elbows and arms and wrists in the ring. Oliva beat Willis of Britain in the semis. Come to think of it, he boxes like the other Willis running up to bowl.

The award to the ungainly Italian, who is now turning pro of course, was nothing less than a slight to the cadre of marvellous Cuban boxers – especially Jose Gomez and Armardo Martinez – who contested eight of the 11 finals and won an unprecedented six gold medals. It was a slight on Rudi Fink, the outstandingly strong and accomplished East German featherweight. It was a slight even on a past award-winner, Stevenson, who equals the legendary Lazlo Papp's record of winning three successive Olympics – though the Cuban's fuse does not smoulder so readily now; he locks away his right and uses the other fist as a far-from-deadly, point-scoring pop gun.

Stevenson's third final was inspired only by a game opponent, Pyotr Zaev of the Soviet Union, a comparatively tiny mite who was not psyched by the big fellow's reputed menace. He fearlessly growled up at Stevenson for all three rounds and even caught the champion enough times to send the crowd into increasing delirium. With the points verdict came a hangar full of whistles like at a world convention of shepherds.

For the rest, the memory of the evening was of the Cuban flag going up and down like a traditional British pro heavy-weight. Oh yes, and the Italian lad weeping with joy at the medal ceremony. Perhaps that's what swayed the old buffers on the voting panel. Ahhh . . .

4 August 1980   **Frank Keating**

The passionate decorators

That pond was the Atlantic Ocean, says Quentin Bell. When we were children it was much bigger. Behind him stands Charleston, the farmhouse where his parents, Clive Bell and Vanessa Stephen and their friends, Duncan Grant and Roger Fry, played adult games for real when Bloomsbury moved to the Sussex Weald 60 years ago.

In the garden, bright fragments of blue and green mosaic are set in moss, which has overgrown the pattern. In a shady corner, where an earth closet stood, they made a terrace. On it stand a table with a ceramic top and wicker chairs, pushed aside as though someone has just got up. But the chairs are rotting, and there is lichen on the neck of a statue of Vanessa. Uncanny absences in a walled wilderness.

But strangest of all is the interior. A Bloomsbury interior in a solid square farmhouse. The rooms painted like a faded stage set. They painted. They painted everything. Not just walls, but door panels, mantelpieces, chimneypieces, screens, table tops. The coal scuttle, even. All four sides of it. And the radiators and the lampshades, too.

They painted them in the joyful way in which the panels on old fairground roundabouts are decorated. But with less draughtsmanship and more artistry. And now the dampness is reclaiming it all. A house more died-in than lived-in, now. And there is just a chance to save it before dilapidation triumphs.

Vanessa Bell took a lease on the house, in 1916, on the advice of Leonard and Virginia Woolf, who lived not far away. Duncan Grant lived there until his death in 1978, and now it hovers between a home and a museum, with Quentin Bell's sister, Angelica, wife of David Garnett, living there as a sort of temporary custodian, while its fate is settled.

'The National Trust have accepted it in principle, but made it practically impossible because they want us to collect such a vast sum,' says Mrs Garnett. There is £50,000 to buy Charleston from the Gage Estate; and at least as much again to dry it out and renovate it. Yet more must be raised for a trust, to provide income for future restoration, and for a curator to live in.

It will be among the strangest bequests which the National Trust has ever received. The only warm room in the house is the studio with its cast-iron stove. 'The atmosphere is dependent on a kind of impressionism. It is very fragile,' says Mrs Garnett. 'If they did too much restoration, they might destroy the atmosphere.' They sit on either side of the stove, an elderly brother and sister whose childhoods are separated by a decade or so, recalling a child's-eye view of Bloomsbury.

Adults painted the furniture simply because it was cheap – they couldn't afford anything better – and ugly, which they could change. 'Duncan Grant and my mother were passionate decorators. Whenever they arrived, they started painting the walls. Every room has got decorations. It's a jumble of styles. but it doesn't seem to matter. It's a place of unique character.'

'They allowed us to join in when we were older,' says Professor Bell, who is art historian, potter, painter and author. The dining room is decorated with chevrons, some haphazardly applied by young hands. The chimney breasts are covered with mock Classical figures; vases of flowers sprout on the backs of doors, and a beefy athlete, all bulging limbs, lolls on that coal scuttle.

It was open house to a fairly closed circle. 'Guests had three fates allotted to them. Painters would go to the studio; or there were literary chaps, who were approved of by my father, and they would be engaged in conversation from breakfast till lunch. Or Desmond (MacCarthy) would read aloud to the painters working in the studio or outside,' said Professor Bell.

It was a very adult place for a child to be. That meant a mixture of precocity and naïveté. 'I think children were

171

treated almost as grown-ups, certainly by Roger Fry and Virginia who had a great mixture of fantasy when talking to you,' said Mrs Garnett. Then she adds: 'But Leonard was a bit fierce.'

And her brother, as though remembering an old truth, says, 'But you soon rumbled his fierceness.' She: 'Lytton didn't like children very much.' He: 'But my memories of him are positively saccharine.' She: 'I thought he was a little bit afraid because he thought we'd do something awful to him.'

There seems to have been remarkably little awfulness. Lytton Strachey, says Professor Bell 'was terribly nice. But that's not what people want to hear. They want to hear that he tried to rape me.' He chuckles into his big white beard. 'But he didn't.' Nor did E. M. Forster, or Maynard Keynes, who wrote *Economic Consequences of the Peace* in Quentin's bedroom.

But there were frustrations for all the inter-generational equality, adults used to monitor their conversation in the presence of the children. 'Latin terms were used for certain activities. Yes, they told me about the facts of life. Several times. But it made no impression. And French was used for talking about secrets. Like birthday presents.'

And further frustrations outside the immediate domain of Charleston. They came to the country, but they were not of it; they didn't fit in. 'I knew we were wrong 'uns. We were really rotters. There was everybody else going off and getting killed in France, but we didn't. We weren't on good terms with local children because we were known as conchies (conscientious objectors) and occasionally a brick would be thrown in one's direction. But things were better when Julian (brother killed in the Spanish Civil War) began to organize the local Labour Party.'

Growing up at Charleston wasn't a particularly enclosed existence for Quentin, who was sent to boarding school and to live in France at 13; more so for Angelica – 'you found it harder to escape,' says her brother. It was self-contained, but not self-sufficient. They made their own pots, but didn't grow their own food. 'They were more concerned with things before their eyes than things for their bellies.'

But gradually, the world intruded. The fame of the Omega Workshops had already spread to the popular pages of the *Daily Mirror* in 1913; the books and exhibitions opened it out still further. Now a whole academic industry is sustained by Bloomsbury. And Quentin Bell, who holds the Virginia Woolf copyright, is bemused by the scale of it. There could be scholars billeted in the loft of Charleston if enough money can be raised to banish the dampness.

12 January 1980   **John Cunningham**

The fat in the foyer

To see it sitting here so calm and stately on the ground floor of the Guggenheim Museum you would hardly think that Joseph Beuys's Tallow represents the severest test of artistic licence ever undertaken.

From a distance the six great white blocks streaked with grey look like marble sliced from the block. As you get closer they loom above you like icebergs. It's only when you get right up to them that you realize what they are: fat. Twenty tons of mutton fat to be precise, with a few barrels of beef fat added for extra firmness.

To date, these blocks of fat have strained the resources of a museum director, a factory floor, scientists, transport companies, and insurance firms. Beuys was absolutely adamant that they should be included in his huge exhibition at the Guggenheim, planned since 1976. When it was discovered that the only way to get the blocks into the museum would be to take out the ground floor façade windows on Fifth Avenue, the director of the museum, Thomas Messer, tentatively inquired whether it was possible to leave them behind in Germany. Beuys's response was: 'No Tallow, no show.' So while Frank Lloyd Wright, architect of this strange spiralling museum, turned in his grave, down came the façade windows and in came the shipped crates on the cranes of Gerosa, one of New York's biggest construction firms.

The contents of 44-foot shipping containers also came into

the museum, along with four air-freighted temperature-regulated containers for 445 drawings and a host of smaller objects. But it was only ever Tallow that posed a real questionmark. It's not the first time the Guggenheim has been challenged. Last time it was another German artist, Hans Haacke, who proposed an analysis of the real estate interests of some of the Guggenheim trustees as part of his exhibition.

The show was cancelled when he refused to withdraw it. This is where the difference between political and artistic licence becomes clear. Although Beuys has often been the centre of violent political controversy in Germany over issues ranging from his espousal of direct democracy within the official education structure to his pursuit of it in independent organizations like the Free International University, founded with Heinrich Böll, Tallow has been more of a challenge to what is artistically and logistically feasible.

The challenge was initially aimed at the follies of modern architecture. In 1977 Beuys was invited to take part in an open air sculpture exhibition in the city of Munster. He despises the idea of sculpture in the open, claiming that nature needs no embellishment. But he accepted because he found an ideal spot to make a point about the inhumanity of the concrete deserts created by modern planning at its worst. While other artists vied for the prime sites, Beuys chose a dead corner in the underpass to the university, a deep wedge-shaped acute angle in which nothing but dirt could collect.

In his work over the past 30 years Beuys has often referred both to the crumbling façade of capitalism and the need to fill the void of materialism with humane and spiritual values. So grot behind the smart façade of a modern city centre becomes a metaphor. So from this underpass a cast was made, a 16-foot-high wooden construction that was set up in a concrete factory outside the city. Then day and night for over a week mutton fat granules were melted in great vats and the liquid fat was poured into the cast.

Fat has been Beuys's most controversial material over the years, partly because for him it symbolizes energy, and partly because it is a material until now unknown in sculpture, fascinating because it can exist in different states.

This is where the scientists first appeared. An approximate cooling time had to be known. The wooden mould was strained. It had burst once under pressure and been buttressed. It turned out that no one knew the answer. The computers were foxed by the calculations. Estimates varied from three days to three months. After a month and a half it was still completely fluid at the centre. After three months it was cool enough to complete.

With the heat of electric current it was sliced into the six sections of the final work and exhibited in the Munster museum. Between then and the transport to New York it was stored in a disused lorry factory while transporter and insurance firms made their calculations: how could it travel?

Scientists were again consulted. Polystyrene foam seemed like the answer. The exotherm method was considered. A skin of polystyrene like the halves of an Easter egg could be cast round the fat to protect it from bumps and temperature change. But this meant a chemical reaction with oxygen and a heat rise to 80 degrees for at least two minutes while the foam solidified. Too risky.

Another scientist came up with a much advertised new method guaranteeing a pressure of five tons per square metre using an injected foam process. But just one week before packing was due to begin he got cold feet, claimed he could only guarantee 800 pounds per square metre in writing and anyway the chemical needed – Tensid – was 'not available'. In the end polystyrene granules did the trick and Tallow arrived unscathed.

That will please the insurance company. Tallow was the key to the tender for this enormous contract – Beuys's market value is astronomical. If the company took the risk of the dreaded Tallow, they would get the rest, though that they did not know at the time. Swiss National and a German company took it on. Lloyd's of London were ruled out.

At the very last moment the German company withdrew, not because of the fragile nature of Tallow, insured at its production cost of over £100,000, at a premium of 15 per cent, but because of 'the subjective risk of Joseph Beuys'. By that they meant a case two years ago when an insurance company played tricky over a claim for damages inflicted on Beuys's Bathtub when it was used as a beer cooler by philistines of the German SPD Party during a boozy night in the local museum. The company finally paid £47,000.

Although the Guggenheim is known for its coverage of European art – Richard Hamilton for instance has shown there – this is the first time a European artist has had such a munificent carte blanche from an American museum. Over the past 15 years or so we've seen a great one way traffic – in the other direction, with little offered in return.

10 November 1979   **Caroline Tisdall**

A fable

Once upon a time, in a city a long way from here, there lived a Father and a Mother and their two enchanting children, Billikins and Millikins. The little fellow was always jolly and smiling, the little maid was always happy and laughing and so they all lived together in the greatest accord in a corner house with two fir trees and a red front door.

But on the day of their thirteenth birthday a wicked fairy, who had not been invited to their christening, disenchanted Billikins and Millikins. Oh, how Father and Mother cried!

'Alas, what ill-luck has befallen us,' said Mother. 'My dearest Millikins has changed her golden curls for purple and has become so clumsy and lazy that I cannot rouse her from her bed in the morning, nor persuade her to sleep at nights.'

'Ah, wretched fate,' said Father. 'My good Billikins is now angry and sulky. He does nought but grunt when I address him, he is dirty as a beggar, and I fear he doth sniff glue. Woe betide us!'

All the livelong day, Father and Mother strove to please Billikins and Millikins. They went out into the town to earn their living and the children spent their gold as fast as it came. They made delicate food but the children did not come home to partake of it. They bought them fine clothes but the children would not wear the clothes and were scornful. They talked merrily of many things but the children were as if deaf.

When Father reproached Billikins, saying to him 'Look, how we slave for you without reward,' Billikins guffawed and replied: 'That be your bag, man.' When Mother lamented to Millikins, saying 'My daughter, what is the matter with you?' Millikins flew into a rage and screamed out with all her might and main, so that Mother was shamed before the neighbours.

Soon, the corner house with the two fir trees and the red front door had become a hideous place, full of loud noise and heavily laden with strange youths who lay about making mock of all that Mother and Father held most dear and would not listen to their good counsel. Now and again, Guardians of the Law came tumbling into the room, amongst the broken glass, with a most dreadful clatter and Billikins and Millikins scampered away as fast as they could. There remained no nook or cranny where Mother and Father could rest their weary heads in peace.

Then Father took his wife by the hand and said 'Since the wicked fairy disenchanted our children, we have not had one happy hour. Billikins is idle and good-for-nothing and Millikins has hardened her heart against us. Even the dog under the table fares better than we, for he often gets a nice morsel. Come, let us wander forth into the wide world.'

So all day long they travelled over concrete pavements, streets and past glittering shops and, by the evening, they came to a large house, all overgrown with briars and brambles. 'What is this place?' asked Mother, trembling with fear. 'Its name is Squat', said Father. 'Sit yourself down here and wait and I will try to break in and get us a bed for the night.' Presently, Father returned and conducted his wife over the doorstep. The two travellers were so wearied with grief and their long walk that they laid themselves down immediately and went to sleep.

The next morning they awoke and set about cleaning and sweeping the house, putting curtains at the windows and wild flowers in a jar on crates that served as tables. Soon, the place looked more welcoming than the house they had left on the corner. Then Mother baked bread in an old oven kindled with sticks and the good smell filled the air and the two were greatly delighted because, after many a moon and much suffering, they were at last peaceful and gay. 'What a fine Squat is this,' said Father. 'Let us stay here as long as we need.' And he and his good wife embraced each other and were happy.

As soon, however, as the other Mothers and Fathers learned of their deed and how happy they had become, and how everything had prospered with them, envy and jealousy were aroused in their hearts and they looked with melancholy upon their own children, who smoked strange herbs and rent the night with the sound of drums and trumpets.

'Should we not report them to the King for their desertion of their children?' said one Father, but his good wife replied 'No, my dear husband. Let us keep our counsel for the moment and forbear.' And, over three more months, the other Fathers and Mothers stayed in their homes, dutifully serving their children and talking spitefully of the two who had left.

But at last, driven to despair by the roaring and the howling and the slothfulness of their children, all the Fathers and Mothers became impatient. The tears fell from the Mothers' eyes and they sat crying the whole day long. Then, one day, a strange music was heard outside in the streets. It was a pied piper who played sweetly on his pipes 'Blow, breezes, blow, let Mothers and Fathers go'. Every one of them felt an itching in their feet and, without further ado, from all the houses thereabouts, they trooped forth and the moans and the plaints of their children could not stop them nor deflect their steps.

Now it came to pass that the great crowd met outside Father and Mother's Squat and stood astonished at how beautiful it looked and what a noble lodging it had become. They knocked three times at the padlocked door and, when it was opened, begged admittance, saying, 'We can no longer bear our lot so, prithee, give us shelter.'

Father and Mother were blessed with the kindest of hearts and so they stood aside and let in the horde and comforted them and a great fire was kindled and everyone rejoiced. As the days passed, each person was apportioned tasks according to their skills and did them with much goodwill and in the evenings they talked of many wise things, or were silent and content.

Their hearts were filled with love towards each other and for the quiet and peace of their humble Squat and they all lived together to a great age in undisturbed tranquillity, while their disenchanted children disappeared beneath an avalanche of dirty dishes, stale takeaway pizzas, old cigarette stubs and unwashed socks.

P.S. The spell of the wicked fairy was broken when Billikins and Millikins and all the other children had reached one score year and one and the maidens had borne children of their own. Thirteen good fairies were invited to the christenings but the wicked fairy was once again forgot and so, upon those children's thirteenth birthdays, she disenchanted them and the whole thing began all over again, for ever after.

3 July 1980   **Jill Tweedie**

World ephemera year

A paper table napkin, signed inscrutably 'Thank You, Elvis Presley,' fetched £500 at Sotheby's yesterday, eight times as much as Queen Victoria's autograph.

It was an auspicious start to World Ephemera Year, which has been designated by collectors, with the enthusiastic collaboration of auctioneers, to celebrate 'the whole spectrum of minor human record'.

The market for pop music ephemera was tested and found to be good. The Presley napkin, a memento of the singer's farewell concert at Las Vegas, brought nearly £400 more than the reserve price set by the auctioneers.

Almost the same level of success was reached by 14 early Beatles' photographs, and an unpunctuated postcard on which Ringo Starr scribbled from a Hamburg tour: 'Arrived here OK The Club is great We are with Little Richard he is fat See you Sunday.'

The catalogue warned that this lot was 'creased, trimmed or marked with adhesive tape', but it sold for £480 to a Covent Garden publican, Mr Brian Brodie, who also bought the Presley relic and paid £220 for four US dollar bills with Beatle signatures. He plans to show off his £1,200-worth of trophies in his upstairs bar. 'I was a Beatles' fan,' said Mr Brodie, using the past tense which dominated the day.

A single Beatles' photo – with the historic inscription 'Odeon Lewisham Sunday December 8 1963' – fetched £120. A Rolling Stones fan got £220, almost three times the reserve price, for a batch of letters and signatures which included a letter from the group's late guitarist, Brian Jones, about his schooldays.

By contrast, Mrs Patrick Campbell's 254 pages of Random Reminiscences, 'written during a period of enforced idleness in Hollywood, 1936,' remained humiliatingly unsold at the reserve price of £280. A three-page letter from King Edward VIII 'hoping that he can go stalking with Lord Fife' and complaining that his own grouse driving has been 'much spoilt by the wind', sold for only £20.

Auction rooms are however used to a plentiful flow of old documents from actresses and royals, and this keeps prices down. It is recognized that the comparatively poorer literacy of pop singers, as well as their greater tendency to die nastily, gives their written memorabilia a rarity value.

World Ephemera Year has the Duke of Wellington as its patron and support from most major British museums. The first international conference, called Ephemera 80, is being held in London in September. The British organizers, the Ephemera Society, say: 'Study items range from tickets to proclamations, trade cards to catalogues, stationery to share certificates, labels to packaging.'

4 March 1980   **John Ezard**

Keep the hooligan juice coming

Government House in Salisbury is decorated and furnished in a manner which makes Versailles seem, well, middle-class. Amid the silken splendour of the chairs and the carpets which are so thick you could lose a cat in them, there are life-size portraits of the last few British monarchs. The Governor has added a homely touch with framed snaps of family and friends – in his case people like the Queen Mother and Winston Churchill.

The servants are immaculately dressed in white, with fitments – sashes, cummerbunds and for some reason fezzes – in bright green. This greenery is trimmed with gold according to the servant's rank, so that the head waiter looks like a gift-wrapped present from Neiman-Marcus, with a gold tassel on top of his head.

The Governor has laid in a plentiful supply of champagne and Havana cigars (the wife of a visiting American congress-man, thinking these were set out for the guests, tried to take one away as a present for Tip O'Neill, Speaker of the House of Representatives. Just as she took it, Soames spotted her. 'Put it back!' he roared.)

Obviously this magnificence is meant to impress somebody, to demonstrate the sheer power and the awesome prestige of colonial Britain (and, for the present month, Zimbabwe, or the British Dependency of Southern Rhodesia as it is officially known, is one of our very few colonies. The others include Belize, Tristan da Cunha, and one or two acres in the Caribbean).

This wealth cannot be to impress the Africans, who, apart from the shimmering servants, barely get a look in. Joshua Nkomo is one who did, and got on very well with the Governor. This is not surprising. Nkomo also has a taste for the high life, and is the Lord Soames of Africa.

After a while, you realize exactly who the trappings are

designed to impress: the Lost Race of Africa, the Tribe That Lost Its Head, the whites of Southern Rhodesia.

If you listen to the British officials who arrived in December on the great silver bird, you realize that they do see themselves as dealing with a backward and primitive people. They swap amusing stories about the childlike white folk they come across; a woman who thought Soames could cancel her parking ticket, another who complained because she did not have two votes in the election. One British official talks about the 'Cheryl and Vomit' society, composed of women who wear their name on gold necklets, and young men on leave from military service who spend their weekends getting drunk in Salisbury and then throwing up in the street.

Even the British squaddies look with faint contempt on the Rhodesians (or 'Rhodies' as they sometimes call them; military slang mushrooms overnight). One private explained to me his alleged success with the local women. 'You see these Rhodies think they can snap their fingers and some bird'll come running. But us Brits give 'em a few cuddles and talk nice to them, and they've never had anything like that.'

No wonder the white Rhodesians resent us. A woman who had, for that part of the world, very moderate views, asked what I thought of Soames. I said he had a reputation for arrogance. 'But all you British are arrogant,' she said, in genuine puzzlement, rather as if I had said he spoke English or had two legs. It was this wish to give the whites a whiff of the old colonial past which probably led to Soames's appointment. Another Foreign Office official explained that his deputy, Sir Anthony Duff, could have done the job standing on his head. 'But he isn't Churchill's son-in-law.'

The corollary of this is that the British are highly impressed by the blacks – possibly in some cases too much so. Many of the Patriotic Front commanders are men of high intelligence and expertise, their education started in mission schools in Rhodesia and frequently finished off in Moscow. This has helped them to run a highly successful guerrilla war and – for the present anyway – follow through politically. But to hear some of the British talking, you'd imagine that the entire physics faculty of MIT had just walked out of the bush.

One British officer in close touch with PF leaders on Nkomo's side blamed the press. 'I thought this lot were all golliwogs with machine guns, but they are very, very different.' And indeed they are, to an extent which would astonish and perhaps appal some white Rhodesians.

A more bluntly phrased view came from a British private who was talking to a PF commander at one of the assembly points. He asked what he had done to pass the time in the bush, and the African said that he had read – Marx, Lenin, that kind of thing. 'I prefer a good western myself,' the squaddie said, adding when the PF man had gone: 'Here, he's pretty clever, innee, for a nig-nog.'

Rhodesian women, black and white, tend to be remarkably good looking. The Shona women have high cheekbones and fine features which make them exceedingly pretty, to European eyes at any rate. The whites have golden hair, lovely toast-coloured skin, and because of the weather, few clothes. There is something particularly disconcerting about hearing those famous racist views expressed in that shrill mounting whine, coming from someone whose rounded figure is straining out of a thin nylon dress.

One such accosted us in a restaurant. 'I heard you were journalists, and I've come over to tell you that Ian Smith is the greatest politician in the Western world. He's so honest and straight. If the blacks could vote for him, they all would. He's the only reason we've had 14 years of civilization.'

Weren't there some people who disagreed with her, who thought on the contrary that Smith had misled them into a worse predicament than ever before?

'They're all turncoats and bastards and fools. You don't understand what savages these black people are. You've never lived here. Answer this, how many blacks are there in the British Parliament? They are all murderers, they just want to kill us. You wouldn't believe the disgusting things they've done.' Surely, though, the whites had mounted some pretty fierce reprisals? 'Yes, but that was in self-defence, that was justified.'

She turned out to be a teacher of English Literature, a fact which might give pause for thought to those who believe in the

183

humanizing effect of great works. Education was exempt from sanctions, and all O and A levels were set and marked in London. 'Now they are being provocative and controversial just to spite us.

'Last year we had *Persuasion* and *King Lear*. Now they've given us Alan Paton, *The Comedians*, which is full of nasty blacks, and *Othello*. I've got a big black buck sitting at the front of my class and I've got to teach him about Desdemona's murder, thanks to you British.'

The casual rudeness to blacks can be astonishing, almost breathtaking if you don't expect it. In a dusty door miles from Salisbury a young woman was working at her accounts while an elderly black servant slowly brushed the carpet. 'Joseph,' she said in the familiar nasal voice, 'Thet dust is gitting strite up my nose.' The pitch rises as if she were about to say 'If you don't stop I shall have you hanged,' but thought better of it at the last moment. Joseph stopped and rested on his broom. A few moments later she turned round and almost spat: 'Oh git on with it, git it over with, will you!'

And yet there has been a startling change over the past few months. Few white people now openly admit to having voted for Smith – to the extent that one imagines one must have met all the 10 per cent of the white population who actually didn't. They feel that they were misled about the military situation and about the political prospects, that nobody prepared them for the inevitable defeat.

To be fair, not all the whites feel like this. Some, while they agree that they have got a worse deal now than they would have got 14 years ago, thank Smith for '14 years of civilization'. Even they now seem to realize that the jig is up; unable to believe that the new black Government might want to hold on to them, they talk of leaving for South Africa, Kenya, South America, even extremist Britain.

They don't like Britain, and popular subjects for dinner-table chat are our shortcomings, strikes, trade unions, vile weather, and general decadence. The steel strike is big news in Rhodesia and a source of much pleasure to the white population.

Yet the effort of the 200,000 whites coming to terms with

'He's got post-flu depression. I'll write out a prescription for some Valium and in no circumstances should you allow him to see any newspapers.'

3 January 1980

the new facts of life is almost audible. Rhodesian culture is almost non-existent – there are no actors, writers, composers, musicians to speak of – but there is one folk-singer, Clem Tholet, who happens to be Ian Smith's son-in-law.

His big hit LP contained the unofficial national anthem, a mendaciously entitled song called *Rhodesians Never Die*, along with a number called *Another Hitler*. In this Rhodesia is depicted as a small nation struggling for freedom against the Communist tide, while a hypocritical Britain and the US stand by.

Tholet's latest record shows a change of heart: its title is *Two Sides to Every Story* and the main track is called *Zambezi Zimbabwe*, a cheerful celebration of the 'new land of Africa' sung to an African rhythm.

A Rhodesian magazine recently prepared its readers for what they might expect with an end to sanctions: wall-to-wall carpets, blenders and digital watches; in fact when the starship Rhodesia is beamed back into the planet Earth, they can expect something much more worrying – exposure to the ideas and the received wisdom of the western world over the past 14 years. They may learn, for instance, that it is perfectly possible to believe that black people deserve the vote without actually endorsing the invasion of Afghanistan.

Because they see the war as invented and run by Communists, they tend to believe that their blacks were happy and content in a white-dominated society. The briefest chat with an African reveals this to be untrue, but then most Rhodesian whites don't have conversations with Africans, except to give them orders.

However, it is easy to see how they have got hold of this idea. Rhodesian blacks are startlingly docile and even courtly. There were about 120,000 of them at Nkomo's homecoming last month, all of them celebrating the success of a guerrilla war against a white enemy. Yet the few dozen white journalists and even Rhodesian Special Branch men were treated as politely and discreetly as a curate at a parish fête. There was no aggression whatever.

This gentility can be surprising. There is possibly nobody

in Rhodesia – black or white – who has not lost somebody in the fighting, the blacks rather more than the whites. Irish people in Ulster tend to relish these deaths, to recount the horrors with something near satisfaction, to draw comfort from each hideous detail. Rhodesian blacks are the opposite, and speak in a deadpan and fatalistic way about the loss of friends and family.

I met General Debengwa, who is Nkomo's senior military leader in Rhodesia itself. Was he going back to his home town, Bulawayo? No, he said, there was no real point since he had no family there. His mother had lived there until a few years ago, but the Selous Scouts had discovered that she had fed a ZIPRA military column which was passing through. They had shot her immediately.

Debengwa described this incident without emotion, as if she had died from a heart attack – something sad but perhaps inevitable. I thought that, like Camus's outsider, he had found coldness his only defence against despair, or that being responsible for many deaths himself, had inured himself against the one which affected him. But later I found that nearly all blacks talk like this; they describe death as we discuss illness or a broken love affair, intolerable only if you let it prey upon your mind.

In a horrible way it matches the whites' unconcern with black mortality; among soldiers prestige can be measured by the number of dead 'terrs' (or 'floppies' – a description of how they fall when shot). 'He and his brother have taken out 58 gooks between them,' one troopie told me in admiration of a friend.

In a war where you have such contempt for your enemy, the idea of mass slaughter becomes attractive, and many whites are now thinking longingly about the idea of bombing the assembly points and so destroying all their enemies and (so they imagine) all their problems. It is not surprising that the guerrillas camped at these points have had exactly the same thoughts. They too are distinctly twitchy.

A week or so ago Josiah Tongamurai, one of Mugabe's senior commanders, visited the 6,000 ZANLA forces at the

Foxtrot assembly point in the east of the country. He was accompanied by the senior British officer in Rhodesia, General Acland. The guerrillas put on an impressive show. They marched in step, ran with their rifles, and while chanting African songs deported themselves with a discipline which would not have disgraced Sandhurst.

Tongamurai spoke to them as they sat around a dirt clearing; he moved about them like a cross between a witch doctor and a Butlin's Redcoat, wheedling, pleading, imploring and inspiring. According to interpreters his speech was fairly routine; how they should behave, how they would be allowed to vote in the election.

However, carried away, they shouted slogans in reply: death to colonialism, death to the British. General Acland speaks no Shona, and so could not understand this chanting, and at one anti-British climax stood up and solemnly took the salute. The 6,000 guerrillas stared in amazement at this astonishing display of phlegm.

Curiously, it is hard not to be a little optimistic about the future for Zimbabwe (as nobody at all calls it yet, except in political speeches). The fear is not that there will be mass slaughter of the whites, followed by their flight to South Africa and the collapse of the economy, but that the need to retain white confidence may mean that the blacks are badly disappointed.

Certainly all the election manifestoes promise the earth (quite literally the earth – all imply that the land will return to the blacks without saying how, when or to whom). They promise new housing, better homes, real social security, secondary schooling for everybody. Yet even if all whites were expelled and their property divided among the blacks (whites are less than 3 per cent of the population) this wealth would be slow in coming.

At the same time all three main parties stress the need for the whites to remain. Muzorewa has suffered badly because his brief rule as Prime Minister brought few tangible benefits to the blacks, who now make of him runic remarks such as 'he is a white man who wears a black skin'.

The problem Nkomo or Mugabe will have to face if either becomes Prime Minister is possibly not the panic of the whites or the sudden collapse of financial confidence but the brutal disenchantment of their own people.

Meanwhile the whites continue to live in a style unimaginable here, but all too familiar to the shop assistants, garage hands and dissatisfied bourgeoisie who have made Rhodesia their home. Around the average Salisbury bungalow is three or four acres of rich land, thick with shrubbery, flower beds, rolling lawns, arboretums: so much greenery you feel you need a platoon of Gurkhas to hack your way through to the front door.

A team of servants irons the grass each morning as the sun rises over the sparkling pool. Later vast dragonflies zoom over the blue water like helicopter gunships as the host and his guests enjoy perhaps a 'wine race' – swimming a length backwards while drinking a glass of wine (Rhodesian wine probably, which is awful. It is the only alcoholic drink to give you bilharzia) – or just pushing each other into the water. Then maybe a few glasses of 'hooligan juice', a large slug of brandy mixed to a slush with a scoop of vanilla ice-cream.

This is what they call civilization, and it is easy for us to mock: after all, they work hard and they have fought hard. It is impossible not to admire the way they have coped with sanctions, the way they have manufactured almost everything from tomato ketchup to armoured cars. Though the cause was perhaps not worth fighting – indeed did not need to be fought – we need not grudge them their mindless pleasures, pleasures we would hugely enjoy if we could.

I recall one faintly pathetic note being struck 150 miles or so north of Salisbury. A young man, just out of the army, asked if there was any chance that the British would stay behind to help the white Rhodesians fight if the settlement went horribly wrong.

I said (fairly) that there was no chance at all, and added – unfairly – that they could expect to see Lord Soames mount the aircraft steps on March 1, write the name of the new prime minister on a scratch pad, throw it on to the tarmac, slam the door and take off for England with a screech of engines.

'Ah, what style,' said the young man. 'When the British wash their hands, they use only the finest soap.'

9 February 1980 **Simon Hoggart**

A step on the Chimurenga road

'Forward with the revolution!' cried the speaker. 'Forward with the revolution!' came the answering cry from 5,000 people sitting on the slopes of a massive outcrop of granite which formed a national amphitheatre.

Two days before the election in the heart of the Gutu tribal trust land, this was the final morale-booster at Chinai for Robert Mugabe's ZANU-PF, the party which believes victory can be denied to it this week only if force or fraud are used by those they refer to simply as 'the oppressors'.

'Forward with ZANU-PF,' called a new speaker standing in the centre of the circle under the shade of a great tree. 'Forward with ZANU-PF,' the crowd roared back. 'Forward with the Mujibas, the boys who helped us in the war,' 'Forward with the mothers who helped to cook for us,' 'Forward with the high command.' 'Forward with the Zanla forces.' 'Forward with the elections.'

Then, moving out of the Shona language, the crowd of simple country people showed their paces in Portuguese. 'Viva Nyerere.' 'Viva Machel.' 'Viva Frelimo.' 'Down with imperialism.' 'Abaixo imperialismo.' 'Abaixo Sithole.' 'Abaixo Muzorewa.'

Perhaps only here, in the depths of the Rhodesian countryside, where the guerrilla struggle was waged most intensely, can one begin to understand the long continuity of Zimbabwe's liberation movement. For the peasant supporters of ZANU, as much as for Ian Smith's Rhodesian Front, this week's election is nothing but a continuation of a war which began with the settlers' arrival in 1890.

The Africans called the Matabele and Shona revolts of the

1890s 'Chimurenga' –'The Revolution'. The armed struggle of the 1970s was Chimurenga Two, and the elections this week are seen as only the latest phase in it, a celebration –so the people here hope –of the military victory which they have won.

Some people had walked 10 to 15 miles to attend this meeting in the small community of Chinai. Many of them would be walking at least that distance to vote. The British are supplying a mobile polling booth, but it will be in the area only for an hour or two, so the speakers at the rally told the crowd that only the very old and the disabled should use the mobile station, men and women must foot it into town, sleeping out in the open for three or four nights.

A young party official warned them of possible intimidation by Bishop Muzorewa's 35,000-strong private army, the Auxiliaries, which has been allowed to patrol in large parts of Mashonaland. 'If you meet any Auxiliaries and they ask you who you are going to vote for, tell them 'Muzorewa' so they don't assault you. Your vote is secret, so you can still vote for ZANU-PF. The soldiers in this country,' he went on, 'are not unpolitical. So if they stop you, say the same thing.'

Chinai, they told us, was the centre of a wartime 'liberated zone'. The people had not seen a Rhodesian Army vehicle come by or a helicopter land since early last year. However much or little one believes the claims of ZANLA and of Joshua Nkomo's ZIPRA that 90 per cent of the country had become no-go areas for the Rhodesians by last year, Chinai's particular claim seemed highly plausible.

This was perfect guerrilla country, densely overgrown mountains and vast boulders of granite, which provide natural cover for ambushes. We had turned off the tarred road home 60 miles east of Fort Victoria, then on to a good dirt road, and covered the last five miles on a narrow bumpy track. The people had dug occasional trenches across it to stop all traffic. The last two miles had been reopened on Sunday, and ours was only the third vehicle to come by, they said. We saw the new earth in the trenches which had just been refilled.

Politically, the area seemed to be solid for ZANU-PF. As the party's minibus, plastered with posters, went ahead of us, every passerby raised his right arm in the clenched-fist salute of ZANU-PF. The Munyikwa area, for which this meeting was called, has an estimated electorate of 20,000. About 4,000 of them, an amazing one-fifth of the electorate, had turned out, plus at least 1,000 teenagers.

'When Muzorewa and company cry, 'Intimidation', what they really mean is that they haven't got the machinery to call a meeting,' Mr Davis Mugabe, the ZANU-PF election organizer for Victoria Province, told us. Mr Mugabe (no relation of Robert Mugabe) spent 10 years in exile in the United States, doing graduate work at Columbia University and teaching politics at the City College of New York.

Eighteen months ago Zanu recalled him to Mozambique where, like every other political commissar, he had to undergo three months of military training ('No joke running up mountains at the age of 46'). Last October and November, while the Lancaster House conference was on in London, he made a secret mission from Mozambique more than 100 miles into Rhodesia's tribal trust lands 'to see if we could afford to accept a ceasefire.'

'What frightens Muzorewa is that he does not have the young people. It's no secret that ZANLA (the Zimbabwe African Nationalist Liberation Army) used to work closely with the ZANU youth. In African areas meetings are called and organized by young people. If they support ZANU, then other parties haven't got the people to walk the necessary miles to call a meeting. That's the real problem for Sithole and Muzorewa.'

Mr Mugabe said that Muzorewa's Auxiliaries sometimes ambush ZANU meetings. At Chikawanda the other day armed Auxiliaries had arrived before ZANU's speakers at a ZANU rally and had started to harangue the crowd against Communism. 'When we asked them to step aside, they refused. We went to the police, and showed our permit for the meeting. The police officer said he had no authority to move the Auxiliaries, but we could hold the meeting somewhere else.'

On another occasion, the Auxiliaries had rounded up people at gunpoint for Muzorewa, he said. Scores of people had been forcibly bused to Salisbury for Muzorewa's weekend rally. Mr Mugabe said he had paid the dollar bus fare home to each of about 50 ZANU people who had managed to escape from the Muzorewa buses in Fort Victoria.

As for the presence outside the assembly points of armed ZANLA men, Mr Mugabe would not commit himself. Unarmed ones, yes. 'It is quite possible that if ZANU had an extra 10,000 men because we've only been given room in the assembly points for 16,000, then ZANU would say, "All political commissars, put down your guns, go to the masses, and spread the political word." That sounds like a very reasonable deployment from our point of view.'

Once again he emphasized the basic continuity of the struggle. 'Guerrillas are not just soldiers. They are politicians.' It was a point made yet again in the final slogans of the enormously enthusiastic and expectant meeting at Chinai. ZANU has given every year of the revolution a name. '1979 was the year of the People's Storming Advance,' cried the speaker. 'Forward!' shouted the crowd. '1980 is the Year of the People's Power.' 'Forward!' came the answer.

Before the meeting could end, torrential rain began to pour. The speakers tried to go on but it became futile. Laughing and shrieking, the crowd rushed under the nearest trees, squashing themselves in under the awnings of the village shop. As we drove off, before the mud made the road impassable, scores of drenched but hopeful people were already starting on the long march to the polling booth.

27 February 1980   **Jonathan Steele**

Eclipse brings silent confusion to Tsavo

Two graceful striped kudu darted out of the bush, heads straining left and right, horns crashing into tree branches as the harsh mid-morning heat turned to evening cool at the beginning of the total eclipse of the sun. Cattle moving across the plain began to jostle, then raced clumsily back and forth, mooing desperately.

To men, in Africa, an eclipse of the sun is the worst of bad omens. Pregnant women must stay indoors, cooking pots must be broken and thrown out. At the last eclipse, visible in northern Kenya, two Turkana tribesmen committed suicide.

At 10.45 a.m. the evening chorus of birds' song was deafening. By then, half the sun had been obscured by the moon and the intense light of the African plains had been drained of its power. Colours were reduced to a pale green.

Japanese and American eclipse enthusiasts at Tsavo Game Park had small planes standing ready to take off and follow the line of the eclipse if clouds threatened to blot out the crucial four minutes of totality just where they were standing.

A pink and yellow sunset ran around the whole horizon at 11.15. Within seconds, Kilimanjaro was completely dark, bright stars were visible in the sky and the sun looked exactly like an advertisement for a Bravington's diamond ring.

The plain was utterly silent – not an animal moved. Waves of shadows (shadow bands to the astronomers) rippled over the red earth and ran strangely over one's feet and hands. What causes them is still unknown. In the second before the sun was gone completely, 'sparklers' shot out of it – Bailey's beads, formed by the last beams of sunlight passing between the mountains of the lunar surface.

In the four minutes of darkness, as dark as a moonlit night, the effect is of a great hole in the sky surrounded by the brilliant pearly pink light of the corona.

During totality, temperatures fell by 26 degrees Centigrade.

As a crescent of the sun, as thin as a new moon, reappeared cocks began to crow from the roofs of the huts of the Taita farmers and women emerged from their huts as though nothing had happened. A frenzy of kissing and champagne cork popping broke out among the American eclipse-watching groups with their hand-built telescopes and batteries of cameras set to record every phase of the eclipse.

'See you in 1986 in New Zealand,' one group leader called to another as he left.

18 February 1980   **Victoria Brittain**

The man South Africa would love to forget

Today Basil D'Oliveira achieves an ambition he first declared 24 years ago. Last night Worcestershire marked the end of his career as one of their most eminent cricketers with a handsome dinner, and this morning he became their full-time professional coach.

The prospect would have amazed him when he was a jobbing printer segregated in a 'non-white' area of South Africa, and not by the wildest stretch of imagination could he have conceived that he would reach his objective by way of Worcestershire county cricket, British citizenship, an England cap, 44 Test matches and the award of the OBE.

In 1955 he wrote from Cape Town, in his immaculate hand and invariable green ink, 'I want to come to England and learn to be a coach so that I can help to bring on young cricketers.' What chance had a man derogatorily classified in his own country as 'coloured' of making his way to England? If he did, who would give him a coaching course? How was he to travel, to subsist, to buy his gear? How, on the other hand, could anyone with a scrap of compassion tell him that his objective was wildly impossible?

The explanation that his only hope was a playing engagement, and the promise to try to find him one, elicited the modestly proffered, but impressive evidence that he had achieved considerable all-round success in what white Africans called 'non-white cricket'.

Those with the power to hire and fire in England were not impressed; they waved aside figures like nine wickets for two runs with leg-breaks in a Cape League match with remarks like 'Must have been a terrible pitch.'

What, then, did they say to an innings of 225 in an hour? What of his selection as captain (and head of the batting averages) of the non-European team against Kenya Asians (who included several Pakistani representative players), and again – with a figure of 46.28 – on a tour of East Africa?

The counties simply smiled: there were no remotely valid comparative figures to measure his ability; and, besides, there was the question of South African racial politics.

So to John Kay, everyman's guide to the Lancashire leagues, whose clubs were at their richest in talent with such players as Conrad Hunte, Chandru Borde, Rusi Surti, Johnie Wardle, Garfield Sobers, Cec Pepper, Sunil Durani and Dattu Phadkar. With Test cricketers from four countries available, why should they engage an unknown?

Time was running short for one with outstanding performances now six or seven years behind him, and then by chance he played in one of the few matches ever permitted in South Africa between white and coloured cricketers. Jimmy Gray and Peter Sainsbury of Hampshire, Alan Oakman of Sussex, pressed to watch him, saw a talented cricketer – a fine striker of the ball, but raw, unsophisticated; his playing experience confined entirely to the mat.

By now, though, John Kay reported that League engagements for 1960 were complete. Regularly, once or twice a year, those courteous letters, instantly identified by the green ink, had arrived, enquiring whether the impossible had been achieved. The time had come, surely, to be frank: to spell it out that England offered no opportunity for the young man – a situation that nowadays, he himself would recognize only too clearly.

Then, by one of these fantastic quirks of event which shatter probability, Middleton, who had parted with their pro, Roy Gilchrist, failed to make their expected signing of Wesley Hall, and with the start of the season so close they had little time for negotiation. By the final stroke of luck, Middleton was John Kay's own club. He telephoned: would the young South African sign for the season? The figure offered – £450 – was meagre; but for the club it was a gamble.

A telegram to the Cape told him: this is your opportunity, a bare subsistence; but there will never be another chance. There was no hesitation. Lately married, with a pregnant wife and no house of his own, he could not afford it; but he accepted.

196

The local non-white cricketing community eagerly, joy-ously, identified with him: they organized raffles, dances, matches, collections, which raised £450, enough with his salary to cover his passage and lodgings for the League season.

So, in April 1960 he arrived in England; shy, amazed at being accepted without question into English company and households for the charming person he was. Urgently, though, he had never played on turf wickets before; nor in the cutting winds of a Lancashire April. For the first three weeks he could barely lay bat on ball.

In his misery, he would have run away, if only he had known how. His position was desperate, but he faced up to it. With the sympathetic aid of Eric Price – the former Lancashire and Essex slow left-arm bowler – he studied and mastered the conditions. By the end of that Central Lancashire League season he had a better batting average – by 48.95 to 48.39 – than Garfield Sobers, and barely inferior bowling figures. In a way, that was an end to the story.

On one of Ron Roberts's Cavaliers tours, Tom Graveney, recognizing D'Oliveira's high potential, persuaded him to join Worcestershire. During his qualifying period he scored 119 for Arthur Gilligan's XI against Bobby Simpson's Australian team of 1964. That was another point of decision.

In just over a twelve-month from spring of the following year, at the age of 33 – though Wisden showed 30 – he first appeared in the Championship, won his Worcestershire cap, became a British citizen, and was chosen for England against West Indies. His willingness to carry the fight to the fast bowlers – at Leeds he hit Hall for a spectacular straight six – and consecutive innings of 27, 76, 54 and 88 against Hall, Griffith, Sobers, Gibbs and Holford, established his Test place.

That was not merely cricketing success. It was the signal of hope to millions of people sentenced to second-class status in his home country that escape to liberty and equality was possible. So Basil D'Oliveira became, almost overnight, a symbol of the evil error of apartheid that the Afrikaner government would have done anything to suppress.

His cricket has always been marked by courage and determination: his batting by straightness in defence and a capacity, through steely forearms, for hitting the ball immensely hard with minimal backlift and little apparent effort.

The demands on a league professional dictated the switch from leg-spin to off-breaks and then to controlled and artfully varied medium swing and cut, with which he proved astutely economical in the over-limit game. A safe catcher, and invariably calm, Basil proved a capable all-rounder, at his best when the game was running against his side.

One of his last major efforts attempted to give Worcestershire their first win in a Lord's final against Kent, in the Benson and Hedges tournament of 1976. Nearly 45 years old, and so restricted by a hamstring injury that he could only stand flat-footed in the crease, he scored an aggressive 50 out of 75 in less than an hour, until, under run-rate pressure, he hit across a straight ball and walked sadly away.

Altogether, he played in 44 Test matches until his last defiant innings against Australia in 1972, when he was rising 41. In the dressing room, his modesty, conviviality, consideration, generosity and – rare on the high levels of competition – humour, gained him completely happy acceptance.

He virtually won the final Test, which drew the rubber of 1968 against Australia, and earned – after some selectorial quirks – a place on the English tour of South Africa in the following overseas season. At the last the South African government thwarted his vision of returning to his native country as a member of an English team, by banning the tour because of his inclusion.

Yet, through all the arguments about the cancellation of that series, and the demonstrations against the projected visit by South Africa in 1970, he behaved with a dignity which revealed his 'masters' for what they were. His behaviour was recognized with the OBE in the New Year Honours.

Throughout his career, he has returned regularly to visit his own people in South Africa, sharing their exclusion from the rights and liberties he enjoys here, in order, as he demanded all those years ago, to help develop cricket among them. He will never settle there, however, because he is determined that his sons shall not grow up under the tyranny of apartheid.

Basil D'Oliveira could yet prove to have had a greater influence on the history of mankind than any other games player.

2 November 1979   **John Arlott**

Tycoon Tony has it taped

What, asked the secretary, do you actually want to talk about? Nothing in particular, I said, I just want to report back to England how their former cricket captain is getting on. Has he grown any taller for instance?

He is just the same. Before we went to lunch Tony Greig had one or two things to do at the new insurance company just across the bridge at Sydney. Just for my benefit I fancied, he bawled out a minion: 'I want figures, man, I don't want your thinks or thoughts. I don't want pie in the sky. I'm back from lunch in two hours and I don't want waffle, I want the real figures, man.'

In the lift going down we were accompanied by a perky little widow in her 70s who had been up in the skyscraper sorting out her life insurance. 'Did they look after you?' asked our beanpole Dale Carnegie. 'Thank you, Tony,' she said. He signed her an autograph for her grandson, held the door open for her and she trotted off like a preening sparrow.

The managing director is alive and well and doing very nicely, thank you. Who wants to be a millionaire? He does and he's well on the way. When he joined Mr Packer and everything hit the fan he insisted on a contract that set him up for life when it was all over. So his friend, the hammerhead shark who bit cricket's Establishment off at the knees, set up a company and made him managing director. A year ago he bought eight big leather books to teach himself all about insurance.

'I planned to learn them word for word,' he says. 'I went to Canberra, to a fellow at University who knows more about

199

insurance than anyone. He told me "throw away those books, just be Tony Greig, and you'll be able to sell more insurance than you've ever thought of".'

He drove me away in his plush big car with reclining seats and a back window which could be opened by electric power. He pushed in his cassette recorder of 'Songs From the Shows' and into his own headbox he turned on the cassette to spew out what he thought was what I wanted to hear.' Kerry and I ... totally vindicated ... more people watching cricket than ever before ... county cricketers have doubled their pay ... he always preached compromise ... I have no regrets ...'

C'mon, Tony. For all your smart blue suits and cold blue eyes there must be some regrets. He switched off the recorder and admitted 'Yes, well, on Sunday at Melbourne with England needing 25 to win and Brearley went in, I thought that could have been me. I wanted to pick up a bat and just go out there. Me going in then, with Knotty to follow, we would have got them for certain. Do you know, I did miss it then. Knotty and I would have got those runs, you know.'

Not that this pillow talk meant anything against Brearley. 'I have a high regard for Mike. He's a bloody good bloke, and a bloody good captain.' 'Name me the last five captains of Sussex,' he asked. After each name, from Mike Griffith to Jim Parks, he said: 'Sawn off at the knees!' Then I had to name the last five captains of England before him – Denness, Illy, Cowdrey ... 'Sawn off at the knees,' he said after each name.

'I did not want to end up at 35 doing radio commentaries like Fred Trueman or writing like Denis Compton. Kerry approached me and it was all very businesslike. I was businesslike back. Inside two years I knew there would be a compromise. I insisted on a contract that gave me some sort of job for life, some new challenge. The first day I played for England I promised Donna I was not going to be all washed up, an ex-sportsman with nothing to do at 35.'

His house in Sydney's swishest suburb overlooks the bay. In the summer his swimming pool is full of the Martini set, in the winters the parquet floor of his ballroom creaks to the footsteps of the very important people. He says he always intended to come to Australia anyway.

He was surprised I wanted to talk about cricket proper rather than cricket politics. He remains the only England player to have scored 3,000 runs and taken 100 wickets: he's proud of that. Only Hammond and Cowdrey have taken more catches for England: he is proud of that too. He remembers practising fielding as a lonely boy in South Africa, practising, practising, practising.

He remembers putting a ball in a sock and hanging it from the branch of a tree and hitting it for hours. To his grave, he says, he will take the memory and pride at his 110 for England at Brisbane in 1974. It was the first time England came up against Lillee and Thomson. E. W. Swanton said: 'No innings was calculated to do more for English morale since Dexter took Hall and Griffith apart on that memorable day at Lord's in the early 1960s.'

Lillee, says Greig, is the best bowler he has ever seen. Of the batsmen he cannot decide on the two Richardses for genius. After them comes Geoffrey Boycott – 'a phenomenal dedicated player. The Richardses pretend they don't care, but they do. The afternoon before last year's Supertest at Perth, Barry asked me to bowl to him in the nets. For three hours I bowled at his off stump. He just wanted to practise playing straight. Every time the ball went backward of square on either side he would drop his bat and do 50 press ups in the crease. Fifty! In that three hours he must have done 600 press-ups. Next day he went out to bat pretending to everyone he hadn't had a net in weeks. He scored the most fantastic century I have ever witnessed.'

It was hard to drag this sort of stuff out of him. He only wants to talk about his friend Kerry Packer, or what he thinks he has done for every ordinary English country pro, or suggest you might like to comment on his latest and blandly boring TV ad for motor cars or breakfast food or insurance. He admits that in the end the criticism he received in England hurt badly. The only difference now is that I know they're real friends.'

He shakes his head at the memory. 'Do you know that one established cricket writer in England wrote a pompous and hurtful piece headlined "The immorality of Tony Greig". The guy honestly thought I was immoral for simply changing my job for four times more money.'

He dropped me at the hotel and revved off to play tennis with Kerry. After that he was due at a board meeting. He would doubtless be rude to a few minions on the way. Of the 50-odd men who have captained England at cricket I bet Tony Greig will be the first to become a self-made millionaire. He looks down at you and laughs at that. A real chortle – but there is not much twinkle in those cold blue eyes.

24 January 1980   **Frank Keating**

Life revives in Neak Luong

As life of a kind revives in Kampuchea, pushing through logged arteries, it bursts out with particularly febrile vigour in such places as Neak Luong, the river-crossing town south of Pnomh Penh. Always a centre of commerce and for 10 years a target of war, Neak Luong is now being reoccupied for perhaps the sixth or seventh time in its battered recent history.

In this pair of dusty market places, one on either side of the broad Mekong, the contradictions of the new Kampuchean existence are easily seen –the burgeoning trade, the determination to rebuild, the uneasy relation between communist leadership and non-communist populace, and beneath all the bustle, the nightmare of the past and the fear of the future.

Backed up along the riverside and into the west bank market are Russian trucks loaded with Vietnamese troops, most of them probably on their way back home for the meagre four or five days' leave a year which they are allotted.

The soldiers stay on board, but the officers dismount and stroll discreetly about. They wear their green tropical helmets at a slightly cocky angle and carry leather map-cases, the badge of rank that goes with the holstered revolver. They speak little, and take no tea in the small food shops, but stare about with their curious, shrewd faces, putting their sun glasses on and off as if by some nervous habit.

The uniform of the vanquished can also be seen – the olive drab of the Lon Nol army, and the thin black cloth which was the trade-mark of the Khmer Rouge. Cut down, patched, re-made, it covers the backs of the hordes of children, and of the squatter families whose cookfires have blackened the ornate balconies of the Chinese shop-houses. Others have made their homes in the roofless warehouses on the east bank, in corners of shattered buildings, or in the mangled cabs of overturned army lorries.

The history of the last decade is all around – in the ruined buildings, the lines of old military entrenchments, the ex-military rags, the rusting steel debris, and, close enough to town, the geometric scars of the long Pol Pot canals in the digging of which so many died. There are not many in Neak Luong who now remember the day – almost ten years ago exactly – when it all began, as South Vietnamese and American troops pushed into Kampuchea in their vain attempts to locate and destroy the North Vietnamese headquarters. That was the first time that Neak Luong was looted – by the South Vietnamese. But the enraged Lon Nol troops ambushed the Saigon column as it left with the booty and the South Vietnamese died amid a clutter of electric fans and air conditioners.

For the next five years Neak Luong, an important strongpoint in the fight for the control of the river lifeline to Pnomh Penh, suffered all the disadvantages of being a strategic place. As the Khmer Rouge closed in, the Neak Luong perimeter shrank to a chinagraph circle on the military maps. So close was the enemy that a misdirected B-52 strike in 1973 ploughed up the main street and the hospital, killing more than 100 people. Finally, in early 1975, the Lon Nol army lost the decisive defensive battle to keep Neak Luong, after weeks in which the town was a hell of incoming fire and screaming wounded. When Neak Luong fell, in Pnomh Penh they knew that the war was irretrievably lost.

But all that is a long time ago, and in another era. Standing on the churned earth of the river bank as he waits for the ferry is one of the middle class survivors of Pol Pot's massacres who now staff the embryo Government.

'It's very difficult to remember what happened before Pol Pot,' he says, 'or to remember England. England . . . it's like a dream.' His eyes search yours for help, reassurance, like those of a child needing to know that the grown-ups won't let the bad things happen again. 'I have a nervous debility, I am going to Ho Chi Minh City to see the doctors.'

He runs his hand worriedly through his hair. 'And I can't see very well. I threw away my glasses – during Pol Pot's time even to wear glasses was to risk death. To speak one word of English would be a death warrant. I saw it happen many times . . . horrible, horrible . . . it is difficult. I cannot sleep at nights. They say I have a nervous debility. Some people seem to be able to put it behind them, but I cannot help remembering.'

Some do remember the old days before Pol Pot, indeed lived on those memories for five years. As we poked about in the market, with its Thai cigarettes, packets of rusty Vietnamese needles, heaps of breadfruit, and trays of freshwater cockles and fish from the river, there is a shout of 'UPI!'. Up comes a tough bouncy little man who used to be a freelance photographer for the United Press International American news agency. In his home he shows us his treasures, drawing them carefully from a plastic bag. 'My books of English language,' he says proudly. 'No, no, I don't lose him, I bury him in the ground during Pol Pot time.'

His name is Siphay and now he produces the most valuable items of all – two worn scraps of paper. The one he hands me has a 1975 date and reads: 'UPI – packed pix to Hong Kong. Used two Siphay. Let us know if any more Pnomh Penh pictures.' He folds them up again as if they were diplomas – which for him, they are.

What people like Siphay and, even more, the truly educated middle class, want back is something like the old Cambodia. What the peasants want is freedom to farm and trade. What the Vietnamese and the Communist Party want is a society moving towards the collective model. The contradictions are obvious, but they are for the future. For the moment, the needs of Kampuchea are obvious to all.

At the back of the crowd of children who follow the rare Westerners around as if they were circus elephants appear two young men waving frantically. They are the schoolteachers of Neak Luong, and they lead us down a lane to the school. The buildings are holed by shells, most of the roofs have gone; along one side a line of old foxholes and in the playground a miraculously intact slide.

The older teacher's English improves with every sentence he speaks until he is finally holding forth quite fluently. 'We have nothing, no tables, no chairs, no paper, no pencils, no books: can you please help us?' Indeed, the 'classrooms' are bare of any equipment whatever, and the lessons are written on the wall in charcoal. One reads: 'If a farmer goes to market to sell his pigs and gets 1998 Riels, how many pigs did he have if each pig sold for 74 Riels?' The question is a bizarre one in a country which has been without money for five years and still has no currency of its own. But the kids bob excitedly about as the teacher translates the 'problem' from Khmer into English. It is the juxtaposition of Neak Luong's and Kampuchea's frightful history and that 'problem', standard blackboard fodder all over the world, which tugs at the heart. Why shouldn't Kampuchean children at last be able to sit and struggle with the intricacies of long division, with pigs and farmers, and half-full baths emptying at such and such a rate?

Nobody knows whether they will be allowed to – not the Kampucheans, nor the Vietnamese, nor the Westerners to whose god-like opinions Kampucheans still defer. The teacher urgently pulls at my sleeve. 'If we can get some help it will be very good . . . we have to have some help . . . chairs, chairs . . . small chairs for children.'

It does not seem too much to ask of a world whose pursuit of larger quarrels helped to plunge this little society into such horror and pain.

13 March 1980   **Martin Woollacott**

Your life in their hands

Robert Winston, senior lecturer at Hammersmith Hospital, has a striking resemblance to Groucho Marx. As he is the narrator of *Your Life In Their Hands* (BBC-1), this could cause consternation among those with subliminal memories of Doctor Hackenbush – horse doctor extraordinaire – 'either he's dead or my watch has stopped.'

However, the value of that fine invention, the surgical mask, is immediately apparent. Once on, it wipes out the more individual features of a face, together with any fears that you are starring in something called, perhaps, *Go West*.

Your Life In Their Hands, back as a six-part series after a 16-year break, begins bravely with an operation for bowel cancer. The patients never did, and, even in colour, do not look like people. The principle of the surgical mask operates. No face is seen. No bare feet pathetically poking out of a regulation gown. No first incision. Only what looks like a good rummage inside a sofa or under the bonnet of a car.

The most disconcerting part of the programme was certainly the American Gun. It's superseding sewing – it shoots staples: 'I am now going to put the instrument in the back passage and push it up. And we're almost ready for firing.'

This is anastomosis, a new word to me of *Call My Bluff* quality. I thou anastomose. He shall have been about to be anastomosed. It means, as far as I can tell, to join tubes and why they can't say so I don't know.

A surgeon's choice of words is, in any case, oddish. 'A nicely mobile tumour, Chris . . . you can see it is on a very nice stalk.' Mr Winston refers to the surgeon throughout as Chris and you wouldn't have got that 16 years ago. I would have liked to hear more from the patient, Mrs McGowan, a woman with her own striking way with words: 'I've heard that cancer is like opening a bag of feathers in the wind.' Apparently it can be, hence the careful tying, twice, of the main vein draining

'*Here is the news – and I'm not telling you who told it to me.*'
31 July 1980

from the bowel to prevent cancer cells spreading. As for that word of fear itself, the cancer, it was quite nondescript to see.

A brisk-half hour – I would have liked the programme longer. I was inclined to applaud and ask Chris to take out something else as an encore
23 May 1980 **Nancy Banks-Smith**

The answer to sex and violence

If one had to produce one fact to put down as evidence against the present health of the British film industry, it would have to be that Ken Loach has not made a film for the cinema for almost a decade. Americans, Australians and Europeans I have talked to are incredulous about this, considering the quality of *Poor Cow*, *Kes* and *Family Life*, the last of which was made in 1971. Robert Altman once told me it was a disgrace. Not, however, on the part of Loach and his associates, who have tried hard to get finance for several projects, notably one about Ireland, over the years.

Now, at last, we are about to see *Black Jack*, which was shown at Cannes last year to very appreciative audiences but was not until recently bought for British distribution. It is an adaptation, very much in the Loach-Tony Garnett style, of Leon Garfield's best-selling adventure story. That was written for children, but found a large adult readership, like many of his books. The film intends as wide an appeal, and judging by the Cannes and Edinburgh Festival reaction, should readily get it.

It is not, of course, that Loach has been idle since *Family Life*, his last film for the cinema. He has done a great deal of television work, most recently the mammoth and widely acclaimed *Days of Hope*, and *The Price of Coal*. But what he achieves on the small screen appears to have cut little ice with film producers, many of whom fear that movies based on Britain and British life will cut no ice on the international market, however moderately budgeted.

Black Jack cost roughly one million dollars, chicken-feed

these days, and is an Anglo-French production, with some German money involved as well. The National Film Finance Corporation had a hand in its making after every major company, on both sides of the Atlantic, had turned the project down.

'If we had agreed to some of the star names that were suggested to us,' Tony Garnett says, 'we could have got the film set up in a week with a much bigger budget and all the time we wanted to shoot it in.' Burt Lancaster was one of those mentioned. But, as Garnett succinctly puts it, 'that's not the way Ken and I work.'

In the end, the film was shot by cameraman Chris Menges largely on Super 16 to cut costs. It was made, also to avoid expense, in six weeks, which Loach says was about two weeks short of the time he would have liked. Jean Franval, the French actor, plays the title role of the highwayman, and three kids from Barnsley, where David Bradley, the boy in *Kes*, came from, are the children whose story is entwined with his.

Stephen Hurst, Andrew Bennett and Louise Cooper proved to be natural performers, and the greatest compliment of all was paid to Louise when Leon Garfield visited the Yorkshire locations midway through filming and presented her with a signed copy of the book with the inscription: 'Thank you for being my perfect Belle.'

Set in the mid-eighteenth century, the story tells how Tolly (Stephen Hurst), a draper's assistant, saves the giant Black Jack after he has been cut down from his hanging, and joins a travelling funfair where he rescues Belle from being returned to the madhouse in York from which she has recently escaped. Hatch (Andrew Bennett), a boy of Tolly's age, schemes to return Belle to her keepers for financial gain.

'I found Garfield's book on one of my children's shelves,' Loach says, 'and I thought it was the perfect answer to all the sex and violence on the screen today. Also, Tony and I had never done an historical subject for the cinema, and the particular background was very intriguing. I wrote the script myself, which is something I don't like doing, because I hate writing and I'm not very good at it. But *Black Jack* is a very articulate book, so I had every chance.

'The language I wanted was one which would evoke the past properly, colloquial without seeming quaint. I also wanted to get on film the extraordinary quality of the pre-industrial revolution English landscape – that and the harshness of the lives of those who lived in it. I also wanted a pace which would seem right and natural. It took a long time, for instance, to get anywhere in those days. Above all, I wanted to get right away from the usual clichés of historical films, to get somewhere near the truth of those lives.'

'In all this, it is not just a children's film. And, I suppose, it is a bit against the current trend, both in films made for the cinema and for television. Anything I say in this respect is bound to sound pompous, but essentially I'm going for a different kind of narration and a changed view of reality. It is difficult now because, especially on television, one's audience isn't as innocent as it used to be. I think it's probably the same in the cinema. And there's a loss in that. We have not always been taught to look at things properly. In fact, the very reverse.

'Besides, there's a big language problem when one is making British films that have to appeal more widely. Subtitles or dubbing are okay for Europe but not for America. There, the same language is spoken but only superficially. Actually, it isn't the same at all.'

Loach tried for years, in between his television prospects, to interest film producers and backers in a Jim Allan story about Ireland. It was written as an adventure story about an Irish flying column before Partition and just after the First World War. 'We tried to say very simply that Ireland is one country and that 700 or 800 years of invasion came before the present troubles. Perhaps that would not be quite adequate as a statement now, but it was found inadequate then for what we felt to be the wrong reasons.

'I sincerely believe that, if we had to set up *Kes* or *Family Life* now, we couldn't get the money. Perhaps I'm just not the man to arouse interest, unless any story I dealt with was very contemporary and pretty sensational. But I don't think it is entirely my way of doing things that's wrong. The system seems pretty inadequate too.

'I don't like explaining what I try to do when I'm making a film. Because it isn't just me, it's everyone else involved too. I work with a team and we share the decisions as widely as possible. But if you force me to explain myself off the screen, I suppose I would say that what I'm generally trying for is to elucidate what is happening, or what did happen.

'And since I believe in certain things politically, it's the way political development affects people and their families. I try very hard to avoid blatant propaganda. But I do think people are less apolitical than a lot of people think. If something overtly affects them, they become political very quickly, even if they relapse back again when the trouble is apparently over.

'Most of my work is certainly political in intent, but hopefully it also touches people personally too. I try to get them to make the inevitable connection, usually against the opinions fed to them elsewhere. Even *Black Jack* does this, if not so obviously.

'The next thing I'm doing for television, for instance, is a Barry Hines play called *The Gamekeeper*. It is the story of a South Yorkshire steelworker who has left that work and become a gamekeeper. And what he is now paid to do is to keep his ex-mates off the estate. The implications of that are considerable.

'What other subjects would I like to do? There are dozens of them. Like the fact that kids are leaving school with no work. That's important, isn't it? I'd like to make more films for the cinema. But I'm not going to change the subject matter, or the objective, or the way I work, in order to get the money. I couldn't do it anyway with any satisfaction.'

Is there anything else in view for the cinema? 'Yes, there is. But it's bad luck to tell.'

In very few other film-making countries would a director of Loach's quality have to cross his fingers so hard before attempting to make another movie. Is there a financier in the house?

16 February 1980   **Derek Malcolm**

Rolling in the aisles

Funny things never happen to me on the way to theatres. They happen in theatres, and most commonly when I'm edging a way crabwise along the row to my allotted place, K19 or L33 or whatever it may be. For whatever it may be it will assuredly be at the very farthest possible point from the aisle. Most people seem to manage this manoeuvre without causing more havoc than a couple of crushed feet. I am rarely so lucky.

Several times I've trodden on what I thought to be a foot, been surprised by the absence of any cry of anguish, and then horrified to find myself dribbling the supposed foot all the way from L9 to L29. The feeling experienced on finding that it's not a foot at all but a lady's handbag might be described as 'relief' were it not for the fast following dilemma; should I kick it into touch under the nearest seat, or boot it back into play along the row?

But even this rates as a mild trauma alongside some I've known. I think my worst was getting the bottom button of my waistcoat entangled in the hairnet of an American lady on the row in front. Naturally I did not know this had happened until her head jerked back and she shrieked in alarm.

It seemed unfair to ask her to remove her net so I set about trying to wrench my button off, aided by the man whose seat I was passing at the time and who kindly struck matches for me to see by. I think the American lady imagined we were trying to burn away the net in order to free the button. Anyway she became very excited, as did several people on the rows behind us for by this time the play had started and what with my writhing bulk and the flickering flare of the matches, the screams of the American lady and the outraged shouts of her friends, they were having some difficulty in following the plot. In the end I took off my jacket and handed it to the companion of the match man, stripped off my waistcoat and left it dangling from the poor lady's hair, and staggered to my seat.

We sorted things out in the interval, but it was a long time before I set foot in a theatre again. Not until last week, in fact, did I find myself once more reciting the familiar litany. 'Excuse me, sorry to disturb you, excuse me, thank you.' I'd got as far as the third or fourth 'excuse me' when something fluttered from my hand, perhaps overburdened with coat, hat and programme. Should I retrieve it, or let it lie?

'Get to your seat,' said one voice, 'But it might be your ticket stub,' said another. 'And you know what will happen if it is. Half-way through the first act someone will turn up and say they are K33 and you won't be able to prove that you are, and you'll be involved in another fracas.' So I scrabbled around on the floor and found it, and I'm glad I did, although it wasn't my ticket stub.

What it was was a slip of green paper that had obviously been tucked inside my programme. It was headed 'Additional Acknowledgements' and underneath it said: 'Cheese and eggs by Express Dairies. Peanut butter by Sun-Pat Products. Tinned vegetables by Danish Bacon Co. Cream puffs by Lyngrave's Bakeries. Digestive biscuits by United Biscuits Ltd.'

I had just about time to absorb this information and to think that it was a funny thing to find inside a theatre programme when the play started. It was about the sexual frustrations and frolics of a grocer, his wife and his friends. It was obviously meant to be a comedy because from time to time a neighbour's backward boy was brought on to get what laughs he could from his diverse afflictions.

I didn't find this the subtlest form of comedy so I switched off and amused myself by musing on the 'Additional Acknowledgments'. 'Stockings by Ballito, Cigarette lighters by Ronson, and Cigarettes by Abdullah' was about as far as I'd seen this sort of thing carried before. 'Peanut butter by Sun-Pat' seemed to be in a different league altogether. I wondered where it had all started; and where it would end.

After the interval I could at least see where they were heading. For reasons not altogether clear to me – unless it was to save on dialogue – the grocer began hurtling the contents of his shelves about his shop.

Cream puffs exploded against the walls, tinned vegetables crashed on to the counter, peanut butter slurped all over the set. As comedy it soon palled, as an indication of the state of contemporary theatre it was depressing, but as background to my green slip of paper it was fascinating and very funny indeed. A Ronson lighter ought to last right through a long-running play, but try putting back together a shattered jar of peanut butter.

Perhaps I should mention that the title of the piece was *Funny Peculiar*. If you feel you want to see it watch out for your 'Additional Acknowledgements.' And, if you can, try to arrange for something funny to happen to you on the way to the theatre.

7 November 1979   **Harry Whewell**

Taxman cometh, Phil

The Archer family of Ambridge, who do such wonderful propaganda work for the Ministry of Agriculture, Fisheries and Food, have incurred the wrath of another Government department. The taxman has been listening anxiously to Radio 4's endless serial ever since Phil Archer started negotiating over an odd-jobbing arrangement with Eddie Grundy.

Phil, the father of the delectable Shula, is a paragon in Ambridge, much given to quoting Min of Ag pamphlets very slowly so that we listeners can have time to note down where to send off for them. He is also a Justice of the Peace and it is this which has particularly upset the members of the Inland Revenue Staff Federation.

Mr Archer's offence has been to offer the surly Grundy, who is unemployed and receiving benefit, payment in cash for doing up the kitchen of one of his tied cottages. This sort of practice is not approved of by the Inland Revenue, which likes to get its proper cut from such deals.

Hence a letter which Mr John Willman, editor of the taxmen's staff magazine, *Assessment*, has just written to the

Magistrates Association. This urges the beaks to lobby the BBC for a fraud squad raid, or at least a visit from the tedious local bobby, Jim Coverdale, in a forthcoming *Archers* script.

This may already be planned but the Diary does not want to spoil any surprises – and, anyway, the *Archers* studio was silent yesterday with everyone off sunbathing or mowing their lawns. In the programme's defence, you might just consider that fiddling by the respectable Phil is probably an accurate reflection of life: and certainly truer than if the crime had merely been allotted to a stock *Archers* baddy like Nelson Gabriel.

27 May 1980   **Martin Wainwright**

Through hell and a hurricane

The American Government is attempting to discourage the massive exodus of refugees from Cuba, who are now pouring into this pleasantly tatty seaside resort. They might just as well try to hold up the Flight from Egypt with traffic lights. No force on earth is going to stop the Floridian Cubans from crossing the 110 miles to Mariel to bring back their relatives to the US and 'libertad'.

The task has an almost religious inevitability about it, a combination of shared folk-loathing of Castro with simple familial piety. The fact that what they are doing is illegal, or that they might be fined and their boats confiscated, is a trivial irrelevance.

Yesterday morning there were more than 1,500 boats from the US waiting in Mariel for the weather to improve, and several hundred more here in Key West preparing to start. Most of the Cubans were waiting in small motorboats of the kind in which three or four people might comfortably cruise the Norfolk Broads. 'I'm gonna bring 10, 12, I don't know how many,' one man who works as a plumber in Miami told us. He had paid $5,000 for the boat and had never been to sea in his life.

Wasn't it extremely dangerous? 'Yeah, but I have to bring

my family back whatever happens,' he said with the air of someone explaining to a dolt who thought it dangerous to rescue a child from a burning house.

Another man, proudly standing on the fibreglass deck of his rickety tub, explained that he had 32 family members in Havana. His wife had 17. 'I guess we'll just have to make seven or eight trips,' he said. Many of the Cubans have lived here since Castro came to power, 21 years ago, and have never met most of the family they hope to bring back.

'Family' appears to include all siblings, parents, grandparents, uncles, aunts, cousins and wives, so there are few people here who feel a responsibility for less than a dozen or so others.

They set off with little or no idea how to steer a boat – the Coastguard helicopters report people at sea holding up cardboard signs saying, 'Which way Cuba?' – dressed in thin cotton beachwear, without radios, life-jackets, and sometimes without even compasses. These are the lucky ones, who have saved enough to afford to buy or rent a boat. They say there is not a Cuban in Florida, and there are half-a-million of them, who would not join the flotilla if he could.

It took the worst weather here for a long time to halt them even briefly. At the weekend the Straits of Florida were visited by what was officially described as a thunderstorm, but which was in fact a baby hurricane. Key West is the last of a 100-mile string of islands stretching from the southernmost tip of Florida, and here windows were smashed and 3ft wide trees uprooted. A good two dozen boats were simply abandoned in the straits, their terrified passengers rescued by other voyagers or by the Coastguard cutters. Several must presumably have sunk. So far only two bodies have been discovered, but many more are expected.

The Coastguard has been stretched to its limits, with the Key West station working on as many as 20 rescues at any one time. They are concentrating on saving life, but even here they face enormous problems. Long after the storm had calmed the waves in the straits were 8ft high and, with thousands of square miles of water splashed with white foam, it was virtually impossible for the helicopters and plane crews to spot the tiny boats. They have stopped picking up empty boats now; they mark them with a red cross and let them drift.

All the boats set off from Garrison Bight, a small concrete marina in the north of the island. At the climax the hurricane on Sunday evening lasted about five minutes, smashing the boats against each other. Yet as soon as it had passed, another handful set out for Cuba on a two-day trip across some of the worst seas south of the Arctic Circle.

'Say, you English?' a man shouted up from a boat, which for its size might as well have been pedal-powered. 'This is Dunkirk!' Along the quay an earnest-looking couple were trying to sell whole-food protein chocolate, which not only keeps you alive but also protects the environment. They found few takers because the Cubans know that what their relatives yearn for is real junk food.

In the receiving centre at the Key West Latin Chamber of Commerce, there were stacks of the stuff: chocolate chip cookies, potato crisps, sugary breakfast cereal, marshmallows, and something called 'snoodles' – a cornucopia of capitalist rubbish donated by the Cuban community to their liberated cousins. There were clothes too but, being Americans now, the Cubans had done the job properly so that instead of looking like an Oxfam fire sale, the racks were crowded with new dresses, suits, and sweaters, flanked by neat piles of clean underwear and scarcely worn shoes which would not have disgraced Selfridges.

In fact, these refugees must be receiving better treatment than any in the world; their processing in Key West is little more than a formality and, two or three hours after stepping shivering and frightened off the boat, they are fed, watered and clothed and whisked to Miami. There US officials do what they can to sort out who they are, before releasing them into the warm, accommodating bosom of the Cuban exile community. Nobody expects any serious attempt to punish them, still less to send them back: this is election year.

The Government is making a belated attempt to stop profiteering and the Customs have impounded three shrimp boats used to bring back a total of 507 people. Usually there is little the authorities can do. The exodus is illegal only if money has changed hands, and both owners and passengers deny that it has. In fact, the going rate is about $1,000 a head, which the Cubans here are happy to pay.

Key West is usually a lazy winter seaside resort, inhabited by fishermen, hoteliers, quite a few gays, and the kind of person who makes a living by painting art deco on driftwood. The Coastguard makes the occasional rescue and devotes the rest of its time to hunting drug smugglers.

At present their weary officers just wish the Cubans would stop. Commander Sam Dennis, who is in charge here, says it is the biggest problem he has ever faced. 'I watched one man who brought a boat on a trailer, trying to launch it. He didn't even know how to get it into the water.' Another Cuban parked his Lincoln Continental on what turned out to be a greased slipway used by seaplanes. It slid gracefully into the water in the general direction of Cuba.

'All we know is that upward of 2,000 boats left for Cuba, and so far 37 have returned. We hope they are in Mariel right now, but we have no way of knowing,' Dennis says. 'The potential for a disastrous situation is extremely high.'

To the Cubans, falling on each other in delight and tears, the weather is a slight irritation. America has become their Israel and everybody – from unskilled labourers who scarcely speak English to lawyers, doctors, and teachers who have branched out into the non-Spanish community – is driven by the same urgent, atavistic necessity.

A softly spoken New England lawyer who came here 22 years ago from Havana as a student, left his prosperous home in Connecticut the day Castro's decision was announced. The next morning he bought his $7,800 boat in Miami. 'I might get fired, but that isn't the point. There are nine or ten of my family over there and they have to be brought in.' How would they exist in the States? 'We'll support them till they find work. They're all industrious people. They'll be okay.'

1 May 1980   **Simon Hoggart**

Burra in Chandler land

Edward Burra's arrival in New York in 1934 might almost have been rehearsed. As he went through Customs his bag was opened to reveal 'an awful mess of Woolworth underwear mixed up with paints and French and Spanish novelettes', which the Customs officer readily passed through. But as Burra stooped to close the bag, the officer noticed a large whisky-bottled shaped bulge in the artist's hip pocket. Leaning over he tapped the offending bulge with a pencil. 'Ed didn't even straighten up. He leered round at the cop and said in that withering voice of his, "It's a growth".'

Burra had obviously arrived in Chandler land with his script prepared. He was ready for the bars and bordellos, the dance girls and sailors, the hooch and the jazz, the gangsters and the danger. It is impossible to look at one of his seething bar-room interiors and not recognize the type who sits in the corner with a cigarette butt jammed impressively between his teeth.

His strident picture of America is being flaunted at the Lefevre Gallery in a stunning collection of watercolours and drawings assembled originally for an exhibition in Boston in 1955. Famous Boston hangouts, like Izzy Orts and the Silver Dollar Bar, have been viewed from our level through the eyes of a fan. The show is Burra's homage to B-movie America.

In his addiction to squalor and toughness, to cheapness and glitter, Burra was a precursor of Warhol's pop world. What differentiates Burra from the generation of English pop artists who followed him into the American dream is his actual presence on the scene. This is no selfconscious peeping, but a full-blooded emotional involvement.

Burra's favourite devices for involving the spectator are the ashtrays full of toasted cigarette ends; the glasses of bourbon which appear on the front lip of the picture, perched on the bar underneath your nose. His schoolboy love of detail and air of intense reality, achieved by harsh, all-revealing lighting, create an air of menace. Rather like the Richard Hamilton illustrations to Joyce's *Ulysses* – which recently appeared at the Anthony d'Offay Gallery – Burra's moment is always an ordinary moment charged with potential. 'Everything looks menacing,' he wrote. 'I'm always expecting something calamitous to happen.'

Sometimes he arrives after the event. In Salome, the Baptist's severed head, shedding tears, sits on the bar beside a dirty ashtray. Salome herself serves behind the bar, a huge, red bird laden down with jewellery. Her feathered customers and potential victims prop up the bar, and wait as we do.

This is Max Ernst country. The giant, incongruous bulk of Salome fills the picture like the Elephant of the Celebes, but somehow it remains an actual bar-room scene.

The ranting, disturbing mood of Burra's interiors is captured perfectly in a letter sent to William Chappell in 1945. 'The very sight of people's faces sickens me. I've got no pity. It really is terrible sometimes. I'm quite frightened at myself. I think such awful things, I get in such paroxysms of impotent venom I feel it must poison the atmosphere. I see that Hitchcock film was actually taken in a California town to save set and money. My God, why don't they always save set and money . . .'

This search for poisoned atmospheres – the identification with Hitchcock – is conducted in the brightest colours. Burra's watercolour technique is constantly fighting against the medium's naturally soft grain. He creates solid forms which radiate a claustrophobic, artificial glow rather than airy daylight. But by pitching his dry, sickly colours in such an intense key, the artist ensures that the spectators' eyes are never allowed to relax.

The more you look at the strange, disquieting images, the more it becomes obvious that Burra's links with his American contemporaries who frequent the same bars are purely superficial. His nearest relatives are not John Sloan, Reginald Marsh or Edward Hopper but William Blake and Stanley Spencer. Burra, the English visionary, makes an undisguised appearance in the handful of religious paintings included in this show; works like Resting Angel and Resurrection, in which it is the landscape's turn to be exposed as an evil.

It is therefore with some relief that you leave behind Burra's tortured colours in a room devoted to his drawings. But suddenly the artist reveals a playful line and a sense of humour that is malicious, but not malignant.

Eugene O'Neill has been endowed with Clark Gable looks and a pair of shoulders worthy of the Minotaur. In between plays, he is being forced to don an apron and hold a tray aloft as he weaves his way through the crowd in his new role of barman. Somewhere at the back, a seedy character with a cigarette butt jammed impressively between his teeth is rubbing his hands with delight at the sight of O'Neill working for a living.

1 January 1980   **Waldemar Januszczak**

Speaking through the static of time

Mexico City is hell on earth; though if you approach like Cortés over the cloud-darkened mountains and see the plateau dissolved in sunshine with light rising from the swamp land beyond the city, you have the illusion of paradise. Strong men are moved to reach for their cameras, but the dream cannot survive translation to film.

This is Earth's most destiny-laden city. The Aztecs understood astral movements and what they portended. The year 1519 was marked out as their year of doom; the year the expelled serpent-god Quetzalcoatl would return from where the sun rises and lay waste to their civilization. And when Cortés appeared with his mounted Conquistadors, the prophecy was fulfilled.

Cortés destroyed the Aztec civilization stone by stone and imposed Roman Catholicism in the approved method by the rack and the gibbet. Tenochtitlan, the Aztec capital, was a New World Venice, set in the centre of a lake and punctuated by canals, bridges, and aqueducts. Cortés razed Tenochtitlan and founded Mexico City. The lake of Texcoco dried up and the city today could be Tokyo or Tel Aviv or Toronto, except that it is bigger and growing faster. Families move into spatchcock buildings before the builders have put the roofs on. People with country houses three years ago are surrounded by shanties now.

In the smart areas where the diplomatic corps and the industrialists live in splendour, the *barrancas*, the valley bottoms fifty feet below the Spanish-tiled swimming pools, are filled with lean-to corrugated iron shacks and waste dumps where Indians and their pigs live together. And ill-refined petrol at 20 pence a gallon means that the streets are choked from dawn to midnight, choked with traffic and choking on fumes.

But Mexico City is not Mexico, any more than London is England. The nation has an uninterrupted indigenous culture rooted in the life of the people that is unparalleled in the western hemisphere.

This Mexico is not the Mexico of desert and scrubland and the smiling, smiling villains of *The Wild Bunch*. It is the country of the rain god Tlaloc where in the rainy season the streets around Chapultepec Park flood within minutes with torrents two feet deep and thunderbolts crash across the face of the 42-storey hotel and lightning strikes in blinding splashes of light. Tlaloc in stone presides massively over the approach to the Museum of Anthropology in Mexico City, and up in the black thunderscape of the Sierra Madre the Catholic peasants still place small offerings of food to appease the mighty rain gods.

This is the Mexico of Popocatapetl, the snow-capped volcano, of valleys so fertile that three crops a year can grow, of banana trees and tall eucalyptus, flamboyant, flaming bougainvillea, and the clear white morning light of Oaxaca. The culture of this Mexico runs north to south, roughly speaking, from the Tropic of Cancer to the Guatemalan border. Between these two parallels were found the strange great Olmec stone heads, the Zapotec tombs, the Avenue of the Dead and the Pyramids of Teotihuacan abandoned hundreds of years before the Aztecs ruled, the Mayan Chacmools – reclining figures with receptacles for the hearts of sacrificial victims – the laughing little god Xipe Totec,

222

hideously clad in the flayed skin of another human but symbolizing re-birth and spring, the exquisite jewellery of the Mixtecs, the vast and awesome realism of the Aztec sculptures to Coatlicue, the Earth Mother, giver and taker of life, the great calendar stone that predicted solar eclipses and the cataclysm that would bring the world to an end.

Now, too, it is the Mexico of petrol and steel and oil slicks on the beaches of Yucatan and in the bay of Veracruz. Some Mexicans predict that their country will become one of the richest in the world within five years. For its poorest *campesinos*, this is a consummation devoutly to be wished, and for its beggars and for the children who work all night between the lines of traffic selling flowers or newspapers, and for the shoeshines and for the blind pedlar of street maps on the corner of Juarez and Juan de Letran and for the legless beggars who pull themselves across the marble floor of the Shrine of our Lady of Guadalajara to pray for redemption.

For them, and surely for us, pre-Columbian art can be nothing but a dead letter, deader than the dead languages of the Mediterranean. For the exotic-plumed culture that Cortes destroyed with his sword was as repulsive to Europeans as the practice of suttee. Before the rule of the Aztecs, there had been four suns. Each had died, and each time a race of Indians had died with it.

The Aztecs were born under the fifth sun, and they kept the sun alive by offerings of blood. Young prisoners who had distinguished themselves in battle were led to the entrance of the temple at the top of the pyramid and there the priest took a knife of sharp-edged flint with turquoise encrusted exquisitely-fashioned handles and tore out the still beating hearts to offer them in triumph to the dreadful deity Tezcatlipoca, the Smoking Mirror. While Leonardo was exploring the meaning of life and Michelangelo was creating the haunting beauty of the *Pietà* and the Medicis were founding capitalism and Giovanni Bellini was painting the tenderest pictures known to Christianity, these savages of Mexico were tearing the living hearts out of dying captives. Their art must be museum fodder, as dead and empty to us as the tombs at Mitla.

And yet it is not so. To the contrary, their art is more alive today than our own fragmented culture.

As it happens the British Council and two of Mexico's government organizations have been sponsoring in Mexico City the Jornadas Culturales Anglo-Mexicanas – and as the culminating event of the festival an exhibition of watercolours and a few oils by J. M. W. Turner has opened. Turner was the last great popular painter of England. The engravings saw to the popularity, and his massive fusion of technique to perception and imagination produced one of the last great flowerings of representational art.

But the industrial and agricultural revolutions had already sundered English society. We talk now of genius to denote greatness where once it meant a remarkable singularity within a social context. Picasso, Henry Moore, Brancusi, Matisse threw up bulwarks in our time against chaos, or perhaps against sameness. They have been working out of a for-midable sensibility, but it is a personal sensibility. They are heroic figures, and to the extent that they are not understood, not they, but society has failed.

Maybe this is why the voice of the art of the period and a race of which we have no real understanding and no sympathetic appreciation speaks through the static loud and clear. There are pre-Columbian sculptures like the best of Moore, of Brancusi, of Gaudier Brzeska, there are little medallions incised with the desperate gaiety of Picasso's fauns. No Dada work could compete with the manic invention of a flute made from a human armbone, nothing by Hans Arp is as taut and powerful as the strong-beaked proud-crested stone macaws of the Toltecs. Picasso never punned better than the sculptor who made a human head simultaneously two coiled serpents, nor was he ever more inventive than the artist who fashioned out of clay the grinning skeleton Mictlantecuhtli, god of death, with his basket-weave torso of ribs and the grape-like group of bones grasped in his fists, the ultimate bunch of fives.

It is not that these artists were better or earlier than our own; but they were working within a popular and well-defined tradition, responding to fact and ever-present myth about life and death, birth and copulation, sickness and health. Their art was not made for the dusty glory of kings and pharaohs – their pyramids are not tombs but bases for temples to the elemental deities. They made art in response to the god-like forces in the mountains and skies and earthquakes and torrents or rain. And it varies from the majestic proportions of the great Pyramid of the Sun, greater than the great pyramid of Egypt, to the carved heads pared down to the size of peas, from the dynamic abstraction of a stone totem to portraits modelled with the sensitive and appealing immediacy of the death mask of William Blake.

If Christian art aspires to ultimate serenity and Buddhist art to ultimate stillness, pre-Columbian art taps the dynamic wells of life and creation. These Indians might almost have invented the notions of functionalism and truth to materials: a sculpture of a god remains simultaneously a god and a block of stone; a slab that might easily be hoisted into place to do duty as a lintel over a tomb's entrance.

It cannot be said that this astonishing breadth of invention survived the invasion of Cortés, but still, there is a discernible line of descent from the first maize-growing farmers of maybe 15,000 years ago to the *campesinos* of today, from the great architects and sculptors and goldsmiths of Monte Alban and Chichen Itza and Teotihuacan to the silversmiths of Taxco and the architects of the university and the muralists Rivera, Orozco, Siqueiros, and O'Gorman.

But when the Indians swallowed Christianity, they produced an indigenous version of Christian art so gaudy that it cannot be mistaken for the European model. The interior of the sixteenth century church of Santo Domingo in Oaxaca is a pullulating miracle of gold, with three dimensional coloured pictures around the walls and life-size figures of the scourged saints in the chapels: a holy relish of bazaar baroque. Good or bad taste is irrelevant. In Mexican art as a whole the notion of taste is beside the point: the art hits you between the eyes with the force of its statement, more or less powerfully, but never with tailored notions of beauty or truth; that is not with any one society's notion of beauty or truth: the truth of Mexican art is its sheer elemental force.

And when painters who emerged from the Mexican revolution of 1910–16 wanted to slough off the degenerate Spanish influences they turned back to pre-Columbian art and to contemporary folk art. Diego Rivera painted Cubist pictures in Paris, but turned to realism and Mexican national subjects on his return home. Between them the great muralists of Mexico covered acres of space depicting Indian suffering and triumph: in the gallery of Cortés's palace at Cuernavaca, in the Prado Hotel, where it offended tourists from the United States and was covered over for many years, in the Ministry of Education, out on the university campus, a self-contained city for a quarter of a million students.

Some of his work seems wilful rather than willed: a painted polemic about the role of art rather than the necessity of art itself. But it is a matter of history that Rivera, Orozco, Siqueiros, and younger followers rejected the temptations of private profit and persuaded successive Mexican adminis-trations to allow them to work on a public scale. They rejected Paris modernism without falling into fey historicism.

And their success is this: that if you visit the Tate Gallery Rothko room, you will see visitors laughing, yes laughing, at the work of Rothko. If you visit any of the great modern murals of Mexico you will see people reading the pictures through. Rothko is a fine artist but who says so? A few painters who know what controlled effort went into his abstractions; a few of the public with the time to care about such things; a few dealers who know the value of scarcity. But the murals of Rivera affect the man in the street and they have no price. They are part of the Mexican heritage, like the stone colossus of Tlaloc the rain god and the tombs on the mountain of Monte Alban. Rothko is the heritage of a few gifted people, a few aesthetes, and that is part of our inescapable tragedy.

It is a matter of fact that this Mexican revolution in art has run into the sand. Its greatest leaders are dead and the world's stupidest television game, *Couples*, can be picked up from Dallas in the meanest hovel on the mountain road between Mexico City and Cuernavaca. Television corrupts and commercial television corrupts absolutely. Siqueiros in his writings foresaw a great future for the artist when he had harnessed modern technology: he saw an integrated architecture and painting and sculpture for our times that might rival the Aztecs and their forebears. In truth Siqueiros, Rivera, and their companions achieved pitifully little measured against the encroaching tide of mass culture and the monstrous sprawl of Mexico City. But at least they heard the rain god speak.

4 September 1979   **Michael McNay**

For artists and simpletons only

For more than 50 years Edward Ardizzone – who died on Thursday night of a heart attack in his 80th year, at his home in Kent – landscaped the long largess of English life, an unruffled vision of town, beach and country populated by fubsy matrons, cooks like cottage loaves, dozy mongrels, pointy-feet children and men who in general seem to be off duty.

As a professional who developed out of a hobbyist he took, in a fairly autobiographical sense, everything that offered and gave back – across scores of books, paintings and commercial art – a personal view: like Cruikshank he was a 'maker-up', working from notebooks at one remove from reality. He sketched constantly in publishers' dummies, and had filled 50 or 60.

His name is perhaps better known as an illustrator of his own and others' children's books than for his water-colours or his works as a war artist. Not a few children have been named after Tim, Lucy and Ginger, the characters in a series which began with a story he told his own progeny that became *Little Tim and the Brave Sea Captain*.

His income was founded on the royalties. And one might call royalties the proceeds of the sketches he loved to make of guests at Royal garden parties.

In his early days he eked out a precarious living from book jackets. Forty years on he still occasionally undertook them. One of these was a pub scene for my own first novel. When I thanked him for it, he reminisced about the pubs and tarts to whom, as subjects, he said, he owed his reputation. He told me he had once appealed to the Inland Revenue for an allowance on them, and that the inspector had graciously conceded validity of the claim, hoping it was mostly for beer.

To visit him in the L-shaped room in the Victorian house in Maida Vale, where he'd lived since the twenties, was to find him working on a wooden stool carved by a refugee in the First World War, set on a dais to keep his feet out of the draught, showering himself in snuff from a little silver box and thus, with Mitchell's Post Office Pens, bought by the gross, he had hatched and cross-hatched several thousand drawings. What he actually saw, he said, was a stage.

It was a worm-in-the-stalls'-eye view that dated back to the Renaissance. He greatly admired Poussin, Cézanne, Daumier and Signorelli, and taught himself by copying them. (He was very impatient with students who declined to copy.) He had trouble with upright shapes, which in any case divide up a book, and much preferred landscape. The fun lay in catching moving figures in a stage setting, their expressive features secondary, and the great hope the noble design.

In outline his life was that of an artist of mixed Italian and English blood, born in Haiphong but who came to England in his infancy and, after a nomadic and troubled youth, settled in London. He travelled a great deal and kept exotic diaries.

The main interval, until he withdrew to his beloved Kent in 1966, was his time as an official War Artist (Lord Clark's choice). Then he saw his job as 'catching the mood' and made 300 pictures, now held in the Imperial War Museum.

That was also the year of his marriage to Catherine Anderson, a former fashion model who kept them going in their impecunious days and who survives him, with two of their three children, and 11 grandchildren.

He has died – after several painful falls that crippled him but did not deter him from working – in the very week before an exhibition of his work opens at Illustrators Art in London, and the publication of *Edward Ardizzone*, a book on his many facets by his brother-in-law Gabriel White.

The book's coda is a wry conclusion quoted from Ardizzone himself: 'One paints for artists and simpletons only.'

10 November 1979 **Alex Hamilton**

Elsinore's Hamlet

'People sometimes say that actors give us their own Hamlets and not Shakespeare's. In point of fact, there is no such thing as Shakespeare's Hamlet. If Hamlet has something of the definitiveness of a work of art, he has also all the obscurity that belongs to life. There are as many Hamlets as there are melancholies.'

So says Oscar Wilde, with the sanity of genius, in *The Critic as Artist*; and his lines are worth quoting at a time when there seem to be as many *Hamlets* as there are actors. But what particularly brought those lines to mind were some recent sniping comments by a couple of television critics – the admired Clive James and Philip Purser – about the concept of the Ghost-less *Hamlet* currently being offered by Jonathan Pryce at the Royal Court. Or rather the *Hamlet* in which the Ghost is some internal, sepulchral demon urging the Prince to revenge.

The first thing to say is that the Ghost is the hardest thing to bring off in *Hamlet*. He tends to come clanking on like the Tin Man in the Wizard of Oz and sounding like Boris Christoff in armour or a pop-spook with his own built-in echo chamber. He has to suggest both the man he once was ('See what a grace was seated on this brow') and the purgatorial resident he now is. For my money the one Ghost I have seen who would have induced me to stick a knife in my uncle's guts was the one presented by Jonathan Miller in a student production at the Arts, Cambridge. Miller gave us a solid, corporeal, untricksy figure who sat next to Hamlet on a bench and told him the full story; the effect was irresistible.

But the real point about the two-for-the-Pryce-of-one

Ghost at the Royal Court is that it entirely suits this particular actor's riven, tortured sensibility. It would be wrong, say, for Derek Jacobi (who brought his own grace, humour and intelligence to the part in the BBC TV version) to try to present Hamlet as a man possessed. But it seems entirely right for Pryce who always looks anyway as if he has been up half the night talking to himself.

Oscar Wilde's point was that, with Hamlet, each actor's own individuality 'becomes a vital part of the interpretation'. And Pryce, with that strange half-moon face, those troubled eyes and that countenance, like Charlotte Brontë's Vashti, 'wasted like wax in flame', is just the man to give us a Hamlet who carries his own Furies inside him.

It would be a pity, however, if the Court production were simply to go down in history as the first *Hamlet* without the Ghost. For a start it wouldn't be true (does no one remember a Zeffirelli-Albertazzi *Amleto* that came to the Old Vic in 1964 and that offered us an ectoplasmic Ghost?). But it would also overlook the point that Richard Eyre's production has cracked one of the crucial problems in presenting this play in any medium: how to keep some kind of balance between the agony of its principal character and the bustle and activity of Elsinore itself. We often forget that at the start of the play, Fortinbras of Norway is claiming back land lost by his father and that Claudius (not unlike Carter with Iran) is looking for a peaceful, diplomatic solution while at the same time secretly planning a quick military strike. Hamlet's 'madness' is the least of many problems.

The one version of the play I have seen to give the action a living, breathing context was the magnificent Russian film directed by Grigori Kozintsev. His Elsinore was both official and domestic: it had courtiers and bureaucrats going about their business, hens and geese in the courtyard, embarrassed soldiers trying to avert their gaze as Ophelia went ostentatiously mad. Suddenly *Hamlet* became what it ought to be and almost never is: a private tragedy being enacted in a public world. This is not only true historically (at the time the play was written, Denmark was a powerful empire ruling over Southern Sweden, parts of Germany and commanding the entrance to the Baltic) but, more important, vital dramatically.

I have always put it down to economics that, in the theatre, we never get much sense of Elsinore. Now I realize it is to do with failure of imagination as much as lack of loot. The Court is a small theatre with a modest budget. But Eyre and his designer, William Dudley, give us a rich sense of unseen activity: the sound of shipwrights 'whose sore task does not divide the Sunday from the week' (no union problems in Elsinore), the buzz of courtiers watching the royal family fall apart in front of their eyes, *trompe l'oeil* doors that make this court an eavesdropper's paradise. After this, it will be hard ever again to take an Elsinore reduced to the usual de-populated palace.

About the character of Hamlet himself, Wilde was right: he takes on the impress of whatever actor is currently playing him. He also brings out the lightning cartoonist in critics: 'a private detective keeping tabs on the Danish Royal Family', wrote one of Wolfit; 'the Duke of Windsor out to get Stanley Baldwin and wife', said George Jean Nathan of Leslie Howard. But such images reinforce the basic point that Hamlet is one of those parts that miraculously transcends differences of temperament, race or gender. Whatever your particular quality, Hamlet can take it.

But while endorsing Wilde's point, we also need to remind ourselves that it is a public and political play about regicide, usurpation, the illegitimate gain of a considerable empire. And just as much as Shakespeare's Histories, it is about the morality of wresting the throne from the *de facto*, if not the *de jure*, ruler. Only when the private and the public worlds interact does one get the full flavour of this amazing play. Eyre-on-a-shoestring pulled it off at the Court. It will be fascinating to see what John Barton and Michael Pennington, with slightly more resources, manage at Stratford in a month's time.

6 June 1980   **Michael Billington**

Top people-watcher

Joyce Grenfell, who claimed in a posthumously published article that she had been a 'people-watcher' all her life, would have had a rich source of material yesterday at her own memorial service in Westminster Abbey.

Well over an hour before the service was due to begin there were queues outside the Abbey. Mostly they were women: women in the sort of angular hats and sensible 1930-ish shoes which the much-loved comedienne and monologuist affectionately sent up and tended to adopt herself. Ladies with prominent pearls and commandingly hooked noses, ladies with unhabitual lipstick on determined lips, ladies with peaked caps and swollen ankles, all made a fitting tribute to that very dignified and funny lady who was Lady Astor's niece and one of the last entertainers to survive from an age in which the middle classes could feel comfortable without feeling uncomfortable about feeling comfortable.

Mr Robin Ray, star of musical quizzes on TV with Miss Grenfell, was there; but the atmosphere in general was delightfully unfashionable and far removed from the tinsel of the present. Sir David Willcocks read the lesson; the Dean thanked God for her 'love of people, for the friendship she gave and fostered with letters to so many friends all over the world'; Paul Scofield, the most distinguished unfashionable actor in Great Britain, read from *Pilgrim's Progress*, and the Reverend Geoffrey White, Joyce Grenfell's village priest, proclaimed the unfashionable sentiment that her art was 'without one cruel, unkind or unclean word or thought.' Princess Margaret set the seal of royal approval on the proceedings.

'This is rather like a service for a Prime Minister,' said the bewildered correspondent of an American newspaper. 'Joyce was a wonderful woman, of course, but she wasn't Prime Minister, was she?' In a congregation of 2,000, with

1,500 reserved seats snapped up as soon as they were offered, her fans obviously thought that she was a lot more than a Prime Minister, and perhaps they may even have been right.

8 February 1980 **Dennis Barker**

The Christmas Pudding that shook the world

A tremendous tale of love and courage, passion, battle, rape and arson, told here now for the very first time by Mr. Alex Hamilton!

Captain Spencer Ponsonby Oliver Nicholas Gore-Eckersley, REMC, known in the mess as 'Sponge' and to his men as 'Bloody-Ecstasy', was brought home on extended leave in the spring of 1913 from his post as district officer in Negri Sembilan. Disturbing rumours filtered back from the East – that he trafficked in opium, that he communed with a local variety of juju and (the proper ghastly indicator that he was due for the cleaners) that he'd sauced London.

Rich tales about him circulated at the Travellers'. Chap apparently wrote the Commissioner, 'When it comes to evil spirits, the juice of the poppy is more blessed than your djinn-and-tonic.' Cut off in the bush he didn't encourage visitors. A couple of Whitehall spies announced a tour of inspection and then received his cable, 'Greetings but advise no bridge at Mile 77.' So they spared him their company. They were back UK-side before they learned there was no river at Mile 77 either. He got it in his head he was being passed over for promotion and indented for 5,000 miles of rubber tubing. When London queried, 'What for?' he telegraphed. 'To help me suck from here.'

So it was plain a mistake had been made. But while totting up severance pay, Whitehall pondered the pity of wasting a good man. With a nuisance developing on the continent, and

233

the muzhiks and Tartars playing silly-buggerskis all the way
from Rasputingrad to the Great Ocean, it would patently be a
nonsense to put a 32-year-old first class sapper out to grass.
An influential Gore uncle urged a sympathetic diagnosis on
the War Office: 'To take timber, nails, cables, and anchors
away from a sapper is like snatching bucket and spade from a
child in a sandpit – it ends in tears. The Captain is suffering
from nothing more serious than pontoon deprivation. Restore
his toys, and I guarantee him amenable.'

· It was a persuasive argument. Intelligence held a hefty
dossier on his exploits in the Yellow War. The secretive
Japanese themselves made no bones about acknowledging
their debt to his genius for improvisation in their victory over
Kuroki's immensely superior Russian First Army at the Yalu
River. Sponge-san it was who rigged the artificial avenue of
trees behind which the Twelfth Division mustered. Sponge-
san devised the decoy bridge to Kinteito on trestles, drawing
the fire of the Russian artillery and disclosing their guns, while
the 10 effective bridges were rapidly thrown across the Yalu
on Chinese junks, anchored in place by means of ploughs
which he commandeered from Korean peasants.

Sponge-san was evidently an honorary Jap in his pleasure at
deception. He had advised that torpedo boats be brought
upriver, though the bottom was here too shallow, because the
threat would keep Kuroki's lines extended. And Sponge-san
was the sporting engineer who, hand-in-glove with the
gunners, as every true sapper must be, nonchalantly rowed
upstream under the very muzzles of the enemy to pinpoint
them as targets for the Japanese howitzers.

The Japanese smiled in reporting the Captain's rapture as
he went about his business. They said they understood why
his following gave him the warrior's title of 'Bloody Ecstasy' –
he was a rare European who had penetrated the emotions
behind the cry of 'Banzai!' All this and more confirmed the
official view that there would be a diplomatic and perhaps
military use in sending Gore-Eckersley to Tokyo, especially if
the Bear broke loose from the Czar and went on the rampage.

But there was nothing in the dossier that explained the
Captain's subsequent sulky mood, nor why he had rusticated

234

himself in the Malaysian forest. Had the Confidential Clerks looked for this cogent truth, they could have had it for the price of a quart of stout bought for one of the gossiping tweenies at the family house in Kensington Gore. Of course, they would probably then have discounted it, as the promptings of minds inflamed by kitchen drawer novelettes.

Their whispered story was indeed one of passion. As a youth their Mr Spencer was known to them as a great ladies' man, and not ungenerous. To gales of giggles they warned any new female recruit below stairs to 'beware of the Last of the Great Spenders'. But his heart remained untouched. He was plain about this – each had heard the same phrase – declaring that 'that organ would no more catch light than a shell filled with sand will explode.' Until, that is, in Tokyo, he fell in love with a young and beautiful hostess named Miss Flourishing Dragon.

Seemingly, she accepted his overtures, saying that her bliss lay in the coincidence that the ideograph that expressed her name meant also 'British Dominion'. Unfortunately, while he was larking at the Yalu River, General Sir Ian Hamilton, ironically his idol from the Boer War, reached Tokyo and was likewise captivated.

In the aftermath, following Port Arthur, the General pulled rank on him, and fobbed him off with another geisha for substitute, the Honourable Miss Sparrow. Poor Sponge did his best to be gallant and said he wished he had a beautiful golden cage to carry her off home. When his compliment was translated the lady immediately turned sour and soon left the company. In fact the intermediary had made a poor job of it, conveying Sponge's words thus: 'As you are a sparrow, I wish you would shut yourself up in a box.' Miss Flourishing Dragon sent Sponge a scandalized note, observing that geishas were not to be treated like Cossacks. And General Hamilton, with the mortifying condescension of his clan, did everything possible to secure him a posting remote from the field of his humiliation.

However, in 1913, Sponge's masters did unwittingly touch on one aspect of this situation. Recognizing from experience that any single man left too long to carry a burden of responsibility in the backwaters of an alien province is likely to go down with a severe case of the greens, they recommended that he spend his sabbatical season in the vigorous pursuit of manly sports, after which they would appoint him as attaché in Tokyo, there being only one condition: that he include among his impedimenta a sensible girl as his bride.

Sponge undertook to swallow the prescription. Actually, he positively soaked it up. It was soon being said of him that 'everything that bounced he struck with a bat; everything that flew he shot; and anything that didn't move fast enough he laid on the nearest convenient platform and ravished.' In the case of Miss Charlotte Vere Hamilton-Blamey, he bagged, notched or perhaps pocketed her on the billiards table of a bijou St John's Wood residence convenient to Lord's, where earlier in the day he had carried his bat for 103 for the Gentlemen. He construed her protests as concern for the flawless green baize of the table and, exclaiming 'Oh damn the expense!' continued his break, or innings.

But Charlotte was no mere notch. She was something more vibrant than a boundary over the head of long off. He was amazed. (They were both amazed.) Her response was an experience akin to having the Pavilion rise to him. In the house of his mind his batman hurriedly pitched the image of Miss Flourishing Dragon into the attic, and nailed up Charlotte's in her place in the parlour.

'Six and out!' he blazed approvingly.

'Come again?' she inquired, puckering her brow as she decanted some vintage port, adding as she passed him the goblet, 'A Whiggish beverage, but needs must . . .'

'For me', he explained, 'it was as if I had clubbed the sphere right out of the ground and into a passing train which did not stop till it reached Land's End. The longest blow in the history of the game!'

'Try to be coherent,' she said.

'I mean,' he said with a sigh, 'that I am the happiest man alive.'

'There was,' she conceded, 'an element of the irrevocable about it.'

(Please don't be alarmed She didn't get pregnant. This is a

Christmas but not a nativity story.)

Now both could admit that, contrary to appearances on the past dozen occasions at house parties when they'd barely spoken to one another, they had privately decided at the outset there could be only one satisfactory outcome. She said she knew him by reputation, beginning with the stories told about him by her mother's cousin, General Hamilton.

He said, 'Your reputation too, Char, goes ahead of you.'

'Not,' she faltered, 'as "Char-a-bang"?'

'I may have heard that, but never understood it.'

'Darling Sponge, it's a wicked joke, based on a lie. Piggish gossips have put it about that I am very accommodating and it's absolutely not true. We all have our cross I suppose, and we on *The Suffragette* are slandered this way, because we argue for Free Love and publicize the best medical opinion on disease.'

'Strong stuff, you know. I hadn't realized you were a penpusher.'

'My by-line is 'One Who Was There".'

'Not my line of country, to be candid.'

'Dearest, I shall take your education in hand. But the imperative news is that before you there was only ever one. I swear it.'

'One, Which one?'

'Not even in this country.'

'The name of my exotic rival?'

'Hardly that. A spiritual mentor. And most respectably married. I met him while at finishing school last year in Switzerland. Such a mind! Quite overwhelming. In some ways quite like you – an élitist, and yet a bit of a Bolshie. His name? Oh well . . . Vladimir Ilyich Ulyanov, but they call him Lenin.'

'Bit of a . . . ? He's *the* Bolshie!'

'Yes, perhaps one might call him that without exaggeration.'

'A great reader no doubt. What's his bedside book – Marx, or Marx?'

'It is not very delicate of you to press the matter, but I wish to clear the air so that we may breathe freely in future. If you must know, it is neither Marx nor Marx, but the timetable of the Trans-Siberian Railway.'

This surprise instantly blew away the cloud. Sponge put his head back and roared with laughter.

'Wonderful!' he cried. 'He must be human. I remember a Christmas in the campaign for Mukden when my entire post consisted of a copy of Bradshaw. Made me quite sick for home. I seemed to see the old haunts and couldn't get at 'em, like a bumblebee against a window pane. Ah, railways. It also caused me to invest in a few shares in that very same Trans-Sib they were laying at the time. Stupendous engineering feat, out in the permafrost, dynamite every yard of the way.'

'I don't know what to say. Except, I'm glad you approve.'

'Certainly. Mr Ulyanov has his priorities right. Can't give him many marks in action though. When the Japs trounced the Czar's lot in '05, that should have let your chap in, but he made a bog of it.'

'He was terribly undercapitalized,' she protested. 'With proper funds, you'll see a difference next time.'

At this point their ardent exchange was interrupted by a party of gentlemen wanting orthodox use of the table, and they decamped to Romano's to lay plans for a summer of entertainments together.

By Jingo, they were busy though. One can't pinpoint every fragment in the kaleidoscope, only a few samples. Ankles, for instance, and the tango craze. Everybody was doing the Turkey Trot, mixed with ominous ragtime. One little number sent up 'That Ragtime Suffragette, – ragging with bombshells and ragging with bricks, Hagging and nagging in politics, That Ragtime Suffragette. She's no household pet.' Russia meant Diaghilev. America meant Miss Pickford. Germany meant the Zeppelin. The Derby brought the death of Miss Emily Davidson.

When not required to be 'One Who Was There' at exploding pillar-boxes and burning houses, Char toured with Sponge in his new bull-nosed Morris – 50 mph and 50 miles to the gallon, petrol 8d. They went to a masked ball in Westminster Council Baths, and both wore one-piece swimsuits. They watched a march by the Union of Clerks, demonstrating for a 15 per cent wage rise – they were masked too, for fear of victimization. There was a rail strike. The postal services, nearing Christmas, threatened to strike. 'You see,' said Char, 'we're on the brink.' Sponge replied, 'Britannia always found the brink bracing, but that's as far as she'll ever go.' Char was having doubts about the strategy of violence, remembering how Lenin despised it.

They married at St Martin-in-the-Fields on December 9, 1913. The society papers naturally spoke of 'an alliance between Venus and Mars'. Char wore white, with a secret scarlet lining, as a compromise with her sense of integrity. The reception was held in the Albany. Everyone said how sensible to beat the Christmas rush to the Continent, and were then staggered to learn they would honeymoon all the way overland to Japan. 'Char's idea,' Sponge blandly answered the critics. 'She has an affinity. And then, it's quicker and cheaper than the old P & O. One lives in pyjamas on the Trans-Sib – with gaiters of course in first class. Besides, I'm a share-holder.'

'But the wolves!'

'We're not going on the old post road. Even political prisoners no longer walk to Irkutsk. I dare say if wolves chase the train they get the short straw.'

A friend of Charlotte, a hack from the *Manchester Guardian*, wondered if he realized Siberia was in ferment, a breeding ground of revolution.

'Oh, matters improve with every Duma,' said Sponge airily.

'A slight improvement in the condition of the wretched,' observed the Mancunian drily, 'is the usual prelude to upheaval.'

'If you say so. But we shall be in Japan.'

'Ah yes, the bulwark. In that last dust-up, the Russians could not fight?'

'They could not. But I'll tell you something for nothing. They could die.'

'And the Cossacks?'

'The Cossacks are all mouth and trousers, as they say in

Whitechapel. You frequent the Whitechapel Russians? It's where all the book-writers on Russia do their research.'

'You feel confident we can carry on as usual?'

'Not at all. A couple of nights ago I watched Carpentier flatten Wells in 73 seconds. I say that the era of the British straight left is over. Now come, don't be a skull, there's a good fellow. This is a wedding.'

The press of guests spilled all down the staircase. There were only two notable absentees. One was Char's editor, Sylvia Pankhurst, who arrived in London on time from Exeter Prison, scorning a stretcher at Paddington, but was straight away rearrested under the Cat and Mouse Act. The other was a favourite Yorkshire aunt, from whom the most sensational present was expected.

However, overcoming the northern snow, there at dawn next day was Lady Violet Hamilton-Groyne, with her ferret-faced huntsman Joby, peering through the steam at Victoria, waiting to see them off on the South Eastern and Chatham, on the first leg of their 12,000-mile journey.

'Charlotte, child,' said the dowager, 'you look radiant.'

'My husband gave me the Russian sable,' said Char.

'Found it advertisèd in the first issue of *The Suffragette*,' said Sponge. 'A snip at £195, and they threw in the matching muff for another hundred.'

'Trust a man to think only of display,' said the old lady. 'You're well off for combinations, I hope.'

'Unshrinkable, in pure white silk with lace tops,' said Char.

'Kind people have seen to everything.' said Sponge. 'We are furnished with rhino-hide bootlaces, Keatings' flea powder, Barbellion's chocolates, visiting cards on cedar, 100 Punch Havanas with humidor, a self-contained Kinematograph with silver screen, a life subscription to the *Manchester Guardian*, a pocket knife for golfers with a six-inch stymie rule, Captain Tharp's sporting silhouettes adapted to hold menu cards, a tiny toast rack with stand and methylated spirit lamp for keeping toast hot, Bibles of all denominations, a bag for carrying loose change .. If I recited the whole inventory we should miss the train, but I must mention that box, which contains four stone of Romney Skin

240

Foods, from another advertiser, with the maker's compliments and the message that "Beauty and Eloquence are powerful factors in making converts." '

'No wonder you look like an army commissariat,' said Lady Violet. 'Joby! Tickle up those porters. Now, have you reading matter and the vital timetables?'

'My husband will read me Lily Waller's *Our Pleasant Vices*, which embodies ideas of profound interest in these days of awakening womanhood. As to the timetable, I had yesterday this treasured gift from an old . . . tutor.'

'Let me see.' Lady Violet read aloud from the flyleaf. "To Charshka. Siberia needs people and electricity. Proceed in peace as fellow travellers. From Vlad." H'm. Not Count Dracula, I hope. I own that I have read more sentimental inscriptions. But, if you've been a naughty girl, it's nice to have an admirer who gives nothing away. Speaking of giving away, I have brought you something so obvious that no one else will have thought of it. May it secure you in love till your Golden Wedding. Joby! Stop fussing, man, and come here!'

As well as he could under his burden, Joby trotted forward. In a linen sheet, bound like a head in a factory haircloth, nestled an enormous sphere, the size of a giant beachball. He thrust it on Sponge, who nearly collapsed with the sudden weight.

'My God!' exclaimed Sponge, 'a cannon ball from Krupp!'

'Your Christmas pudding for Siberia,' announced Lady Violet triumphantly. 'A good pudding is always heavy. I made it myself, and added a bit extra in case you find friends.'

The train whistled. They bundled themselves and the vast pudding aboard and stammered their thanks.

'Look after it,' said the old lady, 'and it will look after you.' The train chuffed out.

'Feeling peckish?' asked Sponge.

'How can you laugh?' Char said indignantly. 'The richest woman in the West Riding, and she gives us a Christmas pudding! I could weep that such stinginess came from my side of the family.'

'The proportions are generous,' said Sponge.

'We'll have to boil it for days!'

However, it amused Sponge to lug it, like a convict his ball and chain, to Ostend, to Copenhagen, to St Petersburg, via many detours to Moscow and the Great Trans-Siberian Express.

It *was* great, like a dream of love in a chrysalis, from that second on December 20, when the express stole silently away on its double thread of iron. It was love in the morning, love with kvass, love in the afternoon, love with bear sausage, love in the evening with the poignant balalaika, love punctuated at all times by the incursions of the samovar lady, in whose boiler the Christmas pudding rode, until a fellow passenger, an Inspector of Prisons, complained about tea flavoured with nutmeg, cinnamon, carrots, currants, beer, candy, and black treacle. So they transferred it to the special ablutions carriage, where it boiled in peace, nobody minding these aromas in their bath.

· It was love up the gentle acclivity of the Urals, and love spanning Asia, which anybody could see was infinite. Marsh under snow, pasture under snow, little wooden houses festooned with firewood, all under snow, great embryonic cities pulsing in the womb of the crystal-feathered taiga. Love parted company with the clock, as the time zones changed, took lunch at midnight, and went to bed at noon. On, on, on – a bridge. On, on, on – a tunnel! On, on, on – sleep. Novosibirsk, Krasnoyarsk, Irkutsk. There were street markets on the platforms.

By Lake Baikal, the diamond of Siberia, on Christmas Eve love was in need of stretching its legs. In the event, actually the crossing of the rock-hard ice, its facilities were stretched to the utmost. It was here that a band of escaped Bolshevik prisoners, with a rabble of malcontents from the mines of Altai, made an onslaught on the train.

They emerged suddenly from the blizzard, just as Sponge was checking the brandy flask with a view to dousing the pudding. They hurled themselves from sleighs on to the rearmost carriages, with the probable aim of first liberating the prisoners, then swarming over the whole train. A tumult of shots and yells could be heard, and in a minute the train braked violently, throwing everyone to the floor.

'There's a thing,' said Sponge, dashing to the carriage entrance. 'We've packed everything but the artillery.'

'What's to be done?' asked Char, in a firm voice.

'Why, save the pudding, I think,' cried Sponge. 'Come on, Charshka. Wait a sec, though. Give us a hand with Romney's blessed Skin Foods.' From the light in his eye she recognized why his battalion had called him Bloody-Ecstasy.

'You're mad,' she said. But she followed him. They jumped down on the ice, and raced alongside the train, past the carriages in a turmoil of despairing passengers, and clambered aboard again on the coach that held baths and pudding.

The Inspector of Prisons was up to his midriff in hot water. 'Out!' commanded Sponge. 'Right out on the ice. We may get away if I can unhitch the waggons here. We'll leave the freedom-fighters to go on their way, since it's Christmas, and we'll go ours. As soon as we're uncoupled, signal the driver to move off. Never mind your trousers. The nuder the better. It'll help attract his attention.'

He turned to Char. 'Now fetch out Auntie Vi's masterpiece, while I build up the pressure.' He snatched up the coal shovel and fed the fire – while Char, with a couple of loofahs, extracted the pudding. Then he swung the shovel against the boiler just above the gutter where the water came out until suddenly a plate gave and steam roared out. He wedged the Pudding in the gap, and clamped it in place with Romney's Skin Foods.

'Charlotte Gore-Blamey,' he intoned, 'you're commissioned Gunner in Charge on the field of battle. That'll hold for about five minutes. Here's the brandy, kiss the pudding goodbye, and light it. To fire, bash Romney away with the spade. You've got one shot. Make it a good one.

He leaped on to the ice.

She could hear the uproar in the prisoners' coaches waxing ever nearer, gradually drowning the clink of Sponge at work. Then came a violent report as the lock to the door of the neighbouring coach was shattered, the door crashed open and a figure from a nightmare, hair shaven on one side, and blood coursing down his furs as if he wore the pelt of an animal just slaughtered, towered menacingly over Sponge, with his cutlass upraised.

With a little yelp, she swept away Romney's Skin Foods. With a noise of erupting steam like a banshee screaming, the flaming pudding was discharged through the opening. It caught the brigand amidships. Propelled back into the arms of his colleagues, he clutched it in astonishment to his belly. In the aching confusion of the next half-minute, Sponge achieved his object, gave the signal, and half the train drew away across the lake, with the Inspector of Prisons scurrying like an animated snowman to rejoin it.

And love resumed its sway to Tokyo. So ends the adventure of the Great Trans-Siberian Christmas Pudding. But there is an epilogue.

In 1918 Charlotte visited her Aunt Vi with her two little Gore-Blameys. As the Christmas pudding was set on the table by the roaring fire, the dowager said: 'You never ate the one I gave you, did you? You wrote that you'd enjoyed it, but I know different.'

'But how?' asked Charlotte.

'You would have mentioned the 500 golden guineas I put inside.'

'Oh!' said Charlotte. Then she gave the true account.

'Lucky it was such a heavy pudding really,' commented Aunt Vi.

'Very,' said Charlotte. She pondered and gradually a lopsided smile settled on her face.

'Tell,' said Aunt Vi.

'Oh, I can't be sure. We got the vote without me, I'm the One Who Wasn't There, but I think that after all I have paid my due to the Revolution. Last year a very old friend of mine went back home. I've heard it said that he paid his fare for the sealed train to the Finland station with English gold.'

'Getting about is becoming very expensive,' said Aunt Vi. 'Now let's have a little toast to absent friends.'

24 December 1979   **Alex Hamilton**

Index